The Lives of the *Miller's Tale*

ALSO BY PETER G. BEIDLER

Murdering Indians: A Documentary History of the 1897 Killings That Inspired Louise Erdrich's The Plague of Doves (2014)

The Lives of the *Miller's Tale*

The Roots, Composition and Retellings of Chaucer's Bawdy Story

Peter G. Beidler

McFarland & Company, Inc., Publishers
Jefferson, North Carolina

LIBRARY OF CONGRESS CATALOGUING-IN-PUBLICATION DATA

Beidler, Peter G.
 The lives of the Miller's Tale : the roots, composition and retellings of Chaucer's bawdy story / Peter G. Beidler.
  p.   cm.
 Includes bibliographical references and index.

 ISBN 978-0-7864-9393-7 (softcover : acid free paper) ∞
 ISBN 978-1-4766-1828-9 (ebook)

 1. Chaucer, Geoffrey, –1400. Miller's tale. I. Title.
 PR1868.M63B45 2015
 821'.109—dc23   2014040163

BRITISH LIBRARY CATALOGUING DATA ARE AVAILABLE

© 2015 Peter G. Beidler. All rights reserved

No part of this book may be reproduced or transmitted in any form or by any means, electronic or mechanical, including photocopying or recording, or by any information storage and retrieval system, without permission in writing from the publisher.

On the cover: Depiction of Geoffrey Chaucer as a pilgrim, Ellesmere Manuscript, folio 153v, 15th century (Thinkstock)

Printed in the United States of America

McFarland & Company, Inc., Publishers
 Box 611, Jefferson, North Carolina 28640
 www.mcfarlandpub.com

For Geoffrey Chaucer, who taught the world
how to make dramatic improvements in a story.

Acknowledgments

I am grateful to Susan Yager for sharing with me her translation of *Dame Sirith*; Bill and Karen Curr for their help in scanning images from books and films; Ellen Fitzgerald at the Seattle Public Library for her help in running down many of the books and articles I refer to; Baba Brinkman and *LATCH* for permission to reproduce portions of my article on Brinkman's rap *Miller's Tale*; Gene Mater for his drawings; the Metropolitan Museum of Art for permission to reproduce part of the Merode Altarpiece; Peter N. Miller and Gareth Machin for permission to reproduce their unpublished versions of the *Miller's Tale* in my Chapter XX; Laurel Broughton for her loving attention to careful proofreading and checking; and Marion Egge once more for her sharp eye, clever mind, and generous spirit.

Table of Contents

Acknowledgments	vi
Preface: A Whiter Shade of Pale	1
Introduction: Dramatizing the Miller's Tale	3

Part One: Chaucer's Transformation of the *Miller's Tale*

I.	Origins	9
II.	Four Genres	15
III.	Seeing and Hearing	30
IV.	Comedic Realism	38
V.	The Structure of John's House	48
VI.	The Shot-Window	60
VII.	Reconstructing John's House	81
VIII.	People and Props	87
IX.	The Pre-Bedroom Sequence	93
X.	The Bedroom Sequence	108

Part Two: Modern Transformations of the *Miller's Tale*

XI.	Early Retellings for Adults: Cobb (1712), Smith (1713), Anonymous (1791)	125

XII. Early Retellings for Young Readers: Johnstone (1895), Darton (1904), Farjeon (1930)	132
XIII. Later Retellings for Adults: Clarke (1870), Haweis (1887), Raffel (2008), Ackroyd (2009)	138
XIV. Later Retellings for Young Readers: McCaughrean (1984), Hastings (1988)	145
XV. In the Modern Missouri Ozarks: Milburn (1956)	151
XVI. In Coloring Books and Cartoons: Adkins (1973), Lorenz (1981), Williams (2007), Chwast (2011)	169
XVII. In Musical Performance: Starkie (1968), Pickering (1988), Brinkman (2006)	183
XVIII. In Theatrical Performance: Woods (1974), Wengrow (1983), Riley (1998), O'Connor (2001), Price (2002), Poulton (2005)	195
XIX. In Filmic Performance: Pasolini (1972), Myerson (2000), Bowker (2003)	217
XX. In San Francisco and Southwark: Miller (2014), Machin (2014)	227
Chapter Notes	251
Bibliography	267
Index	273

Preface: A Whiter Shade of Pale

In the late 1960s a British rock group known as Procol Harum issued a song called "A Whiter Shade of Pale." The song soon was number one on the charts in England. It has kept its popularity down through the years. In 2004 *Rolling Stone* placed it fifty-seventh on its list of the 500 greatest songs of all time. As of 2009, it was the most-played song in public places in the last seventy-five years in England. I mention this song because it bears witness to the widespread knowledge in England of Chaucer's Miller, his drunkenness, and his tale. No one seems to be quite certain what all of the lyrics of "A Whiter Shade of Pale" mean, but the opening seems clear enough: the speaker is a man who has been dancing wildly and drunkenly with a young woman in a public place. Encouraged by an appreciative audience, the couple calls for another drink. The waiter obligingly brings them a tray of drinks. Not long after, as a person identified only as "the miller" was telling his tale, the woman's face, which had before been merely ghostly, turned a whiter shade of pale (line 12). The lyrics go on for another twenty-four lines, but these are the only ones that concern us here. Although the name Chaucer is never mentioned in "A Whiter Shade of Pale," there is no question that the miller referred to is Chaucer's Miller. In the prologue to the *Miller's Tale* the connection between drunkenness, paleness, and tale-telling is made clear. Robyn the Miller is undeniably drunk. The Host sees that he is "dronke of ale" (3128). The Reeve refers to his "dronken harlotrye" (3145). And the Miller himself admits, "I am dronke, I knowe it by my soun" (3138). Indeed, the Miller has drunk so much ale at the Tabard Inn that he can scarcely stay on his horse. Evidence for that advanced drunkenness is his paleness:

> The Millere, that for dronken was al pale,
> So that unnethe upon his hors he sat [3120–21].

That the composers of the lyrics of "A Whiter Shade of Pale" could assume that Chaucer's Miller and his tale were so well-known that the reference to paleness and drinking and a miller's tale-telling would make sense to people who heard their song.

And well they might make that assumption. None of Chaucer's Canterbury pilgrims is better known than the drunken, bagpipe-playing Miller with a tuft of red hair growing out of the wart on his nose, and none of the Canterbury stories has had a richer, more varied, or more enduring life than the *Miller's Tale*. In this monograph I have little to say about the Miller's drunkenness, but a lot to say about his brilliant tale, which I trace from its Continental origins across the English Channel to England in the fourteenth century and, much later, across the Atlantic Ocean to the United States and Canada.

In tracing the development of the tale I shall be answering two large questions. First, how did Chaucer dramatize the story that he found in the Middle Dutch *Heile of Beersele*? How, that is, did he transform the nature of the story that was his central source for the *Miller's Tale* by introducing into the narrative certain elements familiar in the theater: scene division, staging, visual and aural effects, dialogue. The fabliau tale and the secular theatrical farce were relatively recent literary imports from across the Channel. Perhaps because there was little tradition of either in England, Chaucer felt free to bring the two together in the *Miller's Tale* by transforming what he found in his primary Middle Dutch source into a tale that had the feel of a medieval dramatic farce.

Second, how did writers after Chaucer continue to alter the *Miller's Tale* as they adapted it to new purposes and later audiences? In answering that question we will find ourselves considering the tale in various formats: as a short tale, of course, but also as a rap monologue, as a cartoon sequence, as a novel, as a chapter in a graphic novel, as a musical, as a play, as a film.

In answering these two questions we will discover that no story, by Chaucer or anyone else, has lived as many different lives as the *Miller's Tale*.

Introduction: Dramatizing the *Miller's Tale*

I should say right off that by "dramatize" I do not mean what is sometimes called the "roadside drama" on the pilgrimage to Canterbury. That term, which originated with Kittredge,[1] usually refers to the various pilgrims as actors in the grand outdoor theater of the pilgrimage. According to Kittredge, these actors give a series of soliloquies that reveal the personalities of the tellers. The speech spoken by the Knight, for example, is a leisurely military romance set in ancient Athens. Its main characters are almost all, like the Knight himself, of the upper classes—kings, dukes, princes, princesses. Some are of the *really* upper classes—gods and goddesses who control the lives of people. The other "gentils" on the pilgrimage to Canterbury think that the Knight tells "a noble storie" (3111),[2] but the Miller is not pleased. We gradually come to understand that the Miller finds in the *Knight's Tale* idealized, not real, people. He finds in it love but not lust, marriage but not infidelity, bodies but not bodily functions, speeches but not dialogue. He finds missing most of the ingredients of a good tale. He supplies those ingredients in his own "speech."

That kind of "roadside drama" is not the kind of drama that will especially concern me in this monograph. I am more interested in the theatricality of the Miller's story than in the personality of the Miller. In the prologue to the *Miller's Tale* Chaucer tells us that the Miller responds in "Pilates voice" to the Host's invitation to the Monk to tell "Somwhat to quite with the Knyghtes tale" (3119). The drunken Miller jumps in and insists on doing the quitting or matching:

> But in Pilates voys he gan to crie,
> And swoor, "By armes, and by blood and bones,
> I kan a noble tale for the nones,
> With which I wol now quite the Knyghtes tale" [3124–27].

The Miller's swearing by "armes," "blood," and "bones," of course, means that he is swearing by the arms, blood, and bones of the crucified Jesus—that is, to the *corpus Christi*. The allusion to "Pilates voys" is to the voice in which Pontius Pilate calls for the execution of Jesus. I find in the New Testament no mention of the quality of Pilate's voice. We learn there what Pilate said but not how he said it. The allusion, then, must be to the fourteenth-century British Corpus Christi dramas.[3] For Chaucer's reference to Pilate's voice to have any meaning to a medieval audience, he would have had to assume in that audience a certain familiarity with the Corpus Christi plays. Already, then, before the Miller even begins his tale proper, Chaucer has thrust us into the world of the medieval theater.

In the tale itself, Chaucer finds ways of keeping us in that world. There we find two more direct allusions to the medieval theater. The first comes in the initial description of Absolon, the foppish parish clerk who takes a liking to the lovely Alison. To impress her, Absolon tries everything he can think of: he stays up all day and night to woo her, he offers to be her page, he combs his hair in clever ways, he sends a go-between, he sends her sweet wine and mead, he sings like a nightingale, and

> Somtyme, to shewe his lightnesse and maistrye
> He pleyeth Herodes upon a scaffold hye [3383–84].

The "scaffold hye" is the raised stage on which medieval plays were sometimes performed, usually in the center square or marketplace. Chaucer gives us no details about how high the scaffold might have been or about Absolon's performance upon it,[4] but we are no doubt to be amused at the thought of Absolon trying to impress Alison with his "lightnesse and maistrye," which presumably meant that he pranced around a small high stage in the role of the grave, diabolical, baby-murdering King Herod.[5]

The other explicit reference to contemporary medieval drama in the *Miller's Tale* is Nicholas's mention of Noah and his wife.[6] Nicholas mentions them as part of his plan to get rid of old John so that he can enjoy a night of sexual pleasure with Alison. Nicholas plays on John's fears that he and Alison may drown:

> "Hastow nat herd hou saved was Noe,
> Whan that oure Lord hadde warned hym biforn
> That al the world with water sholde be lorn?" [3534–36].

That reference, of course, is ultimately to the Old Testament account of God's destruction of all of mankind except Noah and his family, but it becomes immediately clear that Nicholas has seen of one of the Corpus Christi Noah plays in which the actors would have enacted an entirely unbiblical comic interplay between Noah and his wife:

> "Hastow nat herd," quod Nicholas, "also
> The sorwe of Noe with his felaweshipe
> Er that he myghte gete his wyf to shipe?
> Hym hadde be levere, I dar wel undertake,
> At thilke tyme, than alle his wetheres blake
> That she hadde had a ship hirself allone" [3538–42].

The theatrical tradition that Mrs. Noah refused to leave her gossips and get into the ark, and that Noah had trouble in persuading her to do so, appears in several of the cycles. In the Chester *Noah*, one of Noah's sons forces his mother into the ark. In the York *Noah*, old Noah himself accomplishes the task, but not before he beats his wife until she is too tired and sore to resist any further. That John is convinced by the parallels suggests that he also knew at least one of the Corpus Christi Noah plays, possibly one from a no-longer-extant Oxford cycle. Nicholas apparently later builds on John's knowledge of the desirability for Noah's wife to have her own little ark when he insists that John provide a separate tub just for her. We should not be surprised to discover in the *Miller's Tale* other, but perhaps less obvious, evidence that when Chaucer wrote the tale he was thinking in a theatrical register.

In addition to these explicit allusions to medieval drama, we can detect some less explicit ones. For example, readers familiar with medieval drama might well have seen in Chaucer's portrayal of John and Alison distant reflections of Joseph and Mary. The Miller, we recall, had announced that he would tell "a legende and a lyf / Bothe of a carpenter and of his wyf" (3141–42). The terms "legend" and "life" often refer to the lives of saints. To use "legende" and "lyf" of a carpenter and his wife connects them with Saint Joseph, an old man who worked as a carpenter, and his young wife, the Virgin Mary. Similarly, we are invited to see in Nicholas's singing of *Angelus ad virginem* (3216), a reflection of the angel Gabriel making his annunciation to the Virgin Mary.[7] Probably unlearned and illiterate, the Miller would not have read the scriptures. It is likely, then, that his knowledge of the bible came to him through the Corpus Christi plays. These specific allusive references to medieval biblical drama reinforce the theatrical register of the Miller's narrative.

The Host tries to put the Pilate-voiced Miller off, but the Miller insists. The Host soon relents: "Tel on, a devel wey!" (3134). Just before the Miller begins his tale, Chaucer warns his readers to not to take too seriously the "game" of the tale that follows: "men shal nat maken ernest of game" (3186). That word "game" is usually translated, logically enough, as "joke" or "jest" or "ribaldry" or "mere fun," but it can also mean "play" in the sense of lighthearted drama or farce.[8] Since Chaucer contrasts the "game" of the *Miller's Tale* with the "storial thing that toucheth gentillesse, / And eek moralitee and hoolynesse" (3179–80), he appears to be suggesting that we have in this "game" something far different from the "story-things" or "history-things" that can be found in other Canterbury tales. Part of my purpose in Part One of this book is to suggest that the *Miller's Tale* is, indeed, the most theatrical "game" in the collection.[9]

Chaucer made many alterations to his most likely source, the anonymous Middle Dutch *Heile of Beersele*. Many of those alterations served to make his tale more dramatic by giving his characters different roles to play than they played in his sources, by suggesting that part of the comedy in the tale arises from each of the men in the *Miller's Tale* imagining his role in a different literary register, by adding details of costume to make the characters more easily "seen" in the mind's eye, by adding references to music and other sounds to make the story more "hearable," by adding information about the carpenter's house where most of the tale is enacted, by adding dialogue, and by making the story sufficiently realistic that readers can almost imagine, as they listen to or read the story, that it is being played before them on a medieval stage.

In Part Two I show by reference to some thirty post-Chaucer retellings that the *Miller's Tale* has had a rich and varied afterlife. Writers and publishers have for centuries scratched the itch to retell Chaucer's *Miller's Tale*. I use the noun "retelling" to describe what the revisers variously refer to as their translation, adaptation, improvisation, revisitation, rendering, modernization, and so on. For an excellent analysis of the precise meanings of some of these terms, see Kathleen Forni's *Chaucer's Afterlife*.[10] These retellers generally had one of several reasons for wanting to present the *Miller's Tale* in a new way: (1) to make Chaucer's tale more accessible to readers who were puzzled by his "obsolete" Middle English; (2) to make the *Miller's Tale* less vulgar and so more suitable for women and children; (3) to have fun by experimenting with new twists on an old story; and (4) to offer the tale in a completely different literary genre. I shall of course be particularly interested in the modern versions that build most obviously on the theatrical possibilities that Chaucer built into his *Miller's Tale*.

I try avoid criticizing the various post-Chaucerian authors for departing so widely from Chaucer's *Miller's Tale*. These authors are, like Chaucer in his retelling of the basic plot of *Heile of Beersele*, adapting a story they like to a new audience and to a different literary purpose. There are differences, of course; Chaucer never claimed that he was retelling the Middle Dutch *Heile of Beersele*. Virtually all subsequent writers, on the other hand, claim to be taking their inspiration from Chaucer's tale of an old man, his young wife, and her would-be lovers. They want not to deny or conceal Chaucer's authorship, but to flaunt it.[11]

Along with the *Wife of Bath's Tale* and the *Pardoner's Tale*, the *Miller's Tale* is the Canterbury narrative that most people think of when they think of Chaucer. The *Wife of Bath's Tale* is famous for its often-married teller and its plot about a foolish man who learns to shift his quest from what he desire most desires to what women most desires. The *Pardoner's Tale* is famous for its greedy teller and its plot about three foolish men who seek Death but find death. The *Miller's Tale* is famous for its combative teller and its bawdy plot about three foolish men whose pride brings them a smelly fart, a scorched buttocks, and a broken arm. All three of these tales have been told and retold and "translated" many times. The *Miller's Tale*, however, is the one that was most dramatically altered by Chaucer from its source, and the one that subsequent retellers have most dramatically altered in their renditions. This monograph is an exploration of the ways the story was altered, by whom, to what effect, and why.

PART ONE

CHAUCER'S TRANSFORMATION OF THE *MILLER'S TALE*

I
Origins

The origins of Chaucer's *Miller's Tale* are diverse and complex,[1] but three specific works, all of which Chaucer might well have been familiar with, deserve mention: the Middle English *Dame Sirith*, the Middle Dutch *Lippijn*, and the Middle Dutch *Heile of Beersele*. The first two suggest Chaucer's familiarity with medieval dramatic farces. The third was almost certainly Chaucer's main narrative source for the *Miller's Tale*.

Dame Sirith

The only extant Middle English fablilau before Chaucer was *Dame Sirith*, a short tale of 450 lines written in the last quarter of the thirteenth century. The plot involves Wilikin, a young cleric who wants to make love to Margery, a merchant's wife. She refuses. Frustrated, Wilikin asks for help from Dame Sirith, an older and more experienced woman. For a fee, she agrees to help him. Dame Sirith goes to Margery. Just before she gets there she forces her pet dog to eat hot pepper-mustard. The mustard makes the dog's eyes water. When Margery asks, Dame Sirith says that the dog is actually her own daughter, but that she had been transformed into a dog because she had refused to satisfy the sexual demands of a cleric. Frightened, Margery goes to Wilikin and becomes his lover. *Dame Sirith* has many of the elements of the typical fabliau: it is short, in verse, involves cuckolding, features a cleric propositioning an attractive married woman in a plot that turns on a trick played on someone gullible by someone clever. It is, in other words, broadly similar to the *Miller's Tale*.

Of particular significance is that *Dame Sirith* reads very much like a piece of drama. Although they are not named as such in the text, the tale comprises three distinct scenes with two or three speakers in each:

Scene 1. Wilikin petitions, Margery refuses.
Scene 2. Wilikin asks for help, Sirith asks for payment.
Scene 3. Sirith explains about her daughter, Margery asks for advice, then Sirith fetches Wilikin so that Margery can give him what he desires.

Although there are some lines of narrative, the story is told far less in narration than in dialogue, with the name of each speaker identified in advance of the speech. I give below two of the exchanges (in my modern prose paraphrase). The first exchange (from Scene 1, lines 67–102) comes early in the story when Wilikin first asks Margery to be his lover. The second exchange (from Scene 3, lines 338–70) comes near the end when Dame Sirith plays her trick on the gullible Margery:

Dame Sirith, from Scene 1

WILIKIN: I have loved you for many years, though I have not told you of my love. When your husband was in town, I could not risk private conversation with you. But yesterday I heard on the street that he had gone to the fair at Botolfston, in Lincolnshire. Knowing that he was away, I have come to talk with you about my love. Anyone would be happy to have his way with such a woman as you. Please, madam, if you will grant it, I would like in secret to make love to you.

MARGERY: By our lord, king of heaven, never would I do such a thing. My husband brought me to his house a virgin, and he loves me honorably as I do him. My love for him is without blemish, as true as steel. Even though he is away from home on business, I shall never be a whore and be false to him in bed or on the floor.
[...]

From Scene 3

SIRITH: I once had a lovely and gracious daughter who had the most courteous husband you could find anywhere. My daughter loved him dearly, and that is why I now lament. You see, one day, he had to make a trip, and that resulted in her ruin. While he was away, a bold cleric, with a tonsure, offered his love to my daughter. Despite his pleading, she refused him, ignoring my advice. As a result, he practiced some witchcraft and turned my daughter into this bitch. See how she cries in her lamentation? It breaks my heart to see her so. My heart breaks in two. I advise any young housewife, if a clerk asks for her love, by all means to grant him his wishes.

MARGERY: Oh, Lord Christ! What can I do? Just the other day a clerk came to me and asked me to be his lover, but I refused him. And now he will turn me into a bitch. How, dear woman, can I escape that fate?

Dame Sirith could easily have been acted on a simple stage or scaffold. Some scholars, myself among them, think it probably was performed. The performers would have found little in the text to guide them. The narrator, for example, says only this about the location of Wilikin's opening interview with Margery (lines 19–22): "Wilikin went to her house—it was a fine dwelling—and entered the main parlor where she sat." There is no direct evidence that Chaucer had read *Dame Sirith* or seen it performed, but he could have. It was, after all, in English.

Lippijn

Chaucer is more likely to have seen, on one of his journeys to the Low Countries, a performance of one or more of the four short farces gathered together, along with four longer and more serious plays, in the Middle Dutch Hulthem manuscript, now in the Royal Library of Brussels. These four farces date from the third quarter of the fourteenth century. Chaucer is known to have traveled to the Low Countries and probably knew Middle Dutch. Indeed, one of the four farces, *Lippijn*, might actually have served as a source for the *Merchant's Tale*.[2]

Lippijn is a short play of 200 lines about a henpecked old man who sees his wife (not named in the play) making love with her paramour, then allows himself to be convinced by his wife's godmother, named Trise, that it never happened. No scene divisions are marked in the text, but the play comprises four scenes:

Scene 1. Lippijn's wife gives him some domestic chores to perform while she goes out.
Scene 2. Lippijn's wife meets her paramour.
Scene 3. Lippijn tells Trise that she has seen his wife in the arms of her lover, but she convinces him that he had been tricked by elves.
Scene 4. Lippijn and Trise return home, where Lippijn's wife beats him up for distrusting her.

To give the flavor of the dialogue in *Lippijn*, here is my prose paraphrase of part of Scene 3 (lines 66–103), in which Trise talks old Lippijn out of seeing what he just saw:

Lippijn, from Scene 3

LIPPIJN: Oh, Trise! I am heartsick. I would never have thought my wife would do what I just saw.
TRISE: Lippijn, tell me what you saw.
LIPPIJN: I am ashamed to say that I saw her lying and playing with another man.
TRISE: I cannot believe that. I know she is pure and faithful. She would never do such a thing.

LIPPIJN: You can't talk a man out of what he has seen with his own eyes.
TRISE: Upon my honor, many people have been tricked by their eyes.
LIPPIJN: No, no. I was not tricked. I saw her myself, with her naked knees in the air. She and he both labored hard.
TRISE: Oh, Lippijn, do not dishonor your wife with such talk. Your old eyes made a mistake, perhaps because you've been drinking.
LIPPIJN: What? Are you calling me blind when I saw what happened? I tell you, I saw her lying on her back and he lifted up her skirts.
TRISE: Hush, good Lippijn. It was just your imagination. Haven't you heard that elves trick people? The devil sometimes plays such tricks just to make trouble between husbands and wives. I'd stake my life on it—what you saw was the work of elves.

And so on. In the end, of course, foolish old Lippijn, like foolish old January in the *Merchant's Tale*, allows himself to be talked out of seeing what he saw.

There were, then, dramatic farces in medieval England and across the English Channel, farces that can be thought of either as early secular drama or as dramatized fabliaux. One or more of these might have suggested to Chaucer the possibility of working to dramatize the story he probably heard told or read in a Middle Dutch manuscript, the story that he transformed into the *Miller's Tale*.

Heile of Beersele

Scholars have known for a century that the anonymous *Heile of Beersele* is an analogue to the *Miller's Tale*. Only recently, however, has it emerged as the single most likely source of Chaucer's comic masterpiece. Not only is it one of the very few analogues that is old enough in its manuscript form that Chaucer could have known it, but it is from a land he had visited and in a language he would have recognized. Furthermore, it is the only early analogue to combine the two key plot elements that we find in the *Miller's Tale*—the predicted flood and the burned buttocks—and it unforgettably joins those two plots in the anguished cry of a scorched man for water.[3]

It will be useful to have before us a detailed summary of the short tale which in Middle Dutch comes to 190 lines in octosyllabic rhyming couplets. The tale itself begins after a 13-line prologue in which the teller, apparently a minstrel, speaks directly to the audience about vocal tales accompanied by a harp or a fiddle, and then of the strange story he is going to tell in the Dutch language, a story that happened right there in Antwerp. And then he starts the tale proper at line 14:

Heile of Beersele

In Cow Gate Street in Antwerp lived a lecherous woman called Heile of Beersele who made a living by selling her services to men. One day three fellows came to her separately to ask to visit her that night in her home. Heile was delighted with her good fortune and agreed to satisfy them all, one after the other. She told the first, a miller named Willem, to come in the early evening. She told the second, a priest, to come when he heard the evening bell ring. And she told the third, a smith named Hughe, to come when the night bell rang. All three men eagerly awaited their appointed hour.

In the early evening when Willem came, Heile received him gladly. They made love, for Heile knew that trade well. While Willem was still with her, the time for the evening bell came and the eager priest came and asked to be let in. Willem, not knowing that another visitor was expected, asked Heile who the second visitor was. Heile replied that it seemed the priest had come to say a prayer to cure her ills. Not wanting the priest to know he was with Heile, Willem asked where he could run to. Heile told him to hide in the trough hanging by a rope from the beam. It was a trough that she had found convenient on other occasions. Willem fled to the trough and Heile let the priest in.

After the priest and Heile had made love three times, the priest quoted the gospels and then said that the time would soon come when God would destroy the world with water and fire, and that all the people in the world would be destroyed. Willem heard that from his hiding place in the trough and believed it.

Then Hughe the blacksmith knocked on the door. When Heile discovered who it was, she tried to send him away, saying that she did not feel well. Disappointed, Hughe asked at the very least for permission to kiss her mouth. Then Heile told the priest to let the smith kiss his behind and let him think it was she. The priest got right up and put his bottom mouth out the window, and Hughe kissed it with such zeal that his nose went inside, and he felt caught as in a trap. Realizing immediately that he had kissed a man's arse, not a woman's mouth, the priest silently vowed to get his revenge.

Enraged, Hughe went home to his shop and heated up an iron. Then he ran with the red-hot iron back to Heile's door and called out that he had come back because his love for her was so great. He insisted on coming in, or at least on kissing her mouth again. The priest again put his bottom out, and the smith stuck the red-hot iron into his arse. The priest called out "Water!" long and loud.

Willem from his tub heard the cry and, believing that the priest's prediction had come true, thought that he could save himself by cutting the rope and floating away. He fell to the ground, breaking his arm and his thigh. That frightened the priest, who thought the devil had come. He rushed into a corner, fell into a cesspit, and had to go home in shame with a burned arse and covered with excrement.

There are many obvious similarities between *Heile of Beersele* and the *Miller's Tale*: three men lusting for the same woman; overlapping claims to her; the plan to get rid of one man so a second can visit; the first man above in the tub; the prediction of a terrible flood; the interruption of that second man's visit by a third, less welcome one; the request for at least a kiss; the buttocks at the window; the smithy and the hot iron; the burned behind; the anguished double-cry for "Water, water"; the cutting of the rope by the man in the tub; the fall and the broken limbs; the punishment of the three men and the non-punishment of the lecherous woman.

There are also, of course, many and important differences between *Heile of Beersele* and the *Miller's Tale*: Alison is a wife, not a prostitute; the man in the tub is Alison's husband, not a visitor; the second lover, Nicholas, is a boarder in their home, not a paying customer who comes in off the street; Nicholas predicts the flood before, not after, he makes love to Alison; Absolon is a foppish parish priest, not a blacksmith; there are three tubs, not one; John uses an axe to cut the rope, not a knife, and in his fall breaks only his arm, not his arm and thigh; and so on. And, of course, the *Miller's Tale*, though one of Chaucer's shortest, is much longer than the Middle Dutch one. At 668 decasyllabic lines, excluding the 78-line prologue, it is five times as long as its Middle Dutch counterpart, which has only 177 octosyllabic lines.[4] A consideration of the materials that Chaucer changed from and added to his source will be my central concern in the following chapters.

II
Four Genres

The comedy in the *Miller's Tale* is most obvious in the window scenes. Absolon's silly serenade of Alison in the first window scene primes us for the second and third window scenes when Absolon kisses Alison's "nether eye," when Alison bursts forth with her delightful "Tehee!" just before she claps the window shut on the amazed Absolon, when Absolon gets a faceful of fart, when Nicholas gets his butt burned and cries out "Water! Water!," causing the man-who-would-be-Noah to think the flood has come, to cut the rope, and to come tumbling down. But there is subtler comedy in the overlay of genres in the *Miller's Tale*. Each of the three men who admire Alison imagines his activities as being part of different a literary genre, while Alison herself plays out her role in still a fourth genre.[1] John imagines himself playing a role in a reenactment of an Old Testament biblical narrative. Nicholas imagines himself playing a hero's role in a medieval dramatic farce. Absolon imagines himself playing the role of distressed lover in a medieval romance. And Alison refuses to play her designated role in any of those, but just charges ahead in her role as a fabliau wife.

John in a Biblical Narrative

John draws on his personal inspiration from religion-infused proverbs and from the bible. John is fully acquainted with the proverbial lore of his time. When he hears that Nicholas has not been seen for a day or two, his response is a set of proverb-like truisms:

"Men should nat knowe of Goddes pryvetee" [3454].
"Ye, blessed be alwey a lewed man
That nat but oonly his bileve kan!" [3455–56].
"Thynk on God, as we do, men that swynke" [3491].

John's boarder is smart enough to play into John's trust in proverbs. To help persuade John to do his bidding, for example, Nicholas quotes a couple of proverbs of his own:

> "For thus seith Salomon, that was ful trewe:
> 'Werk al by conseil, and thou shalt nat rewe'" [3529–30].

The irony, of course, is that the "conseil" that Nicholas offers is the direct cause of John's ruefulness; his being cuckolded, maimed, and ridiculed by his neighbors.

John likes not only religious proverbs but religious anecdotes as well. When he hears about Nicholas's trance-like state, John is reminded of an anecdote about another student who neglected Christianity in his pursuit of astronomy:

> "So ferde another clerk with astromye;
> He walked in the feeldes for to prye
> Upon the sterres, what ther sholde bifalle,
> Til he was in a marle-pit yfalle;
> He saugh nat that" [3457–61].

John's speeches bristle with references to God, Christ, and various saints:

> "I am adrad, by Seint Thomas" [3425].
>
> "God shilde that he deyde sodeynly!" [3427].
>
> "Help us, seinte Frydeswyde!" [3449].
>
> "But yet, by Seint Thomas" [3461].
>
> "By Jhesus, hevene kyng!" [3464].
>
> "Awak, and thenk on Cristes passioun!" [3478].
>
> "Jhesu Crist and Seinte Benedight" [3483].
>
> Where wentestow, Seinte Petres soster?" [3486].

John's interest in things religious is readily apparent in his uncritical acceptance of his role as the new Noah, the one good man who is selected by God to be saved when all the wicked are drowned. It is not hard for Nicholas to convince John to play the role of a biblical patriarch:

> "Hastow nat herd hou saved was Noe,
> Whan that oure Lord had warned hym biforn
> That al the world with water sholde be lorn?" [3534–36].
>
> "I wol nat tellen Goddes pryvetee.
> Suffiseth thee, but if thy wittes madde,
> To han as greet a grace as Noe hadde" [3558–60].

John easily is persuaded that he has been selected by God to be saved and to start the repopulation of a renewed Christian world when all the rest of mankind has been drowned.

Old John's literary register, then, is a moralistic, religious, and biblical one. He is egotistical enough to think that he is that rare good man in a world full of evil. He is devoted enough to believe that God would intervene directly to reward him for his goodness. That the biblical Noah did not have to worry about being cuckolded helps to explain why it never occurs to old John to worry about it, either. John is not sufficiently literary, or not literary enough in the proper register, to see that he is really playing a role in an earthy fabliau, not a biblical fable.

The counterpart of John the carpenter in *Heile of Beersele* is a miller named Willem. Willem does not pretend to be anything but just what he is, a miller who wants to buy sex from a prostitute. John is far more complicated. At times he is just a simple, jealous carpenter who loves his wife, wants what is best for her, and feels a certain self-righteous superiority to a college boy who spends so much time studying his books that he has no sense of the practical or the spiritual. John is all right so long as he plays that role. When Nicholas convinces John that he is a new Noah, however, John gets into trouble. Clearly John is attracted by Nicholas's suggestion that the coming flood will transform a common carpenter into a lord after the flood waters recede:

> "And thanne shul we be lordes al oure lyf
> Of all the world, as Noe and his wyf" [3581–82].

John likes the idea of being a lord, so he buys into his assigned role with all the vigor of a simple-minded fool:

> This sely carpenter bigynneth quake;
> Hym thynketh verraily that he may see
> Noees flood come walwynge as the see [3614–16].

Like Noah—or like the new Noah he imagines himself to be—John acquires his three little short-cut arks and builds his three big home-made ladders. He hangs the tubs from the roof beams, carefully following Nicholas's instructions that he must hang his own tub far away from his wife's. John provisions the tubs, then wearily climbs aboard his private ark, hastily says his Paternoster, and immediately falls asleep. Because the real Noah had no need to keep his wife "narwe in cage" (3224), so John in his role as the new Noah assumes that he has no need to be suspicious of Alison any more. Instead of listening in his slumbers for the sounds of his wife's infidelity, he listens for the sound of rain. When he hears Nicholas's cry for water, John wakes up:

> And thoughte, "Allas, now comth Nowelis flood!"
> He sit him up withouten wordes mo
> And with his ax he smoot the corde atwo,
> And doun gooth al [3818–21].

Imagining himself as the biblical Noah, John forgets that he is a simple carpenter with humble virtues and a frisky wife. His downfall comes when he acts out his role in a biblical story.

Willem in *Heile of Beersele*, of course, has his downfall also, but it is not connected with his imagining that he is Noah or a lord. Noah is never mentioned in the Middle Dutch tale. Willem remains a simple miller. He is punished because he consorts with a prostitute, not because he pridefully thinks that he is a new Noah. Willem never acts any other role than his own. He is punished for his foolish lechery, not for his foolish pride or for his foolish aspirations to lordship over an unpopulated world.

Nicholas in a Farce

Nicholas's genre is drama or, more precisely, the theatrical farce. The full flowering of the French farce did not come until the fifteenth century, though it had its origins in earlier centuries. Chambers describes the farce in these terms:

> Because the farces are rather short, rarely exceeding 400 lines, a large cast of characters is unnecessary, and many of them depend only upon three or four characters, although some have as many as six. [...] The characters are essentially stock types, broadly delineated, but often with deft strokes that create some truly memorable personages. Outraged husbands and unfaithful wives, and vice-versa, are everywhere, and jealousy is a common fault of both. The lusty village priest is often the third party in a triangular relationship that abounds in farce. [...] The situations of farce generally revolve around a deception of some sort. Whether practiced by wife and priest upon husband or by roguish youth upon infirm graybeard, trickery and ruses are the stuff of farce. Quite commonly the would-be deceiver is himself deceived by an adversary who proves the smarter. Lusty realism is the order of the day.[2]

That description sounds like the little play that Nicholas rigs up: the stock characters of the greybeard husband tricked by the lusty young man who is himself tricked, if not by someone smarter than he, then by his overconfidence in his own smartness. The unfaithful wife is there in his little drama, as is the lecherous village priest-in-training. And, of course, we have the earthy realism of Nicholas's grabbing Alison by the crotch and his farting on Absolon.

Nicholas almost immediately sets in motion the little play that Chaucer calls a "game":

> And if so be the game went aright,
> She sholde slepen in his arm al nyght,
> For this was his desir and hire also [3405–07].

For Nicholas, the bedding of Alison is to be not just a sex act but a "game," a playlet in which he plays the hero's role. The first scene in the game—the scene designed to set up the big scene in which Nicholas and Alison spend Monday night together in John's bed—is the one Nicholas carefully plans for his own bedroom farce on the preceding Saturday and Sunday. His scheme is masterfully executed, with Nicholas playacting the whole time. First he pretends to be in a death-like trance so that John will miss him and make inquiries. John sends Robyn up to investigate, then goes up himself and helps Robyn open the door. Nicholas then pretends to awaken from a zombie-vision and to have received a message direct from God: "For it is Cristes couseil that I seye" (3504). It is all playacting nonsense, of course, but Nicholas has in John a listener who wants to be duped, and the college boy plays the role of duper masterfully. Nicholas loves playing roles, one after the other. He switches from Gabriel to zombie to prophet of the Lord with the apparent ease of a professional actor.

Nicholas knows about medieval theatrical comedy. When he wants to ensnare his gullible old victim, he is drawn naturally to the troubles Noah in the theatrical version of the Flood story, where the patriarch could scarcely "gete his wyf to shipe" (3540). The theater-oriented Nicholas casts himself not only as a character in a medieval farce, but also as its director and stage manager, the person responsible for making his own farcical game of deception succeed.[3] Nicholas loves to be in charge, telling people what to do, when to do it, and what to say while doing it. As soon as he figures out that the only impediment to sexual success with Alison is her need for assurances that her jealous husband will not find out, Nicholas becomes the stage-director of the drama he has created.

Nicholas carefully sets the "stage" of his own room. He provisions it with food and drink sufficient for a day or two, but before he retreats to it he carefully directs Alison about what to do and especially what to say:

> And to hire housbonde bad hire for to seye
> If that he axed after Nicholas,
> She sholde saye she nyste where he was;
> Of all that day she saugh him nat with ye;
> She trowed that he was in maladye,

> For, for no cry hir mayde koude hym calle,
> He nolde answere for thyng that myghte falle [3412–18].

Having given Alison careful instructions, Nicholas then locks himself into his room and waits for John to figure out that he is not around. When John does figure it out, he becomes the new object of Nicholas's direction. In his long speech, Nicholas gives, in a series of imperative commands, detailed instructions to his gullible Noah-to-be:

> "Fecche me drynke" [3492].
>
> "Upon thy trouthe swere me heere" [3502].
>
> "Thou mayst nat werken after thyn owene heed" [3528].
>
> "Anon go gete us faste into this in
> A knedyng trogh, or ellis a kymelyn,
> For ech of us" [3547–49].
>
> "And han therinne vitaille suffisant
> But for a day" [3551–52].
>
> "Go now thy weye, and speed thee heer-aboute" [3562].
>
> "Go, God thee speede!" [3592].
>
> "Go now thy wey" [3596].
>
> "Go, save oure lyf [3600].

Because he is a good director and stage manager, and because his actors are eager to play their roles obediently, Nicholas's little game works out just fine. Alison says all the right things, John does all the right things, and Nicholas get his sexual reward from Alison in John's own bed the whole night long— well, almost the whole night long.

Nicholas does well until he self-directs himself to play a role in the bedroom farce by presenting his bottom out the shot-window, only to have it scorched. His role as amused farter has backfired for him. Whereas in *Heile of Beersele* the rectally cauterized priest runs madly off into the corner and falls into a cesspit, Nicholas recovers well enough immediately after his scorching to join Alison in summoning the neighbors. He directs them to think John mad. And they do: "he was holde wood in al the toun" (3846).

For Nicholas, then, the play's the thing. He plays the role of the randy younger cuckolder of the foolish old husband in the typical farce, and he himself directs others in their roles in that same farce. Nicholas enters the story as an actor. He begins by playing the role of the angel Gabriel as he sings the Annunciation: "And *Angelus ad virginem* he song" (3216). Nicholas soon makes a more direct approach to his lady the day her husband is away from the house on business. He begins to "pleye" (3273) with Alison. That term "play" need not necessarily refer to acting, of course, but in this context it may carry such overtones. Nicholas tries to play the role of courtly lover, referring to his "deerne love" for his "lemman":

> "Ywis, but if ich have my wille,
> For deerne love of thee, lemman, I spille" [3277–78].

It is all a pretense, of course. Nicholas knows, and Alison knows, that he will not die if he does not have his way with her. When she rejects his romantic little game, throws off his groping hands, and threatens to call for help, Nicholas assumes other roles, including the all-important one as farce-writer. His dramatic versatility makes him more successful than Alison's other would-be courtly lover.

Absolon in a Courtly Romance

If for old John the genre of choice is the bible story, and for Nicholas it is the theatrical farce, then for Absolon it is the romance. Although he is supposedly an ecclesiastic, he dresses and act more like a secular squire. His shoes are finely carved "with Poules wyndow" (3318) traced in the tops. He wears a "kirtle" or fancy-laced tunic:

> Yclad he was ful smal and proprely
> Al in a kirtel of a lyght waget;
> Ful faire and thikke been the poyntes set [3320–22].

The term "kirtle" is mentioned only one other time in Chaucer, as the apparel of the courtly squire Aurelius in the *Franklin's Tale* (line V 1580). Absolon is described in other ways as a romance hero. He has "eyen greye as goos" (3317) and is "a myrie child" (3325), both common descriptors of the romance squire. He dances in the Oxford manner and he plays love songs on his fiddle. He casts his "lovely look" (3342) upon the pretty wives in his parish, and is particularly taken with the lovely Alison whom he thinks of as "so propre and sweete" (3345). He has "in his herte swich a love-longynge" (3349) that he will take no offerings from the women—"for curteisie, he seyde" (3351). He serenades his lady by singing a love-lyric to his "deere lady" and begs, in proper courtly manner, for pity: "I preye yow that ye wole rewe on me" (3362). He tries in every manner, including "gentillesse" (3382), to woo the fair Alison. If we did not know he was the parish clerk, we would assume that this woman-courting, sweet-talking, fancy-dressing young man was a squire trying to get into the good graces of his lord's pretty wife. But because we do know that he is a parish clerk, we smile at his romantic pretensions.

On the fateful Monday night of his final encounter with Alison, the "joly lovere Absolon" (3688) gets up and "hym arayeth gay" (3689). This courtly lover, the "amorous Absolon / That is for love alwey so wo bigon" (3757–58), determines to go to Alison's window again to "tellen al / My lovelongynge" (3678–79). In proper courtly manner, he intends not to ask for anything so gross as sexual congress, but dreams instead of kissing and of being "at a feeste" (3684). In his courtly reticence and indirection, of course, he stands in contrast not only with the grabby Nicholas in the *Miller's Tale*, but also with his counterpart Hughe the smith in *Heile of Beersele*, both of whom are out for immediate sexual gratification. In preparation for his courtly encounter with Alison, the "joly lovere Absolon" (3688) sweetens his breath, combs his hair, and then goes to give his courtly love-speech at Alison's window:

> "What do ye, hony-comb, sweete Alison,
> My faire bryd, my sweet cynamome?
> Awaketh, lemman myn, and speketh to me!
> Wel litle thynken ye upon my wo,
> That for youre love I swete ther I go.
> No wonder is thogh that I swelte and swete;
> I moorne as dooth a lamb after the tete.
> Ywis, lemman, I have swich love-longynge
> That lik a turtel trewe is my moornynge.
> I may nat ete na moore than a mayde" [3698–3707].

Absolon speaks like a true courtly lover, with all foppish politeness. Unimpressed with his courtly nonsense, however, Alison spurns him. Perhaps she thinks his courtly pretensions are nonsense. Perhaps she prefers men like Nicholas who are more direct in expressing and grabbing for what they desire. Perhaps, as an earthy woman who is compared with animals and birds and plants in the natural world, she simply does not understand the romance genre well enough to know what poor Absolon is up to.

Whatever Alison's reasons for spurning the parish clerk, Absolon quite clearly sees himself as the young squire of medieval romance who is playing formal suit to the wife of another man. He tries to play his little game according to the rules as he understands them. He makes no mention of Andreas Capellanus's *The Art of Courtly Love*, but seems to have read some romances based on Andreas's principles and to have envisioned himself as a romance hero paying formal and stylized court to a romance heroine. While he has learned the principles of proper behavior for a love-sick squire, he never quite understands that he is applying the wrong literary register to the wrong woman, and his failure is inevitable.

Hughe, the smith in *Heile of Beersele* and Absolon's counterpart, is what he says he is, a horny blacksmith who wants sex from his neighbor and makes an arrangement to get it. He engages in a bit of playacting only in the third window scene, when he brings his hot iron back and pretends not to know what he has kissed and to demand another kiss:

> "Heile, lieu minne,
> Ic moet nu endelike inne
> Ochtic moew cussin v mondekijn;
> Deen vanden tween moew emmer sijn,
> Ochtic sta hier al den nacht,
> Hier toe dwinget mi uwer minned cracht [137–42].
>> [Heile, my love, I must now either come in or kiss your little mouth. It must be one of the two, or I will stay here all night. The strength of my love for you compels me to do this.]

Having been cured of his love-sickness, Hughe actually hates Heile by now, but he playacts his continued infatuation.

Absolon also camouflages his hatred for Alison under the guise of adoration and sweet talk:

> "God woot, my sweete leef,
> I am thyn Absolon, my deerelyng" [3792–93].

Absolon, however, adds a bit of acting business that Hughe had not bothered with: he offers Alison a special bribe:

> "Of gold," quod he, "I have thee broght a ryng
> My mooder yaf it me, so God me save;
> Ful fyn it is, and thereto wel ygrave,
> This wol I yeve thee, if thou me kisse" [3794–97].

Rising to his acting role, Absolon pretends to have a valuable prop. The only prop he really has, of course, is a hot coulter.

Absolon acts so much that he may no longer be able to distinguish between his true self and his acting self. He is a parish clerk, in training to be a priest, yet he acts the role of the town lush by visiting all of the local brewhouses, and the role of the town courtly lover by "sensyng the wyves of the parisshe" (3341). Perhaps even he is not sure, the night he serenades Alison at the window, whether she is the Virgin Mary to him or the non-virgin Alison.[4]

There is even some reason to suspect that Absolon is uncertain of his own sexuality. He has a voice "gentle and smal" (3360), and he is "a myrie child" (3325). He thinks he wants to be a servant to a pretty woman, but he has no idea how to behave with a woman and so puts on what he thinks is the proper act: singing, combing his curly yellow hair, scenting his breath, and, of course, playacting the role of Herod. Does he really like women as much as he claims to, or is that just an act? Perhaps we see a more genuine Absolon in his brief interaction with the smith Gerveys than we do anywhere else in the tale. There we find, for once, no acting, just friendship and a request for help. It is interesting that one unpleasant incident at the first window scene seems to turn Absolon away from women altogether and forever:

> His hoote love was coold and al yqueynt;
> For fro that tyme that he hadde kist hir ers,
> Of paramours he sette nat a kers,
> For he was heeled of his maladie.
> Ful ofte paramours he can deffie,
> And weep as dooth a child that is ybete [3754–59].

If love is a "malady" that he is so easily cured of,[5] was it ever love to begin with, or was that all just an act?

Absolon's playacting reaches its zenith in the first of the Monday window scenes, where he kneels before the niche of the Alison he pretends to adore. Playing his role as a lover adoring Alison to the hilt, but confusing that role with his role as a cleric adoring Mary, he kneels for his kiss:

> This Absolon doun sette hym on his knees
> And seyde, "I am a lord at alle degrees" [3723–24].

Like John and Nicholas (cf. "And thanne shul we be lordes al oure lyf" [3581]), Absolon pridefully aspires to be a lord. His kneeling—a standard gesture in medieval biblical drama to show religious devotion, subservience, and humility[6]—is comically juxtaposed to his desire to be a lord. And it is just possible that it is part of his lordly aspiration that he wants—or pretends to want—Alison in the first place. Alison is, after all, a flower lovely enough "for any lord to leggen in his bedde" (3269).

Will the real Absolon please stand up? Absolon is so busy acting one role after another that we scarcely know whether he is a man or a maid, a grownup or a child, a cleric or a lecher. We sense that he is not so sure, either. In his day-job he is a priest-in-training preparing for a life of humble devotion to Mary. In his dream-life he is a gentle courtly lover wooing with song, action, word, and gesture the lovely wife of another man. On the stage he is the ranting Herod. It is interesting that this Herod-playing actor seems most at home on a dance floor or a stage. Far more like a showing-off child than like a child-killing Herod, Absolon can nevertheless play the role, thinking absurdly to impress Alison. Immature in his love, he learns the lines of the lover but lacks the feelings:

> "Ywis, lemman, I have swich love-longynge
> That lik a turtel trewe is my moornynge.
> I may nat ete na moore than a mayde" [3705–07].

In the middle of the night, with his ire and his hot coulter raised, he is a vengeful terror.[7] Who can be sure who or what he really is?

None of the three men in *Heile of Beersele* have any pretensions to literature. So far as we can tell, they all "court" Heile in the same way and for the same purposes. That is, they all want to have paid-for sex with a prostitute. The priest, Nicholas's counterpart, is bookish enough to quote the scriptures to Heile after he has sex with her, but he is in no sense the director of the actions in the plot. Willem, old John's counterpart, takes his place in the tub that hangs from the beam, but he never spouts a single proverb, refers to a biblical story, or sees himself as a new Noah about to be the patriarch of a purified race of men and women. Hughe, jolly Absolon's counterpart, is a presumably unlettered blacksmith who shows no evidence of ever having read or heard a romance, or of imagining himself as a romantic squire or Heile as a fitting object of his desires. The idea of having the three men see themselves in connection with three literary registers is clearly the work of the literarily-inclined Chaucer.

Would Robyn the Miller have the interest in or aptitude for literary genres that the tale reflects? We should recall that the Miller reacts so strongly to the Knight's romance that he insists on matching it with one of his own. We should recall that he has seen enough biblical drama to approximate the voice of Pontius Pilate. The *Miller's Tale*, of course, was written by the literarily sophisticated and brilliant Chaucer for the Miller. There is no reason to be troubled by assumptions about the supposed lack of literary sophistication of the teller. Chaucer describes the Miller as a "janglere and a goliardeys" (540)—that is, a man who liked to tell stories. That the stories he liked most to tell were "of synne and harlotrie" (541; cf. 3184) does not mean that he knew no other genres, but merely that he did not like to tell tales in those genres. There is no reason he could not refer to those other genres in one of his harlotries.

Much of the humor of this particular harlotry lies in the disjunction of the different literary registers that these three foolish men associate themselves with. John sees himself as the hero of a set of moral proverbs and biblical narratives in which he is destined to be the patriarch of a purified and newly populated earth. Nicholas sees himself as the hero in and the director of a theatrical farce in which he is destined to cuckold an old husband. Absolon sees himself as the hero of a sophisticated courtly romance in which he is destined to be successful in his pursuit of the love of another man's wife. With three men acting out their heroic roles in plots from three different literary registers, there is bound to be conflict, and in that conflict there is bound to be humor.

Part of the humor is that all three would-be heroes fail to be heroic. John envisions himself as the wise, good, and faithful hero of biblical adventure, but he turns out to be the proverbially foolish cuckold and to be apparently abandoned by the very God to whom he had envisioned himself as the faithful servant. Nicholas directs a farce in which he is to be the hero, but he turns out to be the victim in a quite different kind of farce, one directed by a principle of poetic justice that he does not understand and cannot control. And far from being the hero of a courtly romance, Absolon turns out to be a man who rarely appears in romance—the lover who does not like real women as much as he imagines he does and who receives for his effort first a hirsute kiss that revolts him and then a gaseous eruption that blinds him.

Conflict, of course, abounds, and the conflict is funny. John is so busy being the new Noah that he never imagines that Nicholas is working in a different literary register, and he overlooks Absolon entirely. Nicholas is so busy directing John in his little farce that he fails fully to understand that John wants to play a role in his own genre and that his rival Absolon will seek vengeance. Absolon is so busy being the courting squire of medieval romance that it never occurs to him that plots in two other genres are taking place simultaneously. These medieval Three Stooges are all punished for their self-centered foolishness.

Alison in a Fabliau

Alison plays her role not in a biblical story, not in a theatrical farce, not in a romance, but in a fabliau. She is a bit like Margery, the merchant's wife in *Dame Sirith*. She is young, pretty, and married. When propositioned by a would-be seducer, Alison, like Margery, at first resists:

> "Why, lat be!" quod she. "Lat be, Nicholas!
> Or I wol crie, 'out, harrow' and 'allas'!
> Do wey youre handes, for your curteisye!" [3285–87].

Unlike Margery, however, Alison needs no persuasion by another woman with an absurd tale about a daughter being transformed into a weeping bitch. She yields to Nicholas of her own free will and has the backbone to insist on her own conditions—that Nicholas be patient and discreet:

> And swoor hir ooth, by Seint Thomas of Kent.
> That she wol been at his comandement,
> Whan that she may hir leyser wel espie.
> "Myn housbonde is so ful of jalousie
> That but ye wayte well and been privee,
> I woot right wel I nam but deed," quod she [3291–96].

Brighter and more independent than the gullible Margery, Chaucer's Alison of Oxford is more like the wives in Chaucer's other fabliaux: the resourceful wife of St. Denis in the *Shipman's Tale*, the sharp-witted May of Lombardy in the *Merchant's Tale*, and the staff-swinging wife of Trumpington in the *Reeve's Tale*. Alison knows what she wants—she wants Nicholas—and she gets him.

Alison does a bit of playacting. She pretends to her husband that she is a faithful and loving wife—a role that virtually all fabliau wives play in their marriages. She pretends to Absolon that she will let him kiss her face, but that bit of role-playing ends seconds later with her famous "Tehee!" She is a joyfully eager deceiver of the foolish old John, a joyfully eager bed-partner of the bold Nicholas, a joyfully eager punisher of the persistent Absolon. Her three men cast themselves as heroes of their assumed literary genres and are hilariously brought down to more appropriate roles. Though Alison is somewhat typical of fabliau wives, she does not seem to think of herself as the heroine of any literary genre. She turns out, however, to be the heroine of all three of the genres insisted upon by the others. Perhaps the funniest part of the comedy of the *Miller's Tale* is that Alison, whom the three men think of as the luscious prize in their own plots, manages to take charge of all three plots. She sneaks away from the little ark in John's replay of the Old Testament story, then on her own initiative sticks her bottom out the window in Nicholas's farce, and in doing so boldly turns her back on Absolon's romance. Through her beauty, her intelligence, her quiet insistence on her own needs, and her deep sense of realism, she makes swine of her three literary suitors.

Alison's counterpart in *Heile of Beersele* is of course Heile herself. A prostitute who sells sex for money, Heile does little role-playing beyond a little professional deception. She pretends to be sick when her appointments overlap. When her second client, the priest, comes to visit her, she has to say something in reply to Willem's question about who it is:

> "Willem, in weets niet, maer
> Het dinct mi die pape wesen.
> Hi soude mi ouer thoeft lesen

> Ende beteren mi dat mi deert" [60–63].
>
> ["Willem, I don't know who it is, but it may be the priest. Perhaps he has come to say a prayer to make me better from my sickness."]

Then, when the visit of the third lover, Hughe the smith, overlaps with that of the priest, she must pretend to be sick to get rid of this new complication:

> "Want in ben niet wel ghesont;
> Ghine moget niet in comen nu" [104–05].
>
> ["I am not well; you may not come in now."]

The nature of her supposed illness is not specified, however, and she does not make much of it. That whole scene is at best awkward. Heile's pretending not to want to have Hughe visit her at all is a problem in the Middle Dutch tale, since she needs the money and has, after all, made an appointment with him. The credibility of her response to Hughe is strained even further when she suggests that the priest trick Hughe into kissing his bottom. Hughe, after all, had done nothing more than make an appointment to pay her for sex. The problem is caused by Heile's time management practices, not Hughe's miscalculations. Absolon deserves to be tricked in the ass-kissing scene. Hughe does not.

Alison is more deceptive than Heile, and her deception is far more logical. Alison deceives her own husband, a man who invites and deserves such deception. The motivation for getting rid of her husband is not an issue for Heile, who is not married. Heile deceives paying customers whose business she needs, not a foolish old husband who stands between her and her lover. Alison playacts her faithfulness to John, pretending a love and a loyalty that are false. She fakes a fear of death by drowning to get her old husband out of the way so she can enjoy the embraces of young Nicholas. "Ferde as" in the first line below means "acted as if," the very kind of dramatic pretending that I am speaking of:

> But nathelees she ferde as she wolde deye,
> And seyde, "Allas! go forth thy wey anon,
> Help us to scape, or we been dede echon!
> I am they trewe, verray wedded wyf;
> Go, deere spouse, and help to save oure lyf" [3606–10].

It is all pretense, of course. Alison pretends to be a faithful wife even as she plans to deceive her husband. Her deception does not bother most readers, however, because John, for all his jealousy and his apparent concern for Alison, is a self-deceiving fool who, for thinking he can become a Noah-like lord of the world, deserves to be deceived.

II. Four Genres

Alison's playacting with Absolon is equally justified. She tries to be honest and blunt:

> "Go fro the wyndow, Jakke fool," she sayde;
> "As help me God, it wol nat be 'com pa me.'
> I love another—and elles I were to blame—
> Wel bet than thee, by Jhesu, Absolon" [3708-11].

Only after Absolon refuses to accept her rejection of him does Alison decide to punish him by tricking him into kissing her buttocks. That act is itself a kind of playacting, since she lets her buttocks temporarily masquerade as her face.

Alison playacts again at the very end of the tale when she works with Nicholas to convince the neighbors that her husband is mad. Neighbors play no role in *Heile of Beersele*, but in Chaucer's retelling they serve as the final insult to old John. Convinced by the deception of Alison and Nicholas, they laugh at John's mad foolishness. There is a nice irony in that closing scene. Old John was eager enough to save himself, his wife, and his boarder, eager enough to abandon his supposedly evil neighbors to the rising flood waters. It is fitting that they get the last laugh.

Alison seems not to be aware that she is playing a role in a fabliau. She just does what comes natural to her. In comparison with John, Nicholas, and Absolon, Alison is the least inclined to play different roles. The roles she does play are a part of her nature. She unselfconsciously acts the role of a faithful wife not because she is trying to fit into a genre, not because she wants to be a fabliau wife, but because that is the only way she can think of for a lovely young woman to deal with her jealous old husband. She pretends to be a willing kisser of Absolon, but only because she can think of no better way to get him out of her life. Perhaps because she does not think about the genre of the adventure she is having in Oxford, but just plays herself, she is the only one of the four who is not punished. The *Miller's Tale*, then, is on one level about a conflict of genres and about the humor that results when three foolish men fail to see that their rivals are operating within the traditions of different literary genres than they are. They fail to see that the woman they all desire refuses to play a role in any of their genres. The men in *Heile of Beersele* never quite realize that they are playing roles in a fabliau about the risks to men who engage in lechery with a prostitute. The men in the *Miller's Tale* never quite realize that they are they are playing roles in fabliau about the risks to men who engage in adultery with a married woman. The men in both fabliaux are punished for their shortsightedness. The women, wiser and more resourceful, escape unpunished.

III

Seeing and Hearing

In writing the *Miller's Tale* Chaucer shifted away from his Middle Dutch source to make the experience of the story more like the experience of attending a theater. He made his tale more visible and more audible. That is, he made sure that his reading or listening audience could "see" what his characters looked like and "hear" what they said.

One of Chaucer's changes was to make some of the characters, particularly Alison and Absolon, more easily imagined visually, allowing us to "see" them in our mind as we read the words in the story. Curiously, Chaucer tells us little about what Nicholas or John look like. It may be that, since they are both fairly stock fabliau male characters—the randy young smart-ass college boy and the tired old cuckolded husband—Chaucer felt that it was not necessary to describe them in detail. Chaucer was more interested in the *Miller's Tale* in having his audience visualize the lovely female and effeminate male characters than the manly male ones.[1] In any case, Chaucer tells us more about Nicholas's room than he tells us about his person or his dress. Of his appearance we know only that he is "meke for to see" (3202). As for John, he seems a sufficiently stock character that Chaucer needs for us to know only that he is a "riche gnof" (3118), that he is "olde" (3225), and that he has "wedded newe a wyf" (3221). Our imaginations can fill in the rest. Chaucer wants us, however, to visualize Alison and Absolon quite clearly.

Desiring Alison

We have almost no idea what Heile of Beersele looks like. She is sexually attractive to at least three different men, so we can assume that she is reasonably young and reasonably pretty. That is an assumption only, because the Middle Dutch author gives us no description of what Heile of Antwerp looks like or even how old she is. On the other hand, we have a pretty good idea what Alison of Oxford looks like. Chaucer emphasizes several times her youth. Alison is "eighteene yeer" (3223), is "yonge" (3225, 3233), represents "youthe" (3230) in debate with age. We know her body type. She is tall and slender, with a body as "long as a mast, and upright as a bolt" (3264), and as "gent and smal" "as any wezele" (3234). She is "fair" (3234) and good to the touch— "softer than the wolle is of a wether" (3249). She has "a likerous ye" (3244), narrowly plucked "browes two / And tho were bent and blake as any sloo" (3245–46). Above Alison's brows is a forehead that shines like newly-minted gold:

> Ful brighter was the shyning of hir hewe
> Than in the Tour the noble yforged newe [3255–56].

Her mouth is delicious:

> Hir mouth was sweete as bragot or the meeth
> Or hoord of apples leyd in hey or heeth [3261–62].

Chaucer gives a full account of Alison's dress[2]:

> A ceynt she werede, barred al of silk,
> A barmclooth as whit as morne milk
> Upon hir lendes, ful of many a goore.
> Whit was her smok, and broyden al bifore
> And eek bihynde, on hir coler aboute,
> Of col-blak silk, withinne and eek withoute.
> The tapes of hir white voluper
> Were of the same suyte of hir coler;
> Hir filet brood of silk, and set ful hye.
> [...]
> And by hir girdel heeng a purse of lether
> Tasseled with silk and perled with latoun.
> [...]
> A brooch she baar upon upon hir lowe coler,
> As brood as is the boos of a bokeler.
> Hir shoes were laced on hir legges hye
> [3235–44, 3250–52, 3265–67].

Because he has been so detailed in his description of her, Chaucer has earned the right to call Alison blissful to see:

> She was ful moore blisful on to see
> Than is the newe pere-jonette tree [3247–48].

Chaucer sums it all up with these three lines that emphasize Alison's flower-like attractiveness to any man, be he lord or commoner:

> She was a prymerole, a piggesnye,
> For any lord to leggen in his bedde,
> Or yet for any good yeman to wedde [3268–70].

Chaucer not only tells us in great detail what Alison looks like and how she dresses in those early scenes, but also how she moves, often in animal-like terms:

> Therto she koude skippe and make game,
> As any kyde or calf folwynge his dame.
> [...]
> And she sproong as a colt doth in the trave
> And with her head she wryed faste awey [3259–60, 3282–83].

Because Chaucer describes Alison and her animal-actions so carefully early in the tale, we are able to visualize her athletic movement when, later, she climbs down her ladder, jumps into bed with Nicholas, sticks her bottom out the shot-window for Absolon's kiss, and then quickly turns and slams the shot-window shut.

Laughing at Absolon

Just as the Middle Dutch author is utterly vague in his description of Heile, leaving us totally to our own imaginations, so he is utterly vague in his description of Hughe the smith, the counterpart of Absolon. We know only that Hughe is a smith, which frees us to imagine, if we want to, that he had brawny shoulders from shoveling coal and lifting heavy hammers. Chaucer, however, lets us see Absolon much more clearly. There are more then a few hints that Absolon is effeminate in his physical appearance:

> Crul was his heer, and as the gold it shoon
> And strouted as a fanne large and brode;
> Ful streight and evene lay his joly shode [3314–16].

Chaucer tells us more about Absolon's dress. Not content to wear the simple surplice of a parish clerk, Absolon thinks he must dress for a more worldly role:

> With Poules wyndow corven on his shoos,
> In hoses rede he wente fetisly.
> Yclad he was ful smal and properly

> Al in a kirtel of a lyght waget;
> Ful faire and thikke been the poyntes set.
> And therupon he hadde a gay surplys
> As whit as is the blosme upon the rys [3318–23].

It is significant that to get ready for his confrontation with the lovely Alison on that fateful Monday night, the "joly lovere Absolon" (3688) gets all dressed up: "And hym arraieth gay, at point-devys" (3689). It is almost as if love—at least of women—is not something that comes naturally to him, but something he can playact only after he has dressed for his part.

Chaucer wants us to imagine some of the typical actions of jolly Absolon, but they are the actions of a performing dancer showing off the newest dance steps:

> In twenty manere koude he trippe and daunce
> After the scole of Oxenforde tho,
> And with his legges casten to and fro [3328–30].

His actions are those of the boudoir and the dance floor rather than of the street or the bedroom. We learn that "he kembeth his lokkes brode" (3374) and "cheweth greyn and lycorys / To smellen sweete, er he hadde kembd his heer" (3690–91), and then "cougheth with a semy soun" (3697) to get Alison's attention. These actions are those of a pretty-boy fop whose next action, kissing Alison's bottom, brings him face to face with a reality he does not like and cannot handle. Finally realizing the truth about his chances of succeeding as a lover of the fair Alison, and perhaps realizing that she is the sort of prize he does not want anyhow, he bites his lips "for angre" (3745) and goes to get the means for his revenge. By telling us about his looks, his dress, and his actions, Chaucer lets us visualize this child-woman-man strutting his hair on the stage of the *Miller's Tale*. The descriptions are such that Absolon strikes us as an object of ridicule.

Light and Dark

The author of *Heile of Beersele* tells us only in the most general terms about the lightness or darkness of that fateful night in Antwerp. We know that Willem visits Heile in the early evening ("rechts in den avont" [38]) when it is between day and night ("quan tuschen dach ende nacht" [47]). We know that the priest comes when the evening bell ("slaepcloccke" [54]) is rung, while the smith comes when the night bell ("diefclocke" [43]) is rung. We are apparently to make certain assumptions from those meager descriptions about how dark it is, but we find no explicit mention of light or darkness in the Middle Dutch tale.

Chaucer, on the other hand, serves as lighting engineer for the theatrical setting of his town. In a tale where so many of the key events take place at night, Chaucer feels the need to give his characters at least some moonlight. How, for example, does Absolon find his way through the unlighted streets of Oxford to serenade Alison? Chaucer makes a point of lighting the way for him:

> The moone, whan it was nyght, ful brighte shoon,
> And Absolon his gyterne hath ytake
> [...]
> And forth he gooth [3352–53, 3355].

Not long after that, Nicholas lies in his chamber on a Sunday night after "the sunne gooth to reste" (3422), John sends Robyn up to check on him. Robyn knocks and looks through the hole in a board and sees Nicholas in there. How could he see him in the dark? Well, Chaucer lets us know that he sees Nicholas "capyng upright, / As he had kiked on the newe moone" (3444–45), indicating that there is enough moonlight in the room to let Robyn see him. Nicholas himself reinforces that lighting a few lines later, when he tells John,

> "I have yfounde in myn astrologye,
> As I have looked in the moone bright,
> That now, a Monday next [...] [3514–16].

Chaucer's lighting devices are primitive by modern standards, but at least Chaucer mentions them. For example, when Chaucer dims the candles and the moon. John closes the door of his house that Monday night "withoute candle-lyght" (3634) so that no one outside will know what he and his chosen family are up to. Later we are told that Absolon kisses Alison's bottom when the night is as dark "as pich, or as the cole" (3731). These designations show that Chaucer wanted his characters to see—or, in the specified darkness, not to see—and wanted his readers to see them moving around in the shadows—or to imagine them stumbling around in the dark.

Hearing the Music

I return to Absolon's coughing at Alison's window to get her attention on that Monday night: "And softe he cougheth with a semy soun" (3697). Not only does Chaucer let us "see" the sights of the tale, but he lets us "hear" its sounds. Indeed, it is not such a great exaggeration to say that in writing the

Miller's Tale Chaucer was writing a musical comedy. Certainly music and sounds abound in this tale far more than they do in *Heile of Beersele*. To be sure, we do have in the Middle Dutch story an opening reference to music:

> Ghi hebe gehoert te menegher vre
> Vertrecken scone auonture
> Van messeliken dinghen,
> Beide vedelen ende singhen
> Ende somtijt spelen meter herpen [1–5].
> [You have often heard wonderful adventures about all manner of strange things, sometimes accompanied by singing and a fiddle, and sometimes by a harp.]

We find, however, almost no references to music or sounds in the Middle Dutch tale itself. There are references to the public bells that mark the divisions of the night (lines 40, 43, 54), but they can scarcely be considered music. The only direct reference to music in the tale comes when the priest cries out in the full anguish of a scorched anus:

> Doe sanc hi lude dit vers,
> "Water, water, ic ben doet!" [148–49].
> [Then he sang loudly this verse, "Water, water, I am dying."]

The Middle Dutch author's referring to the call for water as a "verse" that the priest "sang loudly" is apparently meant to be a humorously reductive reference to the priest's anything-but-musical scream for water.

I shall have more to say in Chapters IX and X about our "hearing" the voices of the characters in Chaucer's tale, but for now I want to consider just the music. Many of the sounds that we do hear in the *Miller's Tale* are musical sounds"[3] while other sounds offer humorously cacophonous contrast to that music. It is, of course, interesting that Robyn the Miller, a bagpipe-player with presumably a certain skill in music, is the teller of the most musical of all of the Canterbury tales. It would be tempting to imagine him as a kind of minstrel storyteller of the sort announced at the start of *Heile of Beersele*, but in fact there is no evidence whatever that he sings his tale or accompanies it with any sort of fiddle or harp. Still, Chaucer gives us so many references to music in the narrative itself that it appears that he set out to make his tale a kind of showcase for medieval music and contrastingly unmusical sounds.

Nicholas has "a gay sautrie" (psaltery[4]) on which at night he makes "melodie / So swetely that all the chambre rong" (3213–15). Nicholas is a singer, also, having been blessed with a "myrie throte" (3218). Chaucer even tells us two of the songs Nicholas sings, the *Angelus ad virginem* and the "Kynges Noote" (3216–17).[5] After he gets a promise from Alison that she will satisfy his lust, he pats her bottom and kisses her, then is so pleased with himself that he takes his psaltry and "pleyeth faste, and maketh melodie" (3306).

Nicholas is not alone in his musical aptitude. The lovely Alison likes to sing, with a voice as "loude and yerne / As any swalwe sittynge on a berne" (3257–58). Absolon is also musically inclined:

> [He] pleyen songes on a smal rybible;
> Therto he song som tyme a loud quynyble;
> And as wel koude he ply on a giterne [3331–33].

As part of his courtship of the fair Alison, Absolon serenades her "in his voys gentil and smal":

> "Now, deere lady, if thy wille be,
> I preye yow that ye wole rewe on me,"
> Ful wel acordaunt to his gyternynge [3360–63].

Later he courts her still again with music: "He syngeth, brokkynge as a nyghtyngale" (3377).

All that music, Chaucer tells us, is futile for poor Absolon, because Alison so loves Nicholas that poor Absolon might just as well "blow the bukkes horn" (3387) and "waile and singe 'allas'" (3398). Even sexual activity is described in musical terms. When Alison and Nicholas go to bed, we find Chaucer referring to "the revel and the melodye" (3652). And we know that it is time for Absolon to get up and come to Alison's window that Monday night only because "the bel of laudes gan to rynge, / And freres in the chauncel gonne synge" (3655–56).

The musical sounds are at counterpoint with the other sounds that abound in the *Miller's Tale*. The crowing of the cock (3357, 3675, 3687), the knocking at doors and windows (3432, 3436, 3676, 3764, 3788, 3791), the clapping of windows closing (3746), the coughing (3697, 3788), the farting "as greet as it had been a thonder-dent" (3807), the calls of "water" (3815), and "out," "harrow," "clom," "allas," and "weylaway" (3286, 3398, 3476, 3488, 3522–23, 3575, 3602, 3606, 3638–39, 3714, 3739, 3749, 3753, 3818, 3825), the laughing (3840, 3849), and of course the absurd noises of old John:

> He wepeth, weyleth, maketh sory cheere;
> He siketh with ful many a sory swogh.
> [...]
> For travaille of his goost he groneth soore,
> And eft he routeth, for his heed myslay [3618–19, 3646–47].

All in all, the *Miller's Tale* is one of the most audible of Chaucer's tales. Almost none of these sounds are in *Heile of Beersele*. We find that Hughe "clopte ... stille" [knocked softly] on Heile's door (96), and we find the minimalist expression "Ay" [Ah] repeated six times (58, 64, 98, 100, 106, 110), but beyond those small sounds, *Heile of Beersele* is as quiet as a mouse. By comparison, the *Miller's Tale* roars like a lion. It is apparent that Chaucer transformed the quiet narrative of his source into something that could be heard, something that could be listened to communally, rather than something to be read in quiet privacy. The *Miller's Tale* is not, of course, really a musical comedy in the modern sense, but it is full of music and other sounds, and it is a comedy.

IV
Comedic Realism

A comparison of the Middle Dutch *Heile of Beersele* with the *Miller's Tale* shows that Chaucer wanted to make his story more realistic,[1] more believable, than his source was. One of his reasons was that, because he was thinking theater when he wrote his version of the tale, Chaucer wanted his audience to believe that the characters were not just made-up people in an unlikely narrative, but actors who might actually perform the actions and speeches required of them by the plot. If Chaucer wanted his audience to be able to imagine the actions of the story as if it were being performed on a stage with live actors performing the actions, then he needed to provide the story with a measure of verisimilitude. I give below a series of examples that show Chaucer transforming the generally unlikely fictional materials of *Heile of Beersele* into a more believable series of theatrically imaginable actions.

Hanging a Tub

Heile happens to have hanging from the beams in her house a large trough. We do not know ahead of time that it is there, and the only explanation we get of why it is there is Heile's, to her first customer Willem on the arrival of her second customer, the priest. The explanation is that it comes in handy:

> Heile seide, "daer boven hangt .i. bac,
> Dies ic hier voermaels ghemac
> Hadde te menegen stonden" [67–69].
>> [Heile said, "up there hangs a trough that I have found convenient here on many previous occasions."]

We do not know how it got there and we are left to imagine in what ways it may have been "convenient" to her in the past—presumably to hide other clients who did not want to be discovered in the arms of a prostitute. And we are left to imagine how Willem manages to climb into the tub, which must be pretty high off the floor to make it plausible that he later breaks his leg and his arm by falling to the ground. The Middle Dutch author does not say how high the tub is or how Willem gets into it. Are we to imagine him standing on a high table, or shinnying up a rope, or climbing a ladder? In fact, we do not know because the author does not tell us.

Chaucer leaves far less to the imagination. We know why the three tubs are hanging from the beams—because at Nicholas's direction, foolish old John collects them, provisions them, and suspends them from the beams. As we will see when I discuss the structure of John's house in the next chapter, we know that the tubs are suspended some twenty feet off the floor. And we know how the three characters get into the tubs—by means of ladders that, following Nicholas's instructions, John has built. The realism is there, and we can imagine the actors in the Chaucerian stage-set using the ladders.

Counting the Times

The Middle Dutch author tells us that Heile makes love with the priest three times before the third lover, Hughe the smith, arrives:

> Heile dede den pape te ghemake
> Ende alsi die wiekewake
> Driewerf [75–77].
>   [Heile made the priest happy, and they made love three times.]

That fact may be amusing, but it is pretty unrealistic. We can scarcely imagine the priest to be a randy teenager in the prime of his youth, and whatever his recovery time, it would eat up a lot of the evening for him to perform three times, even with the skilled professional that we may imagine Heile to be. Besides, why would Heile, who knows that she has one client hanging around in the trough and another hanging around outside waiting his turn, let the priest proceed at such an apparently leisurely pace? We can perhaps imagine an explanation—that she is afraid of him, for example, or that she needs his priestly blessing, or that she does not want him to summon her to the ecclesiastical courts—but in fact the text offers no such explanation. Three times is not impossible, but little is gained by giving us an exaggerated number of "wiekewakes" with so unprofessional a prostitute.

By being less specific Chaucer does not strain our credibility:

> And thus lith Alison and Nicholas,
> In bisynesse of myrthe and of solas,
> Til that the belle of laudes gan to rynge,
> And freres in the chauncel gonne synge [3653–56].

We presume that the two young lovers, finally united in bed, are an active pair, but Chaucer does not strain our credibility by specifying precisely how often they make love.[2]

Preaching a Sermon

After he makes love three times with Heile, the priest preaches her a little mini-sermon:

> Ghinc die pape liggen ghewaghen
> Uter ewangelien menech woert.
> Oec soe seidi dit bat voert,
> Dat die tijt noch soude comen
> Dat God die werelt soude doemen,
> Beide met watre ende met viere;
> Ende dat soude wesen sciere
> Dat al die werelt verdrinken soude,
> Grote ende clene, jonge ende oude [78–86].
> [Then the priest quoted many words from the scriptures. He also said that the time would soon come when God would destroy the world with water and fire, drowning everyone in the world, great and small, young and old.]

The priest's motivation is not clear. Why after making love with a prostitute would a priest preach such a sermon? Perhaps we can imagine a plausible reason—for example, that he feels guilty about his sin and so warns both himself and Heile that they should get right with God before death takes them—but the Middle Dutch author gives no such explanation, and the priest's sermon remains a puzzling anomaly.

Chaucer's Nicholas makes a somewhat similar prediction about a coming flood that will drown all the world, but unlike the priest in *Heile of Beersele*, Nicholas has a reputation for being able to predict the weather:

> And koude a certeyn of conclusiouns,
> To demen by interrogaciouns,
> If that men asked hym, incertein houres
> Whan that men shoulde have droghte or elles shoures [3193–96].

John's acceptance of Nicholas's absurd prediction of a one-night flood that will destroy all of mankind is made believable by Chaucer's having made John precisely the sort of old fool who would buy into it. John is foolish enough to imagine that he can cage his wife, even as he accepts into the cage a randy young college boy. He is foolish enough not to imagine that his wife could be attracted to Nicholas or indeed to Absolon, who one night serenades his wife outside their bedroom window. He is foolish enough to imagine that God could select him to be a second Noah, even though God had made a covenant never to send another such flood. John's belief in Nicholas's absurd prediction is believable to us because we know that John is a fool.

Rejecting a Suitor

Heile is a prostitute in need of money who does what prostitutes in need of money do: makes appointments with three different men spaced far enough apart that she can pleasure them all and make a good night's wage. It seems strange enough that an experienced professional would not have spaced them farther apart so that the appointments would not overlap, or that she would not have kept better track of the time so that she had pushed one out the door before the next came a-knocking. The more realistic Chaucer avoids that problem by making Alison a wife rather than a prostitute. Alison makes no appointments. She accepts Nicholas not for money but for fun.

The lack of realism in the Middle Dutch story is even more pronounced when Heile rejects Hughe the smith, her third appointment. He is, after all, a paying customer who should have been good for more business. Instead of apologizing to him or whispering that she is busy and asking him return another time, she cruelly spurns him. When he asks for a kiss at least, she suggests that the priest humiliate him:

> "Ay, here, laet cussen desen knape
> U achterste inde, hi sal wanen wel
> Dat ict ben ende niemen el;
> Sone saeghdi boerde nie so goet" [110–13].
> ["Ah, sir, let this fellow kiss your behind, and he will surely think that it is I and no one else. You've never seen such a fine jest."]

The plot requires the buttocks-kissing so that the smith will be angry enough to go to get the hot iron, but realistically speaking no prostitute could afford to treat her appointed clients so cruelly. It is just bad business.

Chaucer makes the whole scene more believable. Alison rebuffs and insults Absolon with a cruel jest because she does not like him and because she has a man she likes better. She never invited Absolon to come and would not want any money he might offer. He has no appointment with her and is not welcome. When he will not take no as her answer but instead begs for a kiss, she is for that reason motivated to play her nasty trick on him. She behaves just as a frisky young woman, in bed with her real lover, would realistically react to the insistent, uninvited suitor who begs for a kiss.

Listening in a Tub

The Antwerp priest does not know that he has another auditor than Heile when he preaches his illogical little sermon. Willem, sitting in the trough above, overhears the priest's sermon:

> Dit hoerde Willem daer hi sat
> Boven hoge in ghenen bac,
> Ende peinsde het mochte wel waer wesen
> Sidermeer dat papen lesen,
> Ende dewangelie gheeft getughe [87–91].
> [Willem heard this from where he sat high above in the trough and thought it might well be true, since priests read the gospels, and the gospels bore witness to it.]

Immediately, however, there is a problem: if Willem is close enough to the bedroom that he can hear the priest's sermon, how is it that he has apparently not also heard the sounds, however muffled, of the priest's triple-encounter with Heile, and how is it that, immediately after he hears the sermon that is not intended for his ears, he apparently does not also hear the conversation between Heile and Hughe? If he had heard it, and had heard Heile telling the priest to let the smith kiss his buttocks, why does Willem know so little about what goes on that he does not realize, a few minutes later, that there really is no flood? He has, after all, been awake the whole time, has heard no thunder, seen no lightning, observed no patter of rain on the roof over his head. His assumption that the predicted flood has come makes no sense whatever.

Chaucer treats that whole scene more realistically. After his hard day's work of acquiring, provisioning, hanging, and laddering the three tubs, poor old John is exhausted. Almost immediately he falls asleep:

> The dede sleep, for wery bisynesse,
> Fil on this carpenter right, as I gesse,
> Aboute corfew-tyme, or litel moore [3643–45].

Old John does not hear Absolon's conversations with Alison because he is dead asleep the whole time. He sleeps, however fitfully, with his head cocked at a strange angle on the edge of his tub, nervously "Awaitynge on the reyn, if he it heere" (3642). The next thing he hears in his slumber is the "thonder-dent" (3807) of a fart and then Nicholas's cry, "Help! Water! Water! Help, for Goddes herte!" (3815). Having heard nothing of the conversations between Absolon and Alison, he quite understandably assumes from the thunderclap and from the cry for water that the flood has come. It turns out to be a wrong assumption, but Chaucer, unlike the Middle Dutch author, has set things up in such a way that we accept that assumption as believable.

Penetrating I

When Hughe kisses the priest's bottom, he does so with such zeal and force that his nose penetrates the priest's anus:

> Ende Huge waende that Heile ware
> End custe spapen ers al dare
> Met soe heten sinne,
> Dat sine nese vloech daer inne,
> Soe dat die smet, sonder waen
> Harde well waende sijn gevaen
> Gelijc der mese inder cloven [117–23].
>> [And Hughe thought it was Heile and kissed the priest's arse right there with such hot desire that his nose shot inside, so that the smith undoubtedly thought that he was caught like a titmouse in a trap.]

That may be good slapstick comedy, but it is not believable. We all know that the human sphincter would not permit the penetration of even the most Pinocchio-like human nose. This action could not happen on a real stage, but because Heile's men are caricatures, not realistic men, it happens in *Heile of Beersele*.

Chaucer eliminates the impossible nose-penetration:

> And Absolon, hym fil no bet ne wers,
> But with his mouth he kiste hir naked ers
> Ful savourly, er he were war of this [3733–35].

The penetration in the Middle Dutch story we cannot believe; the "savourly" in the English story we can. The "savourly" is, for Absolon, a pretty realistic detail. His mouth has "icched al this longe day" (3682) and at night he has dreamed that he was "at a feeste" (3684). At the window he tells Alison that he yearns for her "as dooth a lamb after the tete" (3704). It is not strange at all that a young man who so consistently associates love with eating, should kiss his beloved "ful savoury." Note that we are not speaking of delicacy here, but of realism. The problem with the Middle Dutch story is not that it is scatological, but that it is unrealistic. Chaucer, who added the fart to the story, was not above scatology, but he wanted it to be realistic scatology. A nose penetrating an anus we cannot believe; a gaseous eruption from an anus we can.

Getting the Hot Iron

Deeply insulted by his misdirected kiss, Hughe angrily rushes home to his smithy and heats up a hot iron:

> Hi liep thuus alse die was erre;
> Hine woende van daer niet verre.
> Een groet yser nam hi gereet
> Ende staect int vier ende maket heet
> Soe dat gloyde wel ter cure [131–35].
> [He ran home as if he were mad. He lived not far from there. He immediately took a big iron, stuck it into the fire and made it so hot that it glowed, just the way he wanted it to.]

On the one hand it seems both logical and economical for a blacksmith in need of a hot iron to run right home and fetch one. On the other, we might realistically assume, though we are not told, that he had let his hearth go cold at the end of the day in anticipation of his visit to Heile, so his returning home to heat up the hearth again would have taken some time—perhaps enough time for his rage to cool, and for him to approach the fateful window the second time with more caution.

Chaucer changed that by having Absolon visit a friend, Gerveys, who already has his smithy up and running, with a hot coulter already there in the forge—"that hoote kultour in the chymenee heere" (3776). He can then, after a very brief conversation with Gerveys, grab the coulter "by the colde stele" of the handle (3786) and rush back with it. In the heat of his anger he knocks again at the window, never thinking that the woman he intends to punish may be cleverer than he, never anticipating that the bottom he scorches may be that of a man rather than of the woman he has come to loathe. He applies his instrument of revenge effectively enough, but does so in such a way that he himself is punished again, this time with a blinding fart in the face. Hughe the smith is not punished a second time. There is no need for him to be punished even the first time because he has done no wrong, unless it is wrong to want to have sex with a prostitute. Absolon deserves not only the first punishment but the second as well, since he is a vow-breaking fraud of a parish clerk who stupidly presses his suit on a woman who has twice rejected him. Chaucer carefully sets the smithy-scene up so that Gerveys has the hot coulter ready, thus permitting Absolon to act quickly and without considering the possible consequences, thereby bringing on his own second and much-deserved punishment.

Penetrating II

When the priest puts his buttocks out the window to receive a second kiss, Hughe thrusts while his iron is hot:

> End die smet stac ongelet
> Tgheloyende yser in den ers [146–47].
>
> > [And the smith immediately stuck the red-hot iron into his arse.]

While it may be funny to have the priest sodomized twice—first by Hughe's nose, then by Hughe's hot iron—it seems, again, a literary contrivance rather than a realistic moment. It is, after all, pitch dark, the human anus is a narrow target, and Hughe has no hint about where to aim his hot iron.

Chaucer treats the second window scene more realistically. For one thing, the weapon is a coulter, the broad plow knife designed to cut the earth vertically before the plowshare cuts it horizontally and turns it over. It is just the sort of implement that a blacksmith would be likely to have heating up in his hearth in the very early dawn of a spring morning, prior to sharpening it for the Oxford farmer who would use it that day.[3] For another, since it is not yet dawn, Absolon's aim cannot be so precise. He has, after all, only the sound of the fart to guide him—itself a realistic element, since Hughe does not have any clue at all to guide his thrust. Even if the early dawn light were beginning to make Nicholas's buttocks visible—and we are not told that it was—Chaucer tells us that Absolon has been blinded by the fart:

> This Nicholas anon leet fle a fart
> As greet as it had been a thonder-dent,
> That with the strook he was almoost yblent [3806–08].

It is realistic enough that, striking blindly, the angry Absolon strikes Nicholas not in the anus, even if he had been aiming for that specific part of the anatomy, but "amydde the ers" (3810). Given the flattened-profile of a plow coulter, it seems appropriate that "hende" Nicholas receives not a puncture wound but, rather, a burn "an hande-brede aboute" (3811).[4] Because in the opening scene Nicholas has his hands on Alison's haunchebones, it is appropriate that he be punished in the closing scene with a different kind of hand on his own. Besides, Chaucer has another role for Nicholas to play, one that requires that he be not so deeply wounded as the priest is in *Heile of Beersele*.

Falling into a Cesspit

The priest in *Heile of Beersele* is double-punished. First, he has his anus scorched by a cauterizing hot iron wielded by Hughe the blacksmith. His shout "Water, water" leads Willem to cut the rope[5] suspending his tub. Willem's crashing down so surprises the priest that he thinks the devil has come. To escape the devil, the fearful priest rushes into the corner, where he receives his second punishment by falling into a cesspit:

> Die pape scoet in een winkel
> Ende waende dat die duvel ware;
> In enen vulen putte viel hi dare,
> Alsoe alsmen mi doet weten
> Quam hi thuus all besceten
> Ende sinen ers al verbrant [172–77].
>> [The priest ran into a corner, thinking [Willem] was the devil, and fell into a foul pit, as I have been told, and then went home all beshitten and with his arse branded.]

Chaucer ma.de a significant change in moving the cleric from the inside of the house, where he is in the Middle Dutch tale, to the outside. Absolon is not yet a full-fledged priest, of course, but this sensor-swinging parish clerk apparently aspires to be one. In any event, he is the recipient of the anticlerical theme so characteristic of the fabliaux. By moving the priest outside and putting Nicholas inside, Chaucer switched the scheme of punishment. Still wanting the priest to receive a double-punishment, Chaucer replaces one scatological element for another—and more realistic—one. How logical is it, after all, to find a "vulen putte" (174) [foul cesspit] inside the house? Certainly we are not told in advance that one is there, and there is no mention of the reek or vermin that must have been associated with such a location.

Chaucer makes no mention of the sanitary facilities associated with John's house in the *Miller's Tale*, leaving us to assume, if we want to, that there was probably the usual outhouse someplace in the back yard. His plot requires no such site, so there is no reason for him to have mentioned it. He does, however, provide a double-punishment for the cleric Absolon. The first is the foul arse-kiss, the second is the foul fart. Both of these are logical enough given the details of characterization that Chaucer gives to the fair Alison who presents her buttocks for Absolon to kiss, and to the raunchy Nicholas, who produces the fart. Both of these punishments, given the preparation Chaucer has given them, are entirely logical in the story that Chaucer has so elaborately set up.

Chaucer's *Miller's Tale*, then, is far more realistic than *Heile of Beersele*. It is so realistic that some readers have even assumed that the story is based somehow on "real life."[6] My own point is not that the events of the *Miller's Tale* actually did happen, either to the pilgrims on the road to Canterbury or to some actual historical people. The events of the tale are, after all, not all *that* realistic, and we are aware always that we are dealing here with fiction, not actual life. My point is that we can in the *Miller's Tale*, far more than in *Heile of Beersele*, imagine the events as actually happening to human beings. Unlike the Middle Dutch author, clever though he was in telling a funny anecdote, Chaucer made a series of narrative moves with that anecdote that help us to imagine the story as being about people whose behavior is in accord with human nature.

More than in his source, then, and more than in any other of his own tales, Chaucer seems to have been thinking "drama" when he wrote the story of John, Alison, Nicholas, and Absolon. Chaucer made his characters more like actors in a play, people whose actions we can readily imagine real actors performing on a stage. Chaucer even provided a "set" that works pretty well as a "stage" for their actions. To understand what I mean, we need to consider what we know or can learn about certain structural features of John's house.

V

The Structure of John's House

Scholars have been understandably vague about the details of the structure of John's house in the *Miller's Tale*. To be sure, every reader knows that Nicholas has a bedroom with a door that John and Robyn smash in. Every reader knows that the house has beams of some sort from which John suspends the three tubs. Every reader knows that the master bedroom has a window out of which Alison and Nicholas present their buttocks for Absolon to kiss. Modern generations of readers have been enjoying the tale knowing only these general facts about John's house. They may, however, enjoy the tale more and better visualize the setting for its nocturnal shenanigans if they pick up from certain details that Chaucer provides a deeper understanding of the structure of the house. What kind of house was it? In what sense do John and Robyn break into Nicholas's chamber? What sort of window is there in John's bedroom, and how do Alison and Nicholas open and close it? What kind of beams are those three tubs suspended from? How far does John fall when he chops his rope in two, and what is the "celle" that he break his arm on? In this section I want to offer answers, some of them a bit tentative, to those questions.[1]

The Timber-Framed House

Virtually all houses in Oxford in the fourteenth century were rectangular or square in floor plan.[2] We can assume that John's house in the *Miller's Tale* was also, if only because Chaucer tells us that John, thinking that Nicholas may be dead, tries to bless his house and make it safe from elves or other evil creatures:

> Therwith the nyght-spel seyde he anon-rightes
> On foure halves of the house aboute,
> And on the thresshfold of the dore withoute [3479–81].

The four sides, as well as the practical realities of building with wood, would make it difficult to imagine anything other than a square or rectangular house.

Almost certainly, John's house was what was called a timber-framed or box-framed building. By Chaucer's time, most domestic buildings were of that sort. The older "earthfast" construction had by Chaucer's time been largely abandoned. In the earthfast form of construction, the posts were set right into the ground two or three feet apart—something like the modern "pole barn." See Figure 1.

Figure 1. The earthfast house, largely abandoned by Chaucer's time for domestic architecture (Gene Mater Studios, www.genemater.com).

Figure 2. A timber-framed house on a raised stone foundation—common building practice in Chaucer's time (Gene Mater Studios, www.genemater.com).

The advantages of such construction were that the earthfast house was quick to build and that the earth itself provided lateral stability against winds, thus reducing the need for bracing. The main disadvantage of earthfast construction was that, in the days before treated lumber and wood preservatives, the posts would rot off at the ground level, so that the house needed to be rebuilt every twenty years or so.

By Chaucer's time the earthfast house had long since given way to the timber-framed house, in which all of the wood was placed above ground. The posts, then, were not set into the earth, but were mortised, that is notched, into a wooden ground-sill or base plate that stretched horizontally around the perimeter of the house and along the bays or structural divisions within the house. See Figure 2.

V. The Structure of John's House

The width of the "bays" was governed by the length and strength of the timbers at one's disposal, but typically were around 12 or 14 feet wide. The walls that edged each side of the bay were bearing walls that supported the construction above. The principle advantages of the timber-framed house are obvious enough. First, they lasted longer, since the wood was kept dry above the ground, with the ground-sill or base plate often resting on short stone columns ("plinths") or on short dwarf walls. Second, the bay walls could be laid out and fastened together horizontally on the ground, then raised vertically into place. See Figure 3.

The third advantage of the timber-framed house is its flexibility. A house could be made taller by the addition of a storey or, more commonly, made longer by the addition of one or more bays to the first one. The assembly of the additional storeys and bays was easiest if done when the building was initially built, but they could be added later, as well. See Figure 4.

The key disadvantage of the timber-framed house was that it lacked lateral stability against the wind. That stability in the timber-framed house was provided by various kinds of angle-bracing. See Figure 5.

Variations of the timber-framed house are still being built in the twentieth century, though the older "post and beam" construction has usually been supplanted by the use of stud walls, and the angle beams for bracing have been supplanted by the use of plywood as the exterior sheath.

Balks, Beams and Soot

How are the rooms in John's house laid out? We cannot be sure, of course, but we know from the storyline that there is a door with a threshold on the main floor, at least one window, and in the peak, a gable. The gable would have been of wattle and daub—a kind of plaster mixture smeared on and reinforced by woven branches. Such a gable would have been easy enough to chop through with an axe. It seems that there are at least three rooms in John's house. First, we know that Nicholas's chamber is on a second floor, with a stairway leading up to it and a door leading into it. Second, the bedroom that John and Alison share on the ground floor has a low window opening to the street. Third, there is a high-ceilinged room wide enough that three tubs can hang there reasonably far apart, with open beams strong enough to hold up the three tubs, each with a full-grown person inside, and with a ceiling high enough that John needs to build ladders so that he, his wife, and his boarder can climb into them, high enough that in his fall John will break his arm.[3]

Anyone familiar with the construction of medieval houses would have recognized that the high-ceilinged room was the open hall. It would have had an open fireplace area in the middle of the room, with no chimney. Chimneys were sometimes found in the fourteenth century, but only in very large structures or in the homes of the very rich.

Everyone else got along with an open fire right in the middle of the earthen floor, something like an indoor campfire. The fire was used primarily for cooking, but it also provided some heat. What happened to the smoke from such a fire? That would have gone straight upstairs into what was called the smoke bay. Indeed, the only reason to have a large, high-ceilinged hall in a medieval house was to provide a lofty place for the smoke to collect and to provide sufficient clearance above the open fire that sparks from it would not set the house on fire. The smoke rising from the fire would collect at the top of the smoke bay before seeping out through the thatch or through small ventilation holes built into the roof. Even with some provision for ventilation, those smoke bays were usually dark from years of smoky fires, and the open beams up there would be sooty and greasy.

Before discussing the nature of those smoky beams in more detail, I pause to wonder whether, imagining the old carpenter hanging alone high in the smoke bay of his own hall, a medieval audience would have imagined that he was quite a different kind of animal from his younger counterparts. He is not a lamb yearning for the teat, as Absolon is. He is not a colt in a trave, as Alison is. He is not a stud seeking to paw a nearby filly, as Nicholas is. He is a different kind of animal—a piece of curing meat[4] hanging, wrinkled with age, from the soot-

Figure 3. Fabricating a timber-framed house on the ground before raising (Gene Mater Studios, www.genemater.com).

encrusted beams of a smoke bay. I do not, of course, think that we are to imagine that the fire is burning in the fireplace on that fateful Monday night. If there were a fire, it would have been too smoky up there for John, Nicholas, and Alison to think of sleeping. Chaucer does not directly specify the season for the tale, but all indications are that it is spring. For example, Gerveys would not have been up all night repairing or sharpening plows in any season but spring. In the spring there would have been no need for a fire in the middle of the night.

It is interesting to note that the high beams of the smoke chambers in medieval houses did become encrusted with soot, and indeed that they were sometimes actually used to smoke meat and even sometimes had iron hooks in

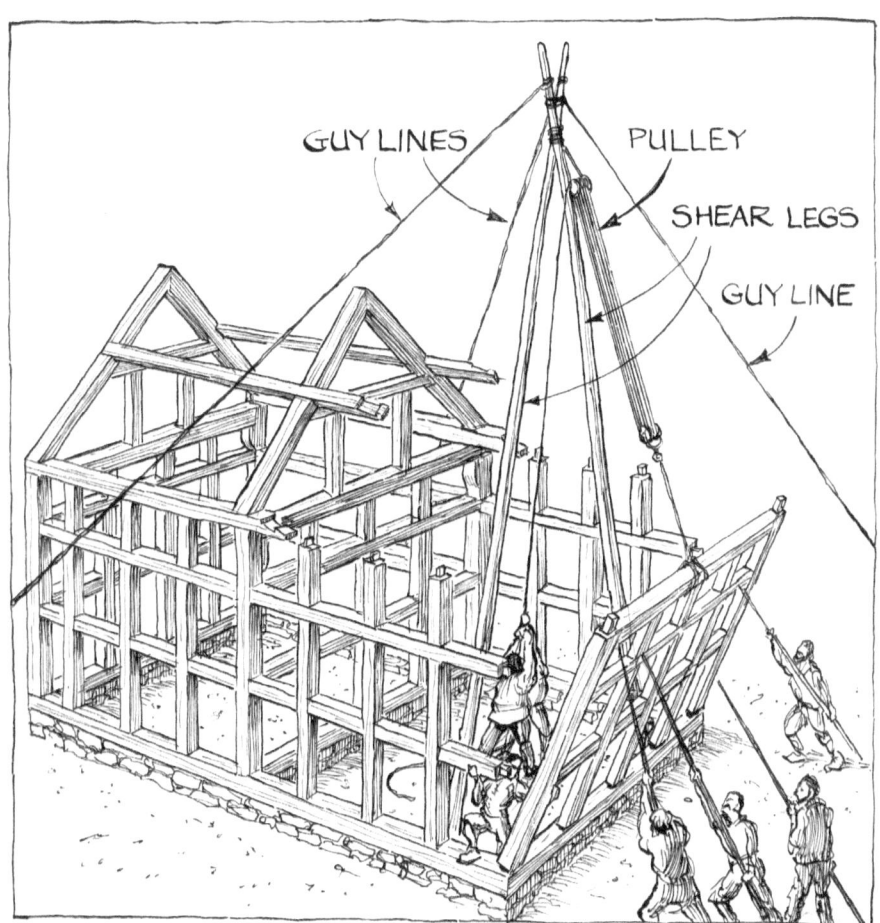

Figure 4. Raising a wall to add a bay to enlarge a timber-framed house (Gene Mater Studios, www.genemater.com).

Figure 5. Braced walls, fire pit, and smoke bay in a timber-framed house (Gene Mater Studios, www.genemater.com).

V. The Structure of John's House

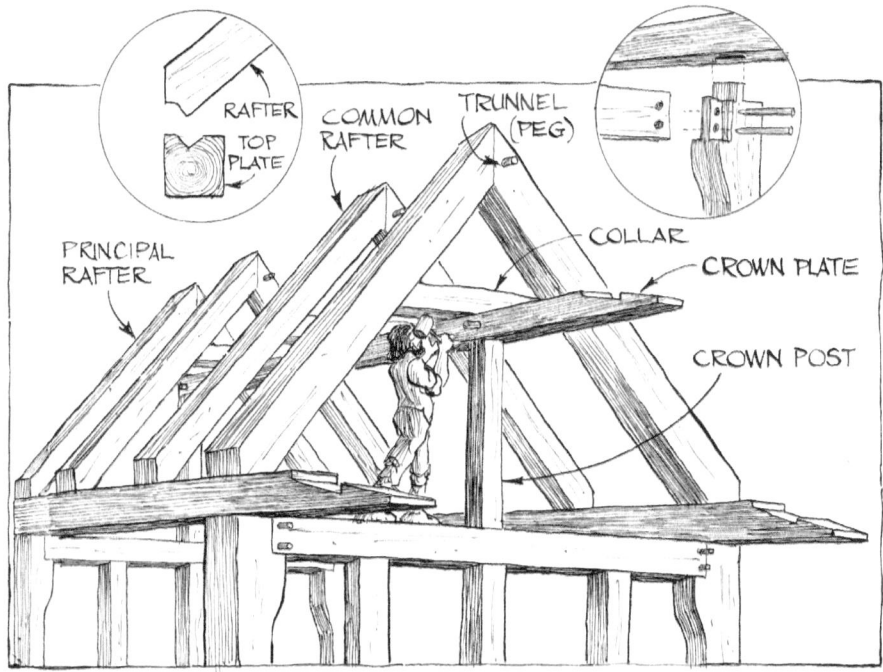

Figure 6. Crown plates, collar beams, and rafters (Gene Mater Studios, www.genemater.com).

them for just that purpose.[5] If we readers are to imagine that John is perhaps a piece of shriveled bacon, then is it any wonder that frisky young Alison seeks elsewhere for fun, or that Oswald the Reeve might have taken particular offense at what he sees as a portrait of himself as smoked bacon in the *Miller's Tale*?

Let's get back to the beams themselves. What were they called? Chaucer calls them "balkes" (3616), a term now largely out of usage except in proverbial expressions like "You see a balk in my eye, but not a beam in your own." Actually, the kind of beam being referred to in the *Miller's Tale* is almost certainly either a crown plate or a collar beam. For illustrations of these crown plates and collar beams, see Figure 6.

The crown plate ran horizontally under the ridge of the roof and parallel to it. The roof was supported by a crown post at the end of each bay. Atop that and perpendicular to it, but also horizontal, were the collar beams. The collar beams would have been fastened to the rafters, which are the sloping beams that held the actual roofing material. The collar beams helped support the weight of the roof.[6] Both the crown plate and the collar beams would have been exposed inside the roof, and so would have provided an easy place for John to lean the ladders and to tie the ropes by which the three tubs are suspended.

At the bottom of that large high-ceilinged hall in John's house is a floor. It would probably have been a clay, brick, or stone floor rather than a wooden one, since it had to support an open fire. If it had a wood floor, the fire would probably have been in a stone-lined pit. At the end of the tale, we recall, John cuts the rope in two and falls until he comes to "the celle / Upon the floor" (3822–23). That expression has puzzled readers and editors for decades.[7] Actually, it gives us important information about the structure of the house.

It would probably have been obvious to any contemporary reader of the *Miller's Tale* that "the celle / Upon the floor" would have referred to the ground-sill, that is the base plate or bottom horizontal timber into which the posts were mortised.[8] They would have known from that terminology that when old John falls all the way down to the "the celle / Upon the floor," he falls clear to the bottom floor of a timber-framed house. He does not fall into its cellar, since timber framed housed rarely had them and Chaucer does not mention one. The "celle" is not a "cellar" but a "sill" or ground-sill—the base plate that supported the walls and perhaps traversed the open bay to tie the base of the house together (see Figures 4 for an example of such a sill cutting across the center of the house between the two bays). To avoid rot, it would have been slightly raised above the surrounding clay, and if so, that is what John would have struck his arm against when he fell do the floor.

How far would John have fallen? We cannot be precise, of course. Chaucer refers to the "roof ful hye" (3565), so we know it is not low. When we recall that Nicholas's chamber is on the second storey, we can assume that the roof would have started above that storey and enclosed what would in effect have been a third storey. If we estimate around eight feet per storey, we can estimate that the peak of the roof would perhaps have been some twenty-four feet above the floor. The crown plate would have been a couple of feet below that. With the ropes tied to that or to the collar beams, the tubs would perhaps have been around twenty feet above the ground floor. Again, we cannot be precise here, but if that figure is even close to accurate, we can well understand why John would have broken his arm from so high a fall. He is lucky not to have broken his neck.[9] Whatever the exact height of the smoke bay, John would have taken quite a fall when he foolishly cut himself loose from the high balk after he heard Nicholas's anguished cry for "Water! Water!"

V. *The Structure of John's House* 57

The Door to Nicholas's Room

No internal door is mentioned in Heile's house in the Middle Dutch analogue. Heile has no boarders' rooms to be closed off from the rest of the house. The door in Nicholas's room in the *Miller's Tale*, then, is Chaucer's addition. It serves the purpose of isolating Nicholas during his pretended death-like trance and of providing a barrier that John and Robyn must overcome before they can gain access to his room. That breaking-and-entering is well-known to readers of the *Miller's Tale*. John, with his knave Robyn in tow, determines to go in and berate Nicholas for ruining himself with so much foolish studying:

> "Get me a staf, that I may underspore,
> Whil that thou, Robyn, hevest up the dore.
> He shal out of his studiyng, as I gesse."
> And to the chambre dore he gan him dress.
> His knave was a strong carl for the nonnes,
> And by the haspe he haaf it of atones;
> Into the floor the dore fil anon [3465–71].

Previous scholars have not quite understood what goes on in that scene. If scholars comment on it at all, it is usually to the effect that Robyn the knave bashes a door in, as Robyn the Miller is said to have done by running at it with his head (550–51). They ignore John's role in opening the door, and they do not understand how medieval doors were made and hung.

I call to the attention of Chaucerians the amazing book by Salzman, *Building in England down to 1540*. After examining more than 1500 manuscripts relating to building and building materials, Salzman has put together a compendium of the materials used by builders and the way they used them. His book helps us to understand the way the doors in John's house were hung on their hinges:

> [T]he majority of doors seem, from the late thirteenth century at any rate, to have been hung by the hook hinge which is practically universal for church doors. In this type the hook, an iron wedge, from the broader end of which a round iron pin rises vertically to carry an eye piece of iron attached to the door, is inserted in the door frame. Normally a pair of hooks is sufficient [Salzman 295].[10]

For a drawing of this kind of hinge and the door attached to a pair of them, see Figure 7.

Such a door had several advantages. It is easy to hang, since all that the carpenter has to do is drive the two hooks into the jamb, prop the door in

Figure 7. A hook-hinged door (Gene Mater Studios, www.genemater.com).

place, drop the eye-strap hinges over the jamb-hooks, and attach the straps to the door with nails or bolts. The other advantage is that the open door can easily be lifted off the hooks and set aside. Lifting the door off its jamb-hooks is more difficult if the door is closed, since the door trim—if there was any— would keep the door in its place. As a carpenter, of course, John would have understood all that. Indeed, he had probably, himself, built and hung that very door.

John would know that with Nicholas's door closed, with the hinges on the inside and the door latched in some way from the inside, it would difficult to lift the door up off its jamb-hooks to gain entrance into the room. He asks for a "staf, that I may underspore" (3465). The staff is apparently a pry bar of

V. The Structure of John's House

some sort, a tool that he can wedge under the door and pry up on the edge of the door where the hinge-eyes are. At the same time Robyn can grab the hasp, or fastener, on the other edge of the door and apply his strength to that side. They do not smash the door in, but they do, with Robyn's sheer strength and John's prying up, raise the door off its hinge eyes so that it falls "into the floor" (3471) of Nicholas's room. The door is apparently not damaged. Some readers think that Chaucer forgets that the door is off the hinges when, a few lines later, Nicholas shuts his door ("his dore faste shette" [3499]),[11] but it would be a simple enough task of no more than a couple of seconds for Nicholas to lift the door back onto its two jamb-hooks and reclose the door. The most that would have been broken is the inside latch or hasp, probably no more than a twist-latch that pivots on a nail in the jam. Having that broken would not have prevented Nicholas from closing his door.

One other structural feature of John's house, the shot-window, is such an important feature of the action and the staging of the *Miller's Tale* that it deserves a chapter of its own.

VI

The Shot-Window

All readers of Chaucer's *Miller's Tale* know that there is a "shot-wyndowe"[1] in Alison's bedroom, but almost no one seems to feel that they know with any certainty just what a shot-window is. Even the magisterial OED is puzzled: "The precise sense of the first element [shot] is difficult to determine." Indeed, the OED devotes more than five large triple-columned pages to the various possible meanings of "shot." Chaucer's is the first recorded use of the term "shot-window," and he uses it only twice, both times in the *Miller's Tale*. It is not recorded again until more than a century later. Because the term "shot-window" quickly became obsolete except in Scottish literature, its meaning is difficult to pin down.

Before I review some possible answers to questions about the window out of which Alison and then Nicholas famously stick their naked buttocks, I note that in the Middle Dutch *Heile of Beersele*, Chaucer's most likely source for the *Miller's Tale*, the window is said only to be "een vensterkijn" (116) [a little window]. The anonymous Middle Dutch author makes no mention of any openings or closings of the window, leaving us to assume that "een vensterkijn" was just an open hole in the wall with no equipment for closing it.[2] One of the most important of Chaucer's innovations is that he lets us know in various ways that the shot-window in Alison's bedroom can be opened and closed.

Many modern editors and glossators have relied on Skeat's early guess that a shot-window was a "hinged" window or "casement,"[3] but they rarely do so with much confidence. And there is no scholarly agreement about the size or shape of Alison's shot-window. As to its shape, Woods, with no evidence, refers to "the round shot window."[4] Chaucer never tells us that the shot-window is round. Bennett supposes, also with no evidence, that it is "a small casement: probably square, about two feet by two feet."[5] Chaucer never tells us that the shot-window is square, and he gives us no dimensions. Actually, we can probably assume that a shot-window, like virtually all windows in medieval timber-framed houses, was rectangular, if only because such windows were easier to build, hinge, and close. As for Bennett's adjective "small," that is of course an imprecise term. Several Scottish literary works suggest that a shot-window was at least large enough to permit a person to enter or exit through it. The early but undated ballad "Lamkin," for example, concerns the way a stone mason gets his revenge against a nobleman who refuses to pay him for building a castle. He slips "in at a little shot window"[6] and murders the nobleman's wife and young son. For other examples of narratives in which someone goes into or out of a shot-window, see "Clerk Saunders" and Sir Walter Scott's *Kenilworth*, both discussed below. Alison's shot-window is also probably large enough to admit a person, for Absolon had apparently hoped to be invited in through it after the kiss. See line 3683, where he takes an itching mouth as "signe of kissyng atte leeste," and line 3725, where he hopes that after the kiss "ther cometh moore." What more might he have hoped for but to be invited to scramble in through the low window? Further indication that Alison's shot-window is large enough to admit a man is Alison's statement that the person knocking at the shot-window is perhaps a robber trying to get in: "'I warante it a theef'" (3791). No robber would have bothered tampering with a window too small for ingress.

But there remains much uncertainty about what a shot-window is and how it operated. One effect of the uncertainty is that translators of the *Miller's Tale* have felt licensed to be creative in translating the two lines in which Chaucer used it: "And dressed hym up by a shot-wyndowe" (3358), "And stille he stant under the shot-wyndowe" (3695).[7] Before I take my own shot at identifying Alison's controversial bedroom window, it will be useful to review here the various other interpretations that have been advanced.

Shot-Window as Jutting-Out Window

The term "shot-window" first appears in the description of Absolon's visit to serenade Alison:

> And forth he gooth, jolif and amorous,
> Til he cam to the carpenteres hous
> A litel after cokkes hadde ycrowe,

> And dressed hym up by a shot-wyndowe
> That was upon the carpenteris wal [3355–59].

The idea of a shot-window as a projecting or "out-shot" one that protrudes past the exterior wall line of a house shows up first, so far as I can tell, in 1791, when an anonymous "modernizer" of the *Miller's Tale* rendered those five lines thus:

> Forth from his chamber stole the amorous spark,
> [Oh deed too ventrous for a parish clerk!].
> His crack'd guittar across his shoulders hung;
> And ere the lark his early mattins rung,
> Where a bay window jutted o'er the street.[8]

A century later, in 1890, Frederick Clarke rendered those same lines thus:

> And forth he went, lively and amorous,
> Unto the dwelling of the carpenter,
> A little after chanticleer had crowed.
> Upon a window ledge he perched himself,
> That jutted like an eave from out the wall.[9]

The idea of a jutting or projecting window appears also in *The Monastery*, one of Sir Walter Scott's Waverly novels. *The Monastery* takes place in the middle of the sixteenth century in the Border regions between England and Scotland. It involves an unlikely plot about angry warriors, kindly commoners, impoverished nobles, impassioned Protestants and Catholics, and a white spirit lady who intervenes directly in the affairs of the living, some of whom she has raised from the dead. The part that concerns us here comes in chapter 14. Two young women, Mysie Happer, the miller's daughter, and Mary Avenel, orphaned daughter of noble parents, are conversing. Suddenly they hear the stomping of horses outside. Excited, "Mysie flew to the shot-window in the full ardour of unrestrained female curiosity" (pp. 115–16).[10] From that window she first sees the handsome man she is destined to fall in love with. She summons Mary Avenel: "Come, dear lady—come to the shot-window and see him" (p. 116). No mention is made of opening or closing the window, so it is apparently already open. The window is described a little later when the laconic Mary joins Mysie: "From the out-shot or projecting window she could perceive that Christie of the Clinthill was attended on the present occasion by a very gay and gallant cavalier" (p. 117).

It seems evident that Scott encountered the term "shot-window" in his own reading of the *Miller's Tale*. Writing in the nineteenth century about events that took place in the sixteenth, Scott seems to have looked to Chaucer in the fourteenth to help lend an air of antiquity to his narrative. He more than once mentions Chaucer by name and even quotes Symkyn the miller in the *Reeve's Tale* (line 4054): "It is an old proverb, used by Chaucer [...] that 'The greatest clerks are not the wisest men'" (p. 91). Scott specifically invokes Chaucer's Robyn the Miller when speaking of Hob Miller, Mysie's father: "But then a miller should always be of manly make, and has been described so since the days of Chaucer" (p. 108). Chaucer's Robyn the pilgrim and Symkyn in the *Reeve's Tale* clearly influenced the character of the miller in *The Monastery*. Like Robyn, who had "a thombe of gold" (563), Hob Miller has a "proverbial golden thumb" (p. 106). Scott's Hob Miller is based also in some ways on Symkyn. Symkyn has "greet sokene" (3987), the right to a monopoly on the grinding to be done in a certain area; Hob has "'sucken,' or enthralled ground" (p. 105). Symkyn's daughter Malyn is "thikke and wel ygrowen" (3973) with "brestes rounde and hye" (3975); Hob's daughter Mysie is "full and round, and firm and fair" and "buxom" (pp. 107, 109).

Because there is no question that Scott knew about Chaucer's millers in the *Canterbury Tales*, it is logical to conclude that he encountered the term "shot-window" in the *Miller's Tale*. Then, not sure what it meant, he apparently decided to define it as a projecting window. I should note that he published *The Monastery* five years before John Brockett published the first edition of his *Glossary of North Country Words*, which does not define the term "shot-window." It was not until the third edition, brought out and expanded by his son, that his dictionary defined a shot-window as "a projecting window, common in old houses."[11] Brockett's definition was quite possibly taken from Scott's *The Monastery*. Wherever the Brockett got it, that definition seems to have been abandoned almost from the start. In his 1879 *Etymological Dictionary of the Scottish Language*, John Jamieson (1759–1838) defines a shot-window as "a window set on hinges and opening outward like a shutter," and goes on to say that it is *not* a projecting window, since that confuses "shot" with "outshot": "In the West of Scotland, such a [projecting] window is called an *outshot* window. The *shot window*, or *shot*, is one that can be opened or shut like a door or shutter by turning on its hinges."[12] It is not clear where Jamieson got the notion that a shot-window swings outward. Surely it does not do so in the *Miller's Tale*, where it would have been awkward for Alison to have to open it out into Absolon's face, then reach out to pull the window in to clap it shut. That would have take too much time, been difficult in the pitch darkness, and been downright dangerous in view of the nasty trick she had just played on the now-angry Absolon.

Whatever Scott's and Brockett's process of coming to the definition of "shot-window" as a projecting window, it does not work well in the *Miller's*

Tale. One of the problems with reading Chaucer's shot-window as a projecting window is that the more the window projects outward from the main wall, the deeper the sill would be and the more difficult it would be for Alison and Nicholas to stick their buttocks out far enough to give Absolon effective access to them. Nicholas, we recall, is specifically said to stick himself out pretty far:

> And up the wyndowe dide he hastily,
> And out his ers he putteth pryvely
> Over the buttok, to the haunche-bon [3801–03].

Indeed, the plot requires that his bottom go out far enough that it almost touches Absolon's face, since his fart then nearly blinds the hapless cleric. How could his bottom stick out that far if there were a wide sill? Nothing, then, is gained by reading Alison's shot-window as one that swings out from a frame that protrudes out past the wall. Besides, while Chaucer tells us twice that the shot-window is low on the wall (3676, 3696; see also 3723), he never tells us that it protrudes out from the wall or that casement windows swing out from it.[13]

Shot-Window as Shut Window

Perhaps in part because the *Riverside Chaucer* hyphenates "shot wyndowe" as "shot-wyndowe," most modern commentators have rejected one simple early explanation: that the window is "shut" as opposed to "open."[14] Both times the term is used in the *Miller's Tale*, the window *is* shut: when Absolon serenades Alison in the middle of the night (3358) and later, on that fateful Monday night, when he asks for a kiss (3695). It seems unlikely, however that a "shot-window" is merely a "shut window." Since it is nighttime in both scenes where it is mentioned, it of course it would be shut. Why would Chaucer need to tell us not once but twice that it is closed? He could have left off the adjective and let the later opening and slamming of it speak for themselves. Besides, later usage of the term in Scotland suggests that a shot-window may originally have been more than just a shut window.

In the late nineteenth century Francis James Child collected a number of English and Scottish ballads, most of which we cannot date with any assurance. The 132-line ballad "Clerk Saunders" is the sad tale of Clerk Saunders and Maid Margaret who go to bed together before they are married. Margaret is reluctant to do so because she knows that her seven bold brothers will take revenge if they find out that she has lost her virginity. Clerk Saunders is insistent, however, and tells Margaret to take his sword to lift the pin that locks the window in her bedroom so that he can climb in:

VI. The Shot Window

> "Then take the sword frae my scabbard,
> And slowly lift the pin;
> And you may swear, and save your aith,
> Ye never let Clerk Saunders in."[15]

The "pin" is apparently an inside bolt or other device that locks the window. The idea is that Margaret can later legitimately say that she did not open the window, because it was *his* sword that did the deed. Margaret obeys him and Clerk Saunders climbs in the open window. Later Margaret's seven brothers find the lovers post-coitally asleep in her bed and kill Clerk Saunders. When Margaret awakes, she finds her father carrying the corpse off to burial. Still later Clerk Saunders's ghost stands outside Margaret's shot-window just before dawn. After they speak, she passes to Clerk Saunders's ghost a crystal wand:

> Then she has ta'en a crystal wand,
> And she has stroken her troth thereon;
> She has given it him out at the shot window,
> Wi' mony a sad sigh, and heavy groan.

The context reveals little of what this shot-window was, but we can infer that it could be locked from the inside with a pin or bolt of some sort, that it was strong enough when locked that a man could not easily or quietly break into it from the outside, that it was large enough to let a man climb in once it was unlocked from the inside, and that it was light enough that a woman could open it—at least enough to hand out a wand. More to the immediate purpose, "shot" here does not mean "shut," since Margaret could scarcely pass a wand out of a window that was closed.

A shot-window later appears in another novel by Sir Walter Scott. *Kenilworth*, originally published in 1821 but set in 1575, is a complicated historical fiction whose main plot need not concern us here. A very minor subplot involves a farmer's daughter named Jane Thackham who elopes and marries a shopkeeper named Goldthred: "She hath jumped out of the shot-window of old Gaffer Thackham's grange."[16] The shot-window does not come up again in the novel and is never defined. Although the reference is late, if we assume some continuity of meaning with Chaucer's shot-window, then the meaning "shut window" does not work. Jane Thackham would scarcely leap out of a window that was closed.

Shot-Window as Bolted Window

Fred N. Robinson suggested that by the term "shot-window" Chaucer may have meant to "designate a window equipped with a fastening bolt."[17]

Robinson probably derived that notion from Gavin Douglas (1474–1522). Douglas was a Scottish bishop and poet best known now for his translation into Middle Scots of Virgil's *Aeneid*. The section that might have suggested the idea of a bolt comes not in Douglas's translation itself but in the quasi-autobiographical prologue to Book Seven, where the poet describes the bitter cold of a late–December morning. When he hears a young falcon's melancholy whistle, the poet gets up, replenishes the fire, lights a candle, gets dressed, goes to a shot-window in his chamber, and opens it a little. Looking out, he sees the frosty weather, the frozen earth, the bleached branches, the icy bark, and the hailstones bouncing off the thatched roof and the pavement. He then closes the shot-window and moves near to the fire, takes up his pen, and proceeds with his translation of Virgil. Here are the key lines—see especially lines 129 and 138—with my translation in italics in alternating lines:

> Fast by my chalmyr, in heich wysnyt treis,
> *Near my chamber, in the tall shriveled trees,*
> 125 The soir gled quhislis lowd with mony a pew:
> *The young falcon whistles loud with many a melancholy chirp:*
> Quhar by the day was dawyn weil I knew,
> *Whereby I knew well that the day had dawned,*
> Bad beit the fyre and the candill alyght,
> *I bade the fire be replenished and the candle lit,*
> Syne blissyt me, and in my wedis dyght,
> *Blessed myself, arranged my clothes,*
> A schot wyndo onschet a littill on char,
> *Opened [un-shut] a shot window a crack [ajar],*
> 130 Persauyt the mornying bla, wan and har,
> *Perceived the morning ice-blue, pale and frosty,*
> With clowdy gum and rak ourquhelmyt the ayr,
> *With an obscuring driven mist overwhelming the air,*
> The sulȝe stythly, hasart, rouch and hair,
> *The soil frozen stiff, grey, rough and hoary,*
> Branchis bratlyng, and blaknyt schew the brays,
> *Branches rattling, bleached on the hills,*
> With hirstis harsk of waggand wyndill strays,
> *The hillsides bare but for the withered stalks of grass,*
> 135 The dew droppis congelit on stibble and rynd,
> *The dew drops frozen on the stubble and bark,*
> And scharp hailstanys mortfundeit of kynd
> *And sharp hailstones, by nature numb with cold,*
> Hoppand on the thak and on the causay by,
> *Bouncing off the thatch and the nearby pavement,*
> The schot I closit, and drew inward in hy,
> *I closed the window and drew inward in haste,*

VI. The Shot Window

>   Chyvirrand for cald, the sesson was so snell,
>   *Shivering with cold, the season was so frigid,*
> 140   Schupe with hayt flambe to fleym the fresyng fell.
>   *Managed with hot flames to expel the freezing cold.*[18]

Finished in 1513, Douglas's work on the *Aeneid* gives us some clues to what a shot-window was, at least for him. First, we know that it had a movable panel. And we know that the panel was not glazed since the poet knows it is dawn only by the mournful song of the falcon. Even to get to the window he has to light a candle. Had there been glass panels in the window he would not have needed to open it a crack on that bitterly cold day to see what was going on outside. The shot-window panel, then, was opaque, shutting out not only the cold but also the light. It is noteworthy that when Gavin Douglas closes the window, he calls it not "the schot wyndo" this time but simply "the schot": "The schot I closit." Whereas "schot" in "schot wyndo" seems to be an adjective modifying the noun "wyndo," here it is a noun, "the schot." That suggests that perhaps "schot" may be a locking device, a bolt or pin or latch of some sort: "I closed the bolt."

That possible meaning gains some support from another early literary work. About the middle of the fifteenth century there appeared a romance called *A Royal Historie of the Excellent Knight Generides*. It begins with a description of a wise, kind, courteous king named Aufreyus who one day goes off with a few men to hunt in the forest. He soon gives chase to a great hart that leads him deep into the forest. As night comes on, the king finds himself lost and cut off from his men, who have fallen far behind. To his delight he sees close by a beautiful palace protected by a pair of ivory gates decorated with gold and precious stones. As he stands admiring the gates, a beautiful woman comes from within and unlocks the gates:

> From within ther cometh a-Ryght
> A goodelie ladie in tirès bright,
> Semelie of person, amyable to see:
> The shottes of the gates opened she,
> And sett open the gates wide
> That the king in might ride.[19]

Those "shottes" are apparently the bolts or other devices that lock the ivory gates. The *Middle English Dictionary*, hereafter referred to at the *MED*, gives as meaning 1(c) for "shot" that it is "a bolt or bar for a door or gate" (p. 759). Something like that meaning could also apply to a window, so a "shot-window" might be simply a window provided with a locking bolt.

Few readers, however, have taken to that interpretation of the shot-window in the *Miller's Tale,* perhaps because neither Chaucer nor any of the other writers who mention a shot-window mentions moving a bolt to open or close it. A possible exception is "Clerk Saunders," but there the locking device is called a "pin," not a "shot," and it needs to be pried up with a sword. Another problem with this reading is that presumably all ground-floor windows in medieval houses, if they could be closed at all, would have been fastened from the inside, so why identify just this one as a bolt-window? In any case, there has been little enthusiasm for this reading. Indeed, the editors of the *Riverside Chaucer*, which is based on Robinson's 1957 edition, drop his idea of a bolt altogether and simply identify the shot-window in a brief on-the-page gloss as "a hinged window (one that opens and closes)."[20]

Shot-Window as Shit-Window

In the only scholarly article devoted entirely to what Chaucer meant by "shot-window," Peter Brown makes a provocative suggestion that the shot-window is a privy window:

> A low, bedchamber window of a certain size giving on to the street, affording an occasional glimpse of bare buttocks—it is within the bounds of possibility that the window in question abutted a latrine. [...] It is in these terms that we might imagine a latrine within John's bower, with the base of the "shot wyndowe" on a level with the seat, and provided with a window for ventilation. [...] Are there any grounds for linking *shot* with *privy*? The most obvious explanation is the most difficult to establish, namely that *shot* is a variant of *chute*. [...] More promising is the occurrence of *shot* as a derivative of both ME *sheten*, to eject or expel, and ME *shiten*, to shit. [...] In the *Miller's Tale* ["shot wyndowe"] may designate [...] a privy window, the window associated with shot in the sense of discharge, shit, or chute.[21]

I appreciate the cautious language with which Brown offers his suggestion—"within the bounds of possibility," "we might imagine," "may designate"—but I must finally turn away from it. It is not clear precisely how Brown thinks this privy would have been constructed. If it is a separate room inside the bedroom with window access to the street, are we to imagine an open-air toilet seat of some sort fastened to the window sill? If so are we to imagine Absolon eagerly anticipating a kiss from Alison who is somehow perched on or just above such a toilet seat? And are we to envision Absolon kneeling next to—or indeed in?—a patch of slick human waste? One can, of course, imagine all sorts of things, but since Chaucer makes no reference whatever to a privy, to a toilet seat, to kneeling in or near a pile of human excrement, or to the odors associated with a privy, I see no textual basis for reading shot-window as shit-window.

I should note that in not mentioning a privy or the material it contained, Chaucer was actively turning away from the privy mentioned in his source. At the very end of *Heile of Beersele* we discover that in the corner is "enen vulen putte" (line 174) [a foul cesspit] into which the priest falls, to emerge "al besceten" (line 176) [all shitty]. The idea of a privy, then, was available to Chaucer. He simply did not want to go that way in his *Miller's Tale*.

To support his case, Brown presents historical evidence that a ground-floor bedchamber "might include a privy, as in the type of house in which Chaucer grew up in the Vintry area of London" (Brown 99). Brown's source for that statement is Edith Rickert's *Chaucer's World*, which itself references an earlier article by Lethbridge Kingsford. Two problems arise with Brown's statement. First, it is a strong assumption indeed that the merchant's house that Kingsford discusses is like the one Chaucer grew up in. The various owners of the merchant's house down through the years tended to be wealthy gentlemen. Visitors to the house came through a large courtyard into a great hall of almost a thousand square feet. The house had three stories above a cellar, as well as a parlor, kitchen, and buttery, not to mention many bedchambers. In other words, to quote Kingsford, this house "will compare not unfavorably with such famous houses as The Coldharbour, Pountney's Inn, or Crosby Hall."[22] Chaucer *may* have grown up in such grandeur, but there is no evidence that he did. Besides, it is a leap indeed to say that because one London merchant's house may have had a ground-floor bedchamber with a privy, Chaucer's nearby boyhood home probably also had a ground-floor bedchamber with a privy.

That brings up the second problem: did the London house that Kingsford studied really have a bedroom with a privy? Brown relied, logically enough, on Rickert's translation of a document recording the dower of a certain Agnes Peckham in 1463. The dower included the house in question, which is said specifically to have a "a house of easement set in the west side of the entry" and "two chambers and a privy on the west side of the entry leading to the said parlor, set betwixt the said hall and the same parlor."[23] Here are the phrases in the original Middle English document as published by Kingsford: "an hous of Easement sette in the West side of the same entre" and "ij Chambres and a withdraught on the west side of the ... entre ledyng to the saide Parlour, sett betwix the saide Halle and the same Parlour" (Kingsford 156). Rickert, working before the *MED* came out, took the term "withdraught" to mean a privy. That is a questionable translation. The *MED* does not give "privy" as one of the meanings of withdraught, but does give this one: "1(b) a place of retirement or retreat within a house, a private chamber ... ; also, a closet or recess within a room" (p. 734). Clearly 1(b) is the applicable definition, especially since the same document gives a different—and unequivocal—term for the privy: "an hous of Easement" located adjacent to the kitchen. Brown's historical example of a London merchant's house with a privy adjacent to a bedchamber turns out, then, to be based on a questionable translation.

Some medieval residences did have indoor privies, but they tended to be residences for the rich, noble, and ambitious. Mark Girouard, in *Life in the English Country House,* mentions several kinds of country-house indoor privies, but these were in the country homes of the ruling class: "basically people did not live in country houses unless they either possessed power, or, by setting up a country house, were making a bid to possess it."[24] That kind of ostentation fits well enough with the wealthy nobleman January in Chaucer's *Merchant's Tale.* January's "paleys" is specifically said to have been "maked as a kynges" (IV 2026–27). January speaks of owning "toun and tour" (IV 2172), and he builds himself a fancy enclosed pleasure-garden. In contrast, John the carpenter of Oxford, though said to be "riche" (2), still works with his hands, has no pretensions to nobility, and even has to take in boarders. He is said neither to own such a country house nor to aspire to the power it gave proof of. "By the later Middle Ages," Girouard says, "a privy usually consisted of a small cell in which a pierced seat was placed over a shaft. That shaft connected to a pit, a drain, or just a slope outside the building" (Girouard 56). So far as we can tell, John's house had none of those features. Nor does Chaucer hint at any of the terms Girouard lists for the room we speak of: "Privy, privy house or privy chamber were the commonest terms in the Middle Ages, but garderobe, withdraught, jakes, latrine, necessary and gong were also current" (Girouard 56). He goes on to say that the term "withdraught" was "applied to any small room attached to a large one, and need not imply a privy" (Girouard 56–57).

Brown cites the privy in the *Merchant's Tale* in support for his view that the shot-window in the *Miller's Tale* is in a latrine:

> Is the existence of a garderobe within John's chamber plausible in narrative as well as linguistic terms? Within the *Canterbury Tales* there is certainly a precedent, or parallel case, of Chaucer's featuring a privy to articulate the plot of a marital deception: in the *Merchant's Tale*, it is a space of privacy, outside January's control, where May can momentarily escape his jealousy and read Damyan's secret love-letter [Brown 99].

There is, however, no evidence in the *Merchant's Tale* that the privy is in the bedroom. Even if it were, the architecture of the "paleys" (IV 1712, 2415) of an Italian nobleman would not set a reliable precedent, or be a parallel case, for the architecture of the mere "hous" (3356, 3481, 3484, 3669, 3694) of an

Oxford carpenter, a "gnof" (3188).²⁵ And even if there were not such a discrepancy in the situations of the two cuckolded husbands, we must not forget the obvious point that in the *Merchant's Tale* Chaucer explicitly *tells* us that there was a privy, whereas in the *Miller's Tale* he does not. Had Chaucer wanted us to think the shot-window was in a privy wall, he could easily have substituted "privee" for "boures" in the crucial lines, "at his wyndowe / That stant ful lowe upon his boures wal" (3676–77). Curiously, Brown says that the shot-window is "close to the bedchamber" in John's house (Brown 98). Chaucer tells us not that it is *close* to John's chamber but *in* it, "upon his boures wal" (3677).

Besides, how likely is it that the fastidiously romantic Absolon, who is specifically said to perfume himself with sweet-smelling herbs and to be squeamish about farting, would court his lady love in the immediate vicinity of the odorous latrine where she and John did their privy business? Medieval privies were notoriously smelly.²⁶ Although it is possible that John and Alison would not have minded the odors of their own ordure, surely Absolon would have been reluctant to attempt a liaison with Alison amid those odors.

Brown, as I say, is impressively careful not to overstate his argument. In the end, however, I must step away from such speculation. The window we speak of is in the wall of John's bedroom, not of a privy that is never mentioned in the tale and that would have been most unusual in the Oxford house of a mere carpenter, one of the "men that swynke" (3491).

Shot-Window as Body Orifice

More recently, Gregory Heyworth reads the shot-window not as a physical object so much as an exegetically symbolic one. Although he finds that Peter Brown "argues convincingly that a 'shot wyndowe' is actually a 'shit window' designed expressly for defecation,"²⁷ his own main concern is with Nicholas's fart, which he takes to be "God's vernacular voice," "politics ventriloquized through an asshole," "a ritual of vernacular consecration" (Heyworth 972, 973, 976), and so on. He has only a little to say about the shot-window:

> In the *Regula monachorum* Jerome adapts Jeremiah 9.21, "For death is come up into our windows and is entered into our palaces," into an injunction against the sensual world that would exert great sway over the medieval notion of the body: "Your senses are your windows and gates. Leave them open and (sin) and death will enter." The same metaphor of the body as an architectural inner sanctum penetrable through the windows of the senses is amplified in the *Ancrene Wisse*,

becoming perhaps the dominant metaphor of anchoritism in the English Middle Ages. The sensual inscape of the Miller's room reflects this hagiographic tradition. It is in itself a metaphor of the body; the "shot wyndowe" is an orifice of sensual intrusion [Heyworth 975–76].

Such readings usually collapse of their own symbolic weight, so I will say no more about Heyworth's brief take on the shot-window. I am, in any case, less interested here in the exegetical possibilities of the window in John and Alison's bedroom than in what it looked like. I am less interested here in the shot-window as a human orifice than in how it opened and shut. I am less interested here in the shot-window's reflection of moral culture than in its reflection of medieval material culture.

Shot-Window as Hinged Wooden Panel

To return for a moment to Peter Brown, he sensibly rejects the usual reading of the shot-window as an outward-opening glazed window:

> Thus, the linguistic, literary, and historical evidence suggests that "hinged window," implying a glazed frame opening outwards, is an inaccurate reading for "shot wyndowe." In the *Miller's Tale* it should be imagined as an unglazed opening with a hinged internal shutter [Brown 100].

While I think he is wrong about where the window is situated, I think he may be right about the kind of window it is—a solid wooden panel hinged inside and thus swinging into the bedroom. I prefer the term "wooden panel" to his term "shutter," however, because the latter term not yet been invented in Chaucer's day (it is not recorded until the late seventeenth century). Besides, a "shutter" for modern readers almost always suggests a useless external architectural decoration with louvers. Chaucer's shot-window was emphatically not that.

Consideration of medieval paintings suggests two possible kinds of hinged in-swinging panels. The first, reproduced here as Figure 8, I take from L. F. Salzman's book on English life.[28] Salzman dates the painting, which he entitles "The Cottager," around 1500. It depicts the sad condition, possibly the death, of a crippled man (notice the crutches to the left of the bed and what I take to be a chamber pot—the only indoor latrine such a house would have had—beneath it). The timber-framed house he lives in, apparently with his devout wife, is in derelict condition, with holes in the roof and the walls, and with the useless, rotting window-panel dangling on one hinge. What is interesting for our purposes is that the window is precisely the kind

VI. *The Shot Window* 73

Figure 8. An in-swinging hinged wooden window panel in a derelict medieval frame house. The drawing is based on the upper right corner of a drawing made about 1500 and reproduced by Salzman in his *English Life in the Middle Ages*. Salzman says that he found the drawing in La Libraire Centrale des Beaux-Arts, Paris (Bill and Karen Curr).

Brown asked us to imagine—an inward-swinging unglazed solid-wood hinged panel. In John's house, of course, it would have been lower in the bedroom wall.

The second kind of in-swinging wooden panel is suggested by the famous Merode Altarpiece in the Cloisters in New York City. The central panel depicts the Annunciation, but of special interest here is the right panel of the triptych, reproduced in Figure 9. It shows two top-hinged wooden window panels held open by small wooden swivel-hooks attached to the ceiling joists. That design shows promise for the *Miller's Tale* because Alison could simply, by flipping back the hook, send the window down with a satisfy-

Figure 9. Joseph in his workshop in the right panel of the Merode Altarpiece, ca. 1425. Notice the top-hinged wooden panels held open by hooks (courtesy the Metropolitan Museum of Art).

ing clap: "'Tehee!' quod she, and clapte the wyndow to" (3740). It also shows promise because, unlike the side-hinged window, it would have to be lifted "up" when Nicholas opened it: "And up the wyndowe dide he hastily" (3801). Most interpreters, by ignoring that word "up" in Chaucer's text, miss the fact that to open the shot-window is to lift or raise it.[29] A sideways swing on side-mounted hinges would bring the panel *in*, not *up*.

This argument that the shot-window was raised upwards gains further traction from a mid-fourteenth century romance in the famous Auchinleck manuscript. In *Of Arthour and Merlin*, young Merlin tells a judge who challenges his legitimacy that the judge himself is the bastard son of the local parson. When the judge brings his mother in to make assurances that she has been faithful to her husband, Merlin directly accuses her of adultery. When her husband came home unexpectedly, Merlin says, she hastily helped the parson to escape out a window. It is not called a shot-window, but notice the language:

> Þo þi lordz com fro Cardoil
> In hert þou haddest gret diol,
> Bi niȝt it ws ar þe day
> Þe persone in þine armes lay
> On þi dore þi lord gan knoke
> And þou stirtest vp in þi smoke
> Wel neiȝe wode for dred and howe
> *Vp þou schotest a windowe*
> And þe persone þou out lete
> And afterward þou schet it sket.[30]

Notice that the window is in a bedchamber, that it is light enough to be opened by a woman but large enough to permit a lover to escape out of it, and that it can be closed quickly—"sket." But notice particularly that the window is not only "shot" open, but specifically shot open *up*wards. Although the window is not said to be a shot-window, the language ("schotest") and the direction of the opening ("vp") give at least indirect support to the notion of an up-and-down moving shot-window in the *Miller's Tale*. Since "sket" means "swiftly," the judge's mother, like Alison, would have gravity on her side as she moved in all haste to close her bedroom window.

Of course, the windows in Joseph's workshop are too high to fit precisely the conditions of the *Miller's Tale*, where the shot-window stands "ful lowe upon his boures wal" (3677). When Absolon stands beneath the window, "unto his brest it raughte, it was so lowe" (3696). Figure 10 shows the top-hinge-and-hook idea adapted to a low window, with the hook attached to the wall rather than the ceiling.[31] Figure 11 shows the way Alison might look presenting her bottom to the foolish Absolon on the other side of such a window.

The shot-window in the *Miller's Tale*, then, might have been a top-hinged wooden panel. But that panel might also have been a sliding window without hinges.

Shot-Window as Sliding Window

In his 1891 precursor to the *MED*, Stratmann defined the shot-window as a "sliding window."[32] Peter Brown mentions the possibility of such a meaning:

> *OED* is of some help here [...] in suggesting a connection with Middle Dutch *schotdore*, sliding door, and *schotpoorte*, portcullis. In each case, *schot* occurs in a compound noun describing an opening and shutting device that is distinctive precisely because it operates *without* a hinge. Thus, *schot* denotes not so much the action of shutting, but the nature of that action. The sliding door and portcullis "shoot" into place, as we would say, with a potential for the action of shutting being a sudden, abrupt movement [Brown 96–97].

Connecting the term in question with the Middle Dutch language is particularly interesting in view of my argument in *Sources and Analogues* that Chaucer had significant professional and personal connections with the Low Countries, knew at least some Middle Dutch, and was operating in a Middle Dutch linguistic register when he reconstituted the Middle Dutch *Heile of Beersele* as the *Miller's Tale*.[33] If I am right, then the Middle Dutch sense

Figure 10. The top-hinged window panel, held up by a wooden hook, similar to the one in the Merode Altarpiece but adapted to a lower position in the wall (Gene Mater Studios, www.genemater.com).

of "schot" as "sliding"—not "shooting"—might well have been familiar to Chaucer. In any case, the linguistic parallels of the Middle English shot-window with the Middle Dutch *schotdor* and *schotpoort* are intriguing, since the use of "shot" in all three applications suggests the possibility of a vertically-sliding door, gate, or window.[34] In the end Brown rejects this notion of a sliding window in favor of a hinged one:

> Yet the arrangement of these events does not *necessitate* a sliding window. Generations of readers have imagined a hinged window without registering any sense that the associated dramatic business is thereby rendered clumsy. [...] In this context, a sliding window is an unnecessary complication, even if there were supporting historical evidence [Brown 97].

Figure 11. Alison presenting her buttocks out a Merode-style top-hinged window (Gene Mater Studios, www.genemater.com).

Unlike Brown, I believe it is entirely possible—indeed, entirely likely—that the shot-window is a slider or, more precisely, that it is an unglazed wooden panel that slides up and down in facing vertical grooves in the window jamb.

How would the panel be raised and lowered? A small rope or cord could be attached to the top of the board (or joined boards) of the wooden panel, run over a pulley near the ceiling, and down in front of or beside the window. The panel could be held down to prevent the entrance of unwanted intruders from the outside with a small removable peg, pin, or bolt inserted into a hole in the groove. With the peg removed, the wooden panel could be pulled up by the rope. Then the peg or bolt could be reinserted into a higher hole to keep the panel in the raised position. Alternatively, the person pulling the rope could hold onto it, then release it suddenly to let the panel bang down. Figure

12 shows how such a window might look. It would makes a satisfyingly loud bang or clap when the rope was released. Figure 13 shows how Alison might manipulate such a window.

There is no question that such an arrangement would have worked in the *Miller's Tale*. Alison could have "undone" the window by pulling the peg or bolt out and pulling the cord down to raise the panel. Then, holding the cord in one hand, she could have turned around and put her bottom out the window for Absolon. Immediately after the kiss, she could have given her famous "Tehee" and, by letting go of the cord, clapped the window down. Reinserting the peg to lock the panel in the down position would have protected her from Absolon's anticipated rage. A few minutes later, on the return of the angry Absolon, the eager Nicholas could have done "up" the window again for his own buttockly presentation by removing the lock-peg and pulling the cord again.

Yes, it would have worked. Brown rejects this reading in part because he was aware of no historical support for it: "a sliding window is an unnecessary complication, even if there were supporting historical evidence" (Brown 97). Actually, there is supporting historical evidence. Archaeologists have discovered precisely the kinds of grooves that the window panel would slide in. In his excellent book on timber-framed buildings, Richard Harris gives us this little disquisi-

Figure 12. Detail of an up-and-down sliding window panel (Gene Mater Studios, www.genemater.com).

VI. The Shot Window

tionon windows that were closed with wooden panels:

> Nowadays we are accustomed to thinking of windows as having frames which are constructed separately from the walls of buildings, usually purchased ready-made from the specialist joiners. Luckily for researchers, however, this was not the case in traditional timber buildings, since window openings and mullions were incorporated directly as part of the frame and can therefore be traced from the mortices which remain, even when—as often happens—the original mullions have been removed and a new window inserted. Before the late sixteenth century very few houses had glass; windows were completely open, but the worst of the weather could be kept out with internal wooden shutters. These shutters seem usually to have been sliding (vertically or horizontally) rather than hinged, and the grooves in which they slid can often still be seen in the timbers adjacent to the window.[35]

Figure 13. Alison positioned for Absolon's kiss and ready to let the sliding panel drop down (Gene Mater Studios, www.genemater.com).

What about the ropes and pulleys I describe above? Again, there is historical evidence that suggests that vertically sliding wood panels might well have been operated by just such equipment. Salzman tells us that a man named Adam Carpenter, hired to fix stuck windows, used ropes and pulleys to help make them work again. Here is the quotation from Salzman's wonderful history of English building practices:

> In some London accounts of 1450 we have: "Adam Carpenter for iij dayys for the turnyng of dyverse wyndowys wych wold nate wele opon nor schot as they hyng

aforetyme ... item ... for polys and ropeys to the same wyndowys." The pulleys and ropes at first suggest sash windows—a distinct anachronism. Harman, in 1519, writes, "I have many prety wyndowes shette with levys goynge up and downe," which is shown to refer to shutters by another of his sentences: "Wyndowe leves of tymber be made of bourdis ioyned to gether, with keys of tree let into them." The "ij newe wyndowis of tymber" at Collyweston in 1500 are also clearly shutters.[36]

Interestingly, the *MED* gives as one of the definitions of the noun "shote" that it is "a rope, cable" (p. 761). If Chaucer knew that meaning, it might well help us to understand what he meant by shot-window.

The shot-window in the *Miller's Tale*, then, was probably a vertically sliding wooden panel or leaf that moved up and down in side grooves to open and close a window opening. The panel was raised and lowered by a rope or cable as shown in Figures 12 and 13. Such a window fits all of the narrative requirements of the *Miller's Tale*: it provides privacy and protection for those within the marital bedroom. It can be operated hastily by a woman working in the dark. It is easily lockable and unlockable from the inside with a pin or bolt. It lifts up quietly and then claps down noisily. Such a window has archaeological and documentary integrity. It also has linguistic integrity since the a "shote" could signify a rope or cable, and since the term "shot-window" is paralleled by the Middle Dutch terms *schotdore* and *schotporte*, both of which indicate doors or gates that slide up and down in side grooves. It would deliver a satisfyingly dramatic clap as it slammed down in Absolon's startled post-osculatory face.

VII
Reconstructing John's House

Because they have not understood some of the architectural and structural features of medieval houses, most literary scholars appear to have imagined John's house inaccurately. Even those who have attempted to work out the design most carefully have gotten it wrong. Bennett, for example, seems to have read key portions of the *Miller's Tale* rather imprecisely:

> The tubs hang from the baulks, i.e. beams of roughly squared timber, probably slightly curved, serving as tiebeams from wall to wall.[...] John eventually crashes down to the "celle" (3822)—the "ground-sel" or ground floor.[...] [I]t is no wonder that he knocks himself out and breaks his arm—and frightens Alison and Nicholas. By the time this happens it is past lauds, so the neighbors would be in any case astir, and would naturally rush in from the street direct to the hall to see what the matter was.[1]

The tubs might perhaps be hung from what Bennett calls tiebeams, but that would mean that they hung pretty far down into the hall. For John, Alison, and Nicholas to hang "in the roof," they would more likely have been suspended from higher up, from the crown plate or the collar beams. As I have indicated, the "ground-sill" is not the same as the floor. Indeed, Chaucer says it was a "celle / Upon the floor," which suggests that it is something *on* the floor, not the floor itself. John lies "aswowne" (3823) but it is not clear that he "knocks himself out," since he speaks almost immediately. There is no evidence that his fall "frightens" Nicholas and Alison. And the neighbors do not rush in to see what all the excitement is about because they are "astir." Rather, Nicholas and Alison run out into the street to summon them in so that they will verify that old John is mad:

> Up sterte hir Alison and Nicholay,
> And criden "Out," and "Harrow" in the strete.

81

> The neighebores, bothe smale and grete,
> In ronnen for to gauren on this man,
> That yet aswowne lay, both pale and wan,
> For with the fal he brosten hadde his arm.
> But stond he must unto his owene harm;
> For when he spak [...] [3824–31].

Bennett tries to reconstruct John's house, but I find it to be based on questionable assumptions. He suggests, for example, that John's bedroom "may have been over a low-ceilinged shop" (p. 38), but he does not say what he thought John would sell in his shop, gives no textual evidence for such a shop, and does not explain how, if here were such a shop under the bedroom, the shot-window could be low enough for Absolon to reach it, either standing or on his knees. He thinks that Nicholas's room is "large," but gives as evidence only the fact that that when Nicholas played his psaltery "all the chambre rong" (3215). On page 28 of his monograph Bennett gives two illustrations. The first (*2a*) he identifies as Pantin's, but it does not appear that Pantin ever tried specifically to reconstruct John's house. He was more interested in describing old Oxford houses in general. The one that Bennett says is Pantin's shows a cellar and an attached stable. There is no evidence that John's house had a cellar or that the stable was attached to the house. I present here Bennett's drawing reconstructing the house. Labeled 2b, it is based, apparently, mostly on the hints in the *Miller's Tale*, but also on some general information about Oxford houses in Chaucer's time. See Figure 14.

There are some obvious errors and some questionable assumptions in Bennett's reconstruction. First, and most obviously, he shows John and Alison's bedroom and the shot-window on the second storey. That is not consistent with the facts of the tale, in which the window to John's bedroom "stant ful lowe upon his boures wal" (3677). Absolon kneels on the street for his kiss. In Bennett's reconstruction Absolon would need a ladder to get up that high, and then there would be no place for him to kneel. Bennett makes other assumptions that are uncalled for. He shows the building to be made of brick, while the evidence suggests that it was a timber-framed building. He shows a cellar and a shop, neither of which is mentioned or even hinted at in the *Miller's Tale*. He shows Gille and Robyn in their own, separate, bedchambers, though no such arrangements are mentioned in the tale. Indeed, it was far more customary for servants to sleep in the hall. Bennett shows a house with four gable ends, while Chaucer mentions only one: "the gable / Unto the gardyn-ward, over the stable" (3571–72). Bennett shows the stable attached to the house, when it was more likely in Chaucer's time to have been a stand-

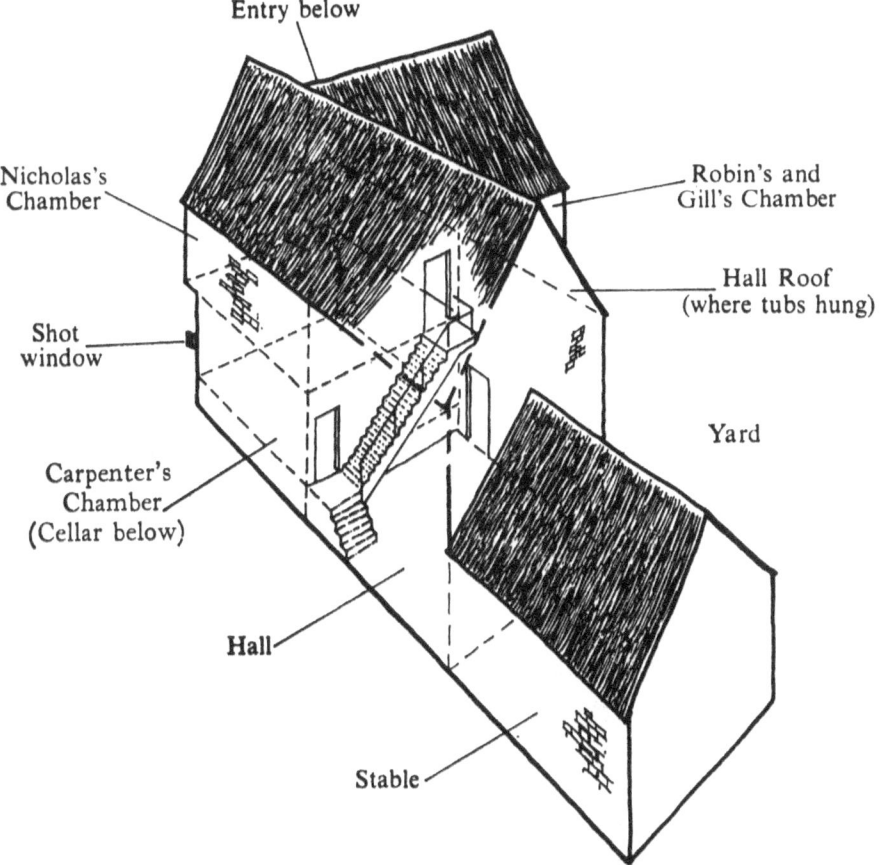

Figure 14. John's house in the *Miller's Tale* as reconstructed by J. A. W. Bennett.

ralone structure at the rear of the property. And even if the stable were where Bennett shows it to be, the three tubs would have had somehow to float through Nicholas's chamber and out the gable, rather than straight to the gable in the end of the hall or smoke bay. Bennett shows that gable on the street side, rather than where Chaucer tells us it is, out back toward the garden and stable.

I hesitate to offer my own reconstruction, since in the end Chaucer does not give us quite enough information that I can offer one with great confidence, but I offer an alternative to Bennett's in Figure 15.

There is much speculation in my reconstruction. We do not know how many other windows there would have been besides the shot-window. We do not know where the door to the house would have been. We do not know how

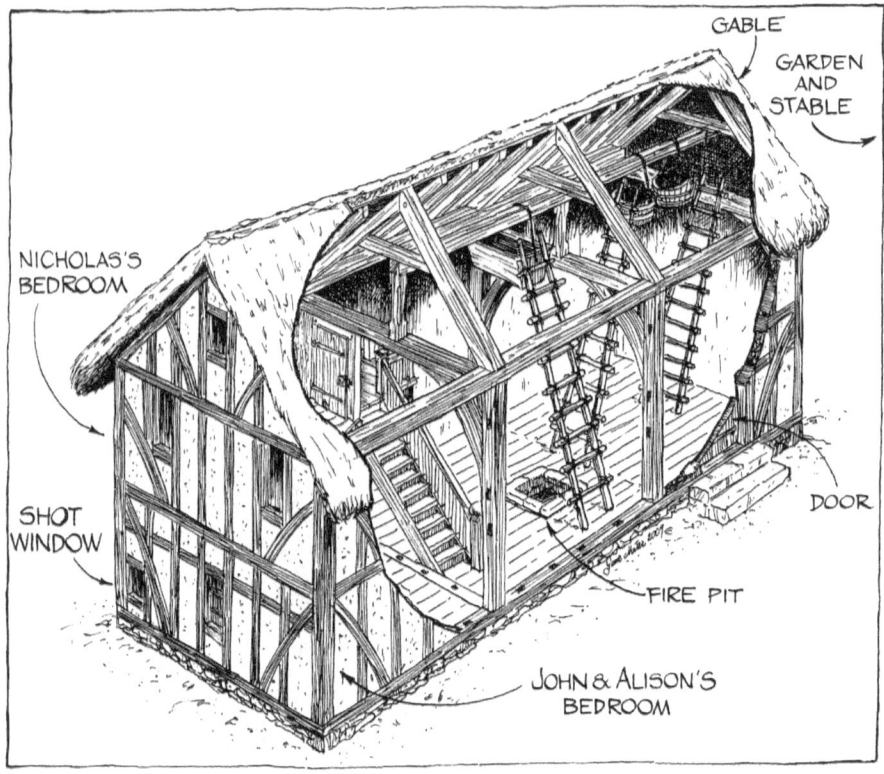

Figure 15. An alternative reconstruction of John's house in the *Miller's Tale* (Gene Mater Studios, www.genemater.com).

many bays there would have been in the house. Still, this drawing shows one possible reading of the setting for the action in John's house.

The House as Stage Set

Of Heile's house we know very little. Actually, we are never even told that she lives in a house. Her three clients just want "Te comen daer si ware" (27) [to come where she was]. We know of the exterior of her house only that it has "die dore" (96) [the door] that the third visitor knocks on, and "een vensterkijn" (116) [a small window] out which the priest sticks his bottom. Neither of these openings in the house is mentioned until it is used by one of the characters as a function of the plot.

Chaucer, on the other hand, wanted us to know at least a little about

VII. Reconstructing John's House

what John's house looks like. In the rest of this section there is some necessary overlap with material covered earlier, but my emphasis here is on the description of the house, and not so much the architecture and structure of houses in general in Chaucer's time. Chaucer calls John's house a "hostelrye" (3203) and an "in" (3545, 3622), but mostly and repeatedly calls it a "hous" (3356, 3481, 3484, 3669, 3694). He tells us early and often that there is a "wyndowe" (3676, 3708, 3727, 3732, 3740, 3789, 3801)—sometimes specified as a "shot-wyndowe" (3358, 3695)—in "the carpenteris wal" (3359, 3787). We know that that window is specifically in the "boures wal" (3367, 3675)—that is, the exterior wall of the bedroom where John and Alison sleep. We know that in one of the exterior walls is a "dore" (3482, 3634, 3674) that John blesses. We know that the house has a "gable" (3571), that there are a "garden" and a "stable" out back (3572). We know that it has a "roof"—sometimes specified as "ful hye" (3564, 3623, 3837, 3841). Typically "roof" is used in the *Miller's Tale* as part of the phrase "in the roof" or "into the roof," where it refers to the interior space below what we now call the roof.

And what is below the roof? Of the inside of Heile's house we know almost nothing. We know that there is "die haenbalke" (70) [the cross beam]. We assume that Heile has a bedroom and a bed, but no mention is made of either, except for the indirect statement that Heile and Willem "laghen si in hare iolijt" (53) [lay in their jolity]. Presumably they are lying in bed, but we have to imagine that bed. We learn at the very end that in the corner is "enen vulen putte" (174) [a foul cesspit]. And that is all we know about Heile's house.

With John's house, it is different. We know that the house has at least at least three rooms: the great hall with a high ceiling and open beams, the "bour" (3367, 3677) or bedroom on the first floor that John and Alison share, and upstairs a private "chambre" (3203, 3410, 3420, 3435, 3468) for Nicholas. We know that there is a stairway going up to Nicholas's room, a door with a hasp and hinges, and a board in the wall with a hole big enough for a cat to go in and out. We assume that Nicholas's chamber contains a bed of some sort, for Nicholas is said to "lay" (3420) in his bedroom and later is seen sitting in it, presumably on his bed rather than on a chair, because almost immediately afterwards, "doun the carpenter by hym he sette" (3500). It is possible, of course, that the chamber has two chairs, but Chaucer mentions none.

We know that John and Alison's bedroom has a low window, and more especially one that "stant ful lowe upon his boures wal" (3677). The lowness of the window, of course, is of some importance in the *Miller's Tale*, and Chaucer carefully sets up the first window scene by reemphasizing it when Absolon gets there:

> And stille he stant under the shot-wyndowe—
> Unto his brest it raughte, it was so lowe [3695–96].

The lowness of the window is important because Absolon kneels before it when he prepares to kiss Alison. The kneeling is important because it reminds us that as a man of the church, Absolon should be kneeling before the Virgin Mary,[2] not the earthy and unvirginal Alison.

Chaucer tells us that there is a "celle / Upon the floor" (3822–23), and in the roof are the "balkes" (3626) or beams from which John suspends the tub. The point is that Chaucer tells enough that we can easily visualize the setting where most of the action of the *Miller's Tale* takes place. Chaucer tells us that old John can with his imagination "see" the coming of Noah's flood:

> This sely carpenter bigynneth quake;
> Hym thynketh verraily that he may see
> Noees flood come walwynge as the see [3614–16].

Just as Chaucer lets John "see" the coming flood, so by giving us readers enough details about the town of Oxford and its people, and about the structure and furnishings of the house, that we may "see" them in our imaginations, "see" them as if they were part of a theatrical set.

VIII
People and Props

Chaucer took pains when composing the *Miller's Tale* to build in the kinds of details that help his audience get a sense that they are not hearing an anecdote but witnessing an event.

Places and People

The adventures of Heile of Beersele take place in a specific street in a specific city, "T'Antwerpen in der Cooperstraten" (14) [in the Cow Gate Street in Antwerp]. Furthermore, Heile is a resident of Beersele, a village just south of Brussels. It is not clear why the Middle Dutch author is so specific about these two towns, since it appears that the tale might just as easily have been set in any town besides Antwerp. And Heile could be from any town besides Beersele. It probably referenced some local situation. Antwerp, after all, is the place where the story of Heile is apparently told: "t'Antwerpen / Hier" (6-7) [here in Antwerp], so it might have made sense to give the local audience a sense of place. It may also be that in the late fourteenth century, Cow Gate Street might have been a street where prostitutes were known to be available. The story itself, however, gives no such details. Nor does the story say why both Heile and Hughe are said to be from the small village of Beersele. That seems curious on several counts. For one thing, Beersele is a suburb of Brussels, many miles to the south of Antwerp. For another, it seems particularly curious that Heile would be so cruel to her own neighbor or former neighbor. I can imagine several back-story scenarios to explain her living as a prostitute so far from her home place and to explain why she might want to gain a cruel revenge against her former neighbor, but none of them are hinted at in the tale itself. And while we do know that the events take place in Antwerp, we have no sense in the tale itself that there are any other people in Antwerp besides the four principles. We assume that the town had a mill, a church, and a forge, but we assume that only because one of Heile's customers is a miller, one a priest, and one a smith.

Chaucer also gives us the name of the town, Oxford. We know why the story takes place there: it is a university town where the local townspeople are known to take in lodgers. Although Chaucer does not give us the name of the actual street where John and Alison live, it is likely that anyone who knew the town in the late fourteenth century would have had a pretty good idea where the blacksmith shops were then located.[1] It may be that the specific street address of John's house was not important enough for Chaucer to give it. Would it help, after all, for us to know that John lives on Catte Street? Other places in Oxford are mentioned. We know that there is a parish "chirche" (3306, 3312, 3429). We know that Oxford has more than one "brewhous" and more than one "taverne" (3334). We know that the town has a "scaffold hye" (3384), presumably in the town square or marketplace, where Absolon tries to impress Alison by playing Herod. We know that in a nearby street is a blacksmith shop occupied, at all hours of the night, by a smith named Gerveys. Chaucer even takes us out of town, to an abbey town named Oseney (4274, 3400, 3659) not far from Oxford, and he lets us know that near Oseney is a "grange" (3667) where John cuts timber. Oseney is close enough to Oxford that John can work there by day and come home at night, close enough that Absolon can visit there for fun, yet still get home at night in plenty of time for a quick nap before starting off to court Alison. We know that London (3632) is far enough away that by sending Robyn and Gille there John will be rid of them for at least a couple of days. Mostly, though, we have a sense that the key events take place in Oxford, which is a town (3334, 3380, 3751, 3846) that has streets (3760, 3825) and other houses, a town in which there are lots of people.

The presence of these people functions in the plot, if only indirectly. Nicholas uses this backdrop of folk when he tells John to be secretive in gathering and provisioning the tubs (italics added, here and in the next several quotations):

> "Thanne shaltow hange hem in the roof ful hye,
> That *no man* of oure purveiaunce espye" [3565–66].

Nicholas invokes the Oxford neighbors again when he tells John that on Monday night, *"whan men* ben alle aslepe, / Into oure knedyng tubbes wol we crepe" (3593–94). Later, when Alison wants Absolon to kiss quickly before he realizes that it is her bottom he is kissing, not her face, she tells him,

> "Have do," quod she, "com of, and speed the faste,
> Lest that *oure neighbores* thee espie" [3728–29].

And when Nicholas and Alison need the neighbors for real, and not just as a threat, the neighbors are right there:

> *The neighebores*, both smale and grete,
> In ronnen for to gauren on this man [3826–27].

We do not need to know the name of the street John lives on, but we need to know that his shenanigans take place in a town full of people. The people go to church, go to market, watch plays, worry about the weather, are friends of the college students, are enemies of the college students, beat down doors, buy charters and haircuts, have their blood let, get drunk, flirt with barmaids, lend hot coulters to their friends, sing, dance, go to Oseney, go to London, build fires, pray, sleep, sharpen plowshares, gossip, laugh, and form a chorus to be amused at the mad actions and foolish words of an old carpenter. None of this backdrop of people is mentioned in the tale that takes place in Antwerp.

Props and Provisions

In *Heile of Beersele* there are four props: ".i. bac" (67) [a trough], hanging by "enen vasten zele" (71) [a strong rope] from the beam, "een groet yser" (133) [a large iron], and Willem's "mes" (161) [knife]. None of these is mentioned before it is needed in the plot. That is, the trough hanging by the rope from the beam is not mentioned until it is time for Willem to hide from the priest by fleeing into it, and the knife is not mentioned until he uses it to cut the rope at the very end of the story.

Chaucer changes all that. Most importantly, the three troughs do not just appear when the plot requires them, but they are carefully provided for by Nicholas's detailed instructions to John:

> "Anon go gete us faste into this in
> A knedyng trogh, or ellis a kymelyn.
> For ech of us, but looke that they be large,
> In which we mowe swymme as in a barge" [3547–50].

Nicholas even tells John what to do with them:

> "But whan thou hast, for hire and thee and me,
> Ygeten us thise knedyng tubbes thre,
> Thanne shaltow hange hem in the roof ful hye" [3563–65].

The point is that the tubs do not just happen to be there when the plot requires them. Rather, Chaucer provides us information about them so that we know what they are and how they got there before the plot requires them.

And what about getting into the tubs? The Middle Dutch author is vague about the manner of that action. He tells us merely that Willem "in den bac geuloen" (74) [fled into the trough]. Are we to imagine that he leaps into it by jumping first onto the dining room table? Perhaps, but of course the Middle Dutch author does not tell us that any such table exists or that Willem jumps onto it. Chaucer, of course, has the carpenter not only acquire the three tubs, but also has him build the three ladders by which the three climb into them:

> His owene hand he made laddres thre,
> To clymben by the ronges and the stalkes
> Unto the tubbes hangynge in the balkes [3624–26].

In addition to the tubs and the ladders, we find all sorts of smaller props mentioned in Chaucer's tale. In Nicholas's chamber are a number of items[2]:

> His Almageste, and bookes grete and smale,
> His astrelabie, longynge for his art,
> His augrym stones layen faire apart,
> On shelves couched at his beddes heed;
> His presse ycovered with a faldyng reed
> And al above ther lay a gay sautrie [3208–13].

Not all of these items figure directly in the tale, though some of them do. They serve to establish Nicholas as a bookish man who can predict the weather, and of course his psaltery comes into play soon enough. After Alison agrees to become his lover, he "taketh his sawtrie, / And pleyeth faste, and maketh melodie" (3305–06).

In addition to his fancy clothes his comb and his spices, Absolon has his own share of props. He has a "rubible" (3331) and a "giterne" (3333, 3353), the latter of which he uses to serenade Alison. He has a "sencer" (3340), as well, that he uses in "sensynge" (3341) other men's wives.

We even have in the *Miller's Tale* several false props, such as the stone that Alison threatens to throw at Absolon if he does not go away: "Go forth thy wey, or I wol caste a ston" (3712).³ Another false prop is the ring that Absolon pretends to have so that he can bribe the fair Alison to open the window a second time to receive a second savory kiss:

> "Of gold," quod he, "I have thee broght a ryng.
> My mooder yaf it me, so God me save;
> Ful fyn it is, and thereto wel ygrave.
> This wol I yeve the, if thou me kisse" [3794–97].

John has his "staf" (3465) to pry up the door and, at Nicholas's bidding, "an ax" (3569) to cut the rope and hack his way through the gable. And of course Absolon, like Hughe in the Middle Dutch tale, acquires a hot iron with which to punish his antagonist. Instead of running home to his own smithy to get the iron, one that Hughe has illogically preheated in a fire he leaves burning when he goes off for his appointment with Heile, Absolon goes off to his friend Gerveys's smithy to get one that Gerveys, more logically, has already heated preparatory to sharpening it. I find it telling that we know more about Gerveys's smithy than we know about Heile's house. We know that it is close to John's house—house: "over the strete" (3760). We know that it has a "dore" (3786) that Absolon "knokketh" at (3764) and later "gan to stele" (3786) away from. We know that it has a "forge" (3760) and a "chymenee" (3776) or hearth. We know that Gerveys has a "shaar" (3765) and a "kultour" (3765, 3776, 3785). Chaucer provided even for an unimportant setting more details than the Middle Dutch author provides for the important one.

No discussion of the "props" in the *Miller's Tale* can ignore the culinary provisions. Not a hint of any food or drink appears in *Heile of Beersele*, but we find in the *Miller's Tale* almost enough food and drink to provision a small corner pub. Absolon, for example, has a whole arsenal of delectables with which to bribe Alison:

> He sente hire pyment, meeth, and spiced ale
> And wafres, piping hoot out of the gleede;
> And, for she was of town, he profred meede [3378–80].

When Nicholas gets ready to play dead in his bedroom, he carries with him "Bothe mete and drynke for a day or tweye" (3410). When he comes out of his pretended trance, the first thing he tells John is, "Fecche me drynke" (3492). John obligingly runs down and brings him "of myghty ale a large quart" (3496). Nicholas instructs John to provision the tubs with "vitaille suffisant" (3551, 3568) for a day. Never one to pass up a chance for enlivening detail, Chaucer tells us what kinds of provisions John buys:

> And hem vitailled, both trogh and tubbe,
> With breed, and chese, and good ale in a jubbe,
> Suffisynge right ynogh as for a day [3627–29].

Even in the account of John's fall from the tub we find food imagery:

> And doon gooth al: he foond neither to selle,
> Ne breed ne ale, til he cam to the celle
> Upon the floor [3821–23].

It is a strange expression: to fall so rapidly that he has no time to sell the bread and ale, but Chaucer seems to want to close out even the food references by letting us know that the provisions that John takes into the ark with him he never gets to eat and cannot even sell.[4]

Chaucer, then, transforms a tale with remarkably little information about the setting for the story, the structure and furnishings of the house, and the implements and provisions that the characters use. He adds enriching details that let us see the town of Oxford and its people, let us see the house and its contents, let us know what the folks eat and drink and hear and smell and feel. In doing so he helps us to create a theater in our minds, a theater in which we can take in, far better than in *Heile of Beersele*, the actions in the story and the people who perform them.

To further explain my point that Chaucer was working toward a more dramatic work of literature than the one he found, let us consider the way he invents and develops the various scenes that are the *Miller's Tale*, and the way he uses dialogue to enliven those scenes.

IX

The Pre-Bedroom Sequence

Heile of Beersele has essentially only one sequence of scenes, what I refer to as the bedroom sequence, where the three lecherous men visit the lecherous Heile in her home. The thirteen-line introductory material really has little to do with the actual narrative itself. Roughly parallel to the Miller's prologue, those thirteen lines recount the reasons for the narrator's telling this tale. Then at line 14 the narrator begins the story proper with a brief thirty-three-line narrative summary of the events that prepare for the action of the tale in the bedroom sequence: the locale in Antwerp where Heile lives, the three fellows who one day make separate arrangements to visit Heile in her home that night, their anticipation of the pleasures ahead of them that evening, and Heile's delight at the chance to make so much money. And, then, at line 47 we start what I call the bedroom sequence, beginning when Willem goes to Heile's place at his appointed hour: "Alst quam tusschen dach end nacht" [When dusk came, the time between day and night]. That sequence runs to the end of the tale and amounts to 132 lines, or 80.0 percent—four-fifths—of the 165 lines of the tale proper. The "tale proper" excludes not only the thirteen-line prologue but also the twelve-line moral interpretation at the end.

That bedroom sequence, of course, is also a key part of the 663-line *Miller's Tale*. Corresponding roughly to the bedroom sequence in the Middle Dutch tale, it starts at line 3633 in Chaucer: "And on the Monday, whan it drow to nyght." Chaucer's bedroom sequence, which runs to the end of the tale and amounts to some 217 lines, is nearly twice as long as the corresponding scene in the Middle Dutch source.[1] There is no question, then, that Chaucer saw the importance of that scene to the tale. But we should notice, even more importantly, that for Chaucer, the bedroom sequence is not four-fifths of the

Chart 1. Major divisions of *Heile of Beersele* and the *Miller's Tale*.

	Heile of Beersele	Miller's Tale
Total number of lines in the tale proper	165 lines	663 lines
The pre-bedroom sequence	33 lines (14–46) 20.0 % of tale proper	446 lines (3187–3632) 67.3% of tale proper
The bedroom sequence	132 lines (47–178) 80.0 % of tale proper	217 lines (3633–3849) 32.7% of tale proper

tale, but less than a third. To put the matter differently, Chaucer takes the small introductory thirty-three-line setup for the bedroom sequence from his source and expands it to 446 lines in his own tale. That expansion makes Chaucer's pre-bedroom setup more than two-thirds of the tale, or nearly seventeen times as long as it was in his source.[2]

Perhaps it will be helpful to put some of these numbers in table or chart form. In Chart 1, I exclude the prologues to the two tales (thirteen lines or 6.8 percent of the total 190 lines of *Heile of Beersele*, and seventy-eight lines or 10.4 percent of the total 746 lines of the Miller's prologue and tale). I also exclude the closing moral summary (twelve lines or 5.8 percent of the total 190 lines of *Heile of Beersele*, and five lines or 0.7 percent of the total 746 lines of the Miller's prologue and tale), since that closing summary is not part of the actual story line in either tale. In the Chart 1 include information only about the tales themselves—what I call the "tale proper"—the narrative of the woman and her three admirers, without the opening prologue materials or the closing moral interpretation. The tale proper amounts to 165 lines in the Middle Dutch tale and 663 lines in the English one.

The Pre-Bedroom Sequence

It is useful to consider the three larger narrative units of the opening two-thirds of Chaucer's *Miller's Tale* proper: **1. Nicholas approaches Alison**, that is, the descriptions of Nicholas and Alison followed by Nicholas's attempted seduction of Alison, 120 lines (3187–3306); **2. Absolon approaches Alison**, that is, the description of Absolon followed by his nocturnal serenade of Alison, ninety lines (3307–96); and **3. Nicholas tricks John**, that is, Nicholas's

Chart 2. Major divisions of the pre-bedroom portion of the *Miller's Tale*.	
	Number of lines and their percentage of the Miller's Tale
Total number of lines in the tale proper	663 lines
1. Descriptions of Nicholas and Alison and Nicholas's approach to Alison	120 lines (3187–3306) 18.1% of tale proper
2. Description of Absolon and his approach to Alison	90 lines (3307–3396) 13.6% of tale proper
3. Nicholas's tricking of John with prediction of a coming flood	236 lines (3397–3632) 35.6% of tale proper

encounter with John to set up the bedroom trick, 236 lines (3397–3632). See Chart 2 for percentages.

Before considering in more detail each of the Chaucerian scenes in the pre-bedroom sequence, we should note that the opening two scenes in the pre-bedroom sequence in the *Miller's Tale* are longer than the whole of *Heile of Beersele*.[3] That is, Chaucer devotes considerably more space to descriptions of Nicholas, Alison, and Absolon and to their initial encounters than the Middle Dutch author does to the whole of his tale. We should note also that Chaucer devotes as much space to Nicholas's effort to trick John into thinking that a second Noah's flood is coming as he does to the whole bedroom sequence. Clearly, then, Chaucer was interested in preparing through the early scenes in his tale for the big sequence at the end. He wanted us to know, by the time the climactic bedroom sequence comes, who the characters are, what they do, why they react as they do, and why the punishments meted out are appropriate. As we consider in more detail the three pre-bedroom scenes in the *Miller's Tale*, we should keep in mind that there is virtually no equivalent to these scenes in *Heile of Beersele*.

Nicholas Approaches Alison

Chaucer is not much interested in describing John. We know that he is rich, that he is a "gnof" (3188) or churl, that he is a carpenter, that he is jealous. John does not play a large role in the bedroom scene. He snores through most of it, so we need to know less about him than about the other characters. Besides, his small role in the pre-bedroom scene comes after the two shorter scenes in which Nicholas and Absolon approach Alison. In these first two scenes, Chaucer describes the three younger characters in considerable detail.

Chaucer starts off with Nicholas, the English counterpart of the Middle Dutch priest. In *Heile of Beersele* we are told merely that the priest is one of the three men who approach the lecherous Heile. We know nothing more about him than that he is a priest. We have no idea what he looks like or how old he is. We know nothing more about his motives for approaching Heile than that he is horny. Perhaps he lusts for any pretty woman, not specifically Heile, and perhaps she just happened to be a willing and affordable prostitute who is available when he wants some action, but in fact we are simply not told.

Nicholas in the *Miller's Tale* is the counterpart of that priest in *Heile of Beersele*. We are not told what he looks like, except that he looks "lyk a mayden" (3202), presumably a reference to his shy and innocent demeanor. But we learn a great deal about him: he is a poor young scholar, he knows astrology, he predicts the weather, he is sly and secretive, he lives in Alison's house, he has many books, he plays a psaltery, he sings, and he knows about secret love and about lust, he spends time with his friends, and so on.

In *Heile of Beersele* we are told initially almost nothing of Heile herself except that she is a lecherous prostitute who will have sex with anyone and everyone who offers her money. We assume that because she is an in-demand prostitute, she is young and pretty, but that may be merely an assumption. The author never tells us. Chaucer tells us much more about Alison: she is pretty, young, weasel-like in her slender body. She wears a belt and a white apron, an embroidered shift and black silk collar, a white cap with black ribbons and a silk headband. She has a lecherous eye and plucked brows. She is prettier than a pear tree, softer than lambswool, and so on. Through Chaucer's attention to details of description, Nicholas and, especially, Alison take form on the page before us. We can "see" them in our mind's eye, almost as if they were in front of us. When they start to talk, we know something of what they look like, and what kind of people they are.

We find several theatrical elements in this first part of the tale where Nicholas makes his bold approach to the lovely Alison. There is nothing in *Heile of Beersele* even close to Nicholas's bold attempted seduction of Alison. In the Middle Dutch source, we are told that three fellows come to Heile to make arrangements to see her later. We do not see the scene, we merely hear about it, and then in the most general terms:

IX. The Pre-Bedroom Sequence

> Eens geuielt, hoerdic vertellen
> Dat ane hare quamen .iij. gesellen
> Op enen dach. [21–23].
> > [I heard tell that once it chanced that three fellows came to her in one day.]

We know that one is a miller (corresponding roughly to John), one a priest (corresponding roughly to Nicholas) and one a smith (corresponding roughly to Absolon). They have separate interviews with Heile, but these are not shown directly. Rather, they are joined together and summarized in a few words:

> Deen vore ende dander na,
> Ende die hare alle om vrienscape baden
> Dat si hem wilde ghestaden
> Te comen daer si ware [24–27].
> > [One after the other they all asked for her love, asked that she would let them come to see her where she lived.]

The scenes are not individualized. They are not made visual through description or action, or made audible through dialogue. We learn only, through summary narration, that Heile agreed to see them all at different times of the night, the miller first, the priest second, the smith third. The narration of those arrangements takes place in nine short lines:

> Dat ierste was, des geloeft,
> Een moeldre hiet Willem Hoeft.
> Dien hiet si comen ter selver stont
> Rechts in den avont.
> Dander was .i. pape; dien hiet si comen
> Alse hi die slaepclocke hadde vernomen.
> Terde was hare gebuer, .i. smet;
> Dien hiet si comen al ongelet
> Alse die diefclocke geluut ware [35–43].
> > [The first was a miller named Willem Hoeft. She told him to come in the early evening. The second was a priest. She told him to come when he heard the evening bell. The third was her neighbor, a smith. She told him to come when he heard the night bell rung.]

In contrast, in the first pre-bedroom sequence in the *Miller's Tale*, which takes place when John is out of town, Nicholas tells Alison what he wants. Nicholas is a man of direct action, so his first act is to grab Alison: "And prively he caught hire by the queynte [...]. / And heeld hire harde by the haunchebones" (3276, 3279). Nicholas balances that crude action with sweet love-talk, hoping apparently that either the grabbing or the gabbing will get him what he wants:

> "Ywis, but if ich have my wille,
> For derne love of the, lemman, I spille."
> [...]
> "Lemman, love me al atones,
> Or I wol dyen, also God me save!" [3277–78, 3280–81].

We see and hear Alison, his stage-partner, as well. Anyone who knows about barnyards can "see" the sprightly young woman:

> And she sprong as a colt dooth in the trave
> And with hir heed she wryed faste awey [3282–83].

And we can hear her voice as she speaks:

> "I wol nat kisse thee, by my fey!
> Why, lat be!" quod she, "Lat be, Nicholas,
> Or I wol crie 'out, harrow' and 'allas'!
> Do wey youre handes, for your curteisie!" [3285–88].

This little exchange is interesting in part because Alison's speech looks ahead to later scenes. Though Nicholas has not asked for a kiss, she refuses to give him one, anticipating the window scene later, when she does grant her other suitor a kiss, but on a place that surprises him. Her threat to "crie 'out, harrow' and 'allas'!" also looks forward to the end of the bedroom scene, where she and Nicholas both cry "Out" and "Harrow" (3825) in the street to call in the neighbors so that they can laugh at old John's absurd behavior. Most important, this scene is a dramatized exchange, with action matched with action and speech matched with speech. Nicholase grabs, Alison throws his hands off. He threatens to die, she spurns him. He begs, she refuses. We have here a real scene, not a narrator's hasty summary of a scene. To be sure, there is some summary narration in the *Miller's Tale*, as Chaucer gets on with the scene, and some of the conversation is presented in narrative summary rather than through direct dialogue:

> This Nicholas gan mercy for to crye,
> And spake so faire, and profred him so faste,
> That she hir love hym graunted atte laste,
> And swoor hir ooth, by Seint Thomas of Kent,
> That she wol been at his comandement,
> When that she may hir leyser wel espie [3288–93].

Although not every word is revealed through dialogue, the important words are, as when Chaucer takes us immediately back to direct reporting of the words that Nicholas and Alison speak:

IX. The Pre-Bedroom Sequence

> "Myn housbonde is so ful of jalousie
> That but ye wayte wel and been privee,
> I woot right wel I nam but deed," quod she.
> "Ye moste been ful deerne, as in this cas."
> "Nay, thereof care thee noght," quod Nicholas.
> "A clerke hadde litherly biset his whyle,
> But if he koude a carpenter bigyle" [3294–3300].

And then we get some actions to match the words we have just heard:

> Whan Nicholas had done thus everideel
> And thakked hire aboute the lendes weel,
> He kiste hire sweete and taketh his sawtrie
> And pleyeth faste, and maketh melodie [3303–06].

These two characters reveal themselves through their words and their actions. Nicholas shows himself to be horny, full of life, bold, willing to take risks, knowledgeable about the forms of courtly love, forthright in his approach to women, lying (they both know that he is not really going to die if he does not get Alison), willing to bide his time to get what he wants, and pridefully confident that as a college student he can beguile a mere ignorant tradesman. Alison shows, through action and speech, that she is lively and spirited, able to hold her own against aggressive men, aware that men do not value what they get too easily, willing to use threats she does not mean, eager for love, and willing to take risks to get it—but cautious risks, taken with all the necessary caution and secrecy.

The Middle Dutch storyteller tells us virtually nothing about his characters except that they arrange to meet later for paid sex. Chaucer shows us what they look like, what they do, what they say, why they do what they do, how they react to situations, what turns them on and off, what they know, and what risks they are willing to take to get what they want. Chaucer, shows us people doing and saying. Having said that, however, I hasten to point out that this first pre-bedroom scene, while more dramatic than the corresponding lines in the source, is not Chaucer at his most fully dramatic. The first 120 lines of the *Miller's Tale* are, finally, more narrative than drama. The action is vivid, to be sure, but it figures small in the total. The dialogue is revealing, to be sure, but skimpy. In the first scene, where Nicholas approaches Alison, we have more description of people and actions than we have dialogue. Of the 120 lines in that first scene, 105 lines are spoken by the narrator, seven lines by Nicholas, and eight lines by Alison (see Chart 3).

In Chart 3 I show the number of "speeches"—that is, the number of times the narrator and each of the two characters begins a new speech. The narrator's words, of course, are not speeches in the same sense as those of the characters

Chart 3. Speeches in the scene where Nicholas approaches Alison in the *Miller's Tale*.

	Number of speeches	Total number of lines	Average number of lines per speech	Percentage of total length of scene
Narrator	5	105	21 lines	87.5%
Nicholas	3	7	2.3 lines	5.8%
Alison	2	8	4 lines	6.7%
Totals	10	120		100%

themselves, but the data are interesting. The narrator "talks" five times. His 105 lines, average twenty-one lines each. Nicholas and Alison speak less often and have shorter speeches.[4] We see what they look like, we see them in their initial encounter, but we don't hear them much. Without any question, the narrator dominates in the first pre-bedroom scene. He does in the second, also.

Absolon Approaches Alison

In *Heile of Beersele* the third lover, a smith named Hughe, is individualized no more than the other two men. Like them, he approaches Heile and she makes an appointment with him, just as she had made with the others. We have no idea what the depth of his affection for Heile is. Except for his name, his occupation, and the fact that he is or has once been a neighbor of Heile's in Beersele, we know nothing about him. We have no idea what he looks like, unless we want to imagine that as a blacksmith he is probably large of arm, smoky of complexion, and scarred of face from the sparks of his fire. But that is us imagining a stereotype, not the author describing him. The Middle Dutch author was simply not interested in our knowing what the smith looked like or what sort of personality he had. With Chaucer, it is different. Chaucer wants us to know, wants us to see, wants us to hear.

Absolon is probably in almost every way the opposite of our imagined blacksmith who was his counterpart in *Heile of Beersele*. But at least we see Absolon. Delicate and a bit effeminate, Absolon has curly yellow hair that shines like gold, combed out like a large broad fan with a nice straight part. He has a rosy complexion set off by grey eyes. And what lovely clothes he wears—red stockings and shoes with fancy carving in the leather. With his tight-fitting clothes, his lace, and his ecclesiastical gown, he is as pretty as a white blossom on a springtime twig (3324). He is a man of many talents. Not only is he a sensor-swinging parish clerk, but he augments his slender income by letting blood, shaving, cutting hair, and writing contracts. He can act in a biblical drama and dance in the Oxford style, casting his legs to and fro. He plays songs, accompanying himself on a fiddle or a guitar, and he sings in a high-pitched treble. He surely does get around, particularly to the pubs with jolly barmaids. He makes it a point to frequent any place he might expect to encounter one of the pretty young wives of his parish. He is fastidious in his speech and—oh yes—a bit squeamish about farting.

Why in the world does Chaucer want us to know so much about this unlikely lover? The Middle Dutch author had already proved that a teller could tell the story with no details of appearance or occupation or character at all, and then along comes Chaucer and changes all that. Why does Chaucer want to pump in all the details? The obvious answer is that Chaucer is not merely setting Absolon up to be the character most appropriately punished in the bedroom scene,[5] but that he wants us to see and hear, not merely imagine, Absolon cavorting on the high scaffold where he foolishly plays Herod to impress his lady love. Chaucer is writing here fictionalized drama, and for that we need to hear and see the important characters.

We see Absolon in action just outside Alison's bedroom window. Chaucer sets the scene nicely. It is late into the night, just after the crowing of the cock, but the moon is shining brightly. The action in this scene is minimal, but we are told that Absolon takes "his gyterne" (3333) with him "and forth he gooth" (3335) to the carpenter's house. Then he "dressed hym up" to the shot-window (3338) and there "syngeth" (3360). The verbs "takes" "goes," "moves," and "sings" are not the most vivid of action verbs, but they get Absolon to where he needs to be, and with the right equipment. The important thing in this scene is that we get to hear, "gentil and smal" (3360), his voice singing to Alison:

> "Now, deere lady, if thy wille be,
> I praye yow that ye wole rewe on me" [3361–62].

The actual "deere lady" that Absolon sings to, of course, is Alison, but because he is the parish clerk, gullible old John, hearing him, wakes up and thinks Absolon is chanting a prayer to the Virgin Mary asking her to take pity on him. Jealous though he is said to be, it seems never to occur to John that in Absolon's plea for spiritual pity from Mary there is a veiled plea for a more physical or emotional kind of pity from Alison. John speaks to his wife:

> "What! Alison! Herestow nat Absolon,
> That chaunteth thus under oure boures wal?" [3366–67].

She hears, too, and makes only a brief answer:

> "Yis, God woot, John, I heere it every deel.
> This passeth forth; what wol ye bet than weel?"[6] [3369–70].

That little scene at John's window does not amount to much. Each of the three characters sings or says two lines, but those lines are revealing. In his lines Absolon reveals himself to be foolishly resourceful in his approach to Alison, trying to pass off a seduction attempt as a morning prayer to the Virgin Mary.[7] For a man who is supposed to be jealous and suspicious, old John reveals himself to be foolishly blind to the motives of the parish clerk who serenades his wife so late at night. And in her sleepy reply to him, Alison reveals herself to be bored with her foolish would-be lover: "This too," she sighs, "will pass." In that brief scene Chaucer not only informs us about three of the four principle characters, but also builds our expectations about what is to come. We have, on the basis of this scene, plenty of reason to expect that the supposedly jealous John will never suspect his wife no matter what she does, that Absolon will get his just desserts for his refusal to accept the truth about Alison's boredom with him, and that Alison will have a chance to repay Absolon for his persistently unwelcome advances. Chaucer uses this short scene—little more than a vignette, really—to develop his characters and move his plot toward its inevitable conclusion at that same window a few nights later.

In the second pre-bedroom scene, we have even more narrative and even less dialogue than in the first one. Of the 90 lines, 84 are spoken by the narrator. Two are spoken by Absolon, two by John, and two by Alison (see Chart 4).

Note once again, in Chart 4, the sheer dominance of the narrator. The action is there, but it is minimal. The dialogue is there, but it also is minimal. The descriptions and the actions of the characters, of course, are important

	Number of speeches	Total number of lines	Average number of lines per speech	Percentage of total length of scene
Narrator	4	84	21 lines	93.4%
John	1	2	2 lines	2.2%
Alison	1	2	2 lines	2.2%
Absolon	1	2	2 lines	2.2%
Totals	7	90		100%

Chart 4. Speeches in the scene where Absolon approaches Alison in the *Miller's Tale*.

in helping to understand the characters and "see" them in the theater of our minds, but they are not fully dramatic. For the dialogue that will make the tale more fully dramatic, we look to the third of the of the scenes that make up the pre-bedroom sequence.

Nicholas Tricks John

The third scene in what I am calling the pre-bedroom sequence in the *Miller's Tale* is the wonderful scene in which Nicholas convinces John that a second Noah's flood is coming and that John can save himself, his wife, and Nicholas by hanging three tubs from the roof beams. There is nothing even remotely equivalent to this scene in *Heile of Beersele*. The second lover in the Middle Dutch tale is the priest. To be sure, he does predict that a flood may come, but the circumstances are entirely different. He makes his prediction not as part of his plan to get Heile into the sack but rather, quite strangely, after he has enjoyed her professional services three times:

>> Ghinc die pape liggen ghewaghen
>> Vter ewangelien menech woret.
>> Oec soe seidi dit bat voert,
>> Dat die tijt noch soude comen
>> Dat God die werelt soude doemen,
>> Beide met watre ende met viere,
>> End dat should wesen sciere
>> Dat al die werelt verdrinken soude,
>> Grote ende clene, ionge ende oude [78–86].
>>> [Then the priest started to quote words from the gospels and said also that the time would come soon when God would destroy the world with water and fire, that all the people would drown, great and small, young and old.]

One of the central flaws in *Heile of Beersele* is that we never understand why a priest would, after three times making love to Heile, suddenly preach her a little sermon and predict the end of the world. One can imagine several possible motivations: that he feels guilty for his unpriestly lechery and wants at least to sound like a priest even if he does not act like one, that Heile puts him up to it to convince Willem in the trough above that the priest really is there to say a prayer for her, or that he really does think a flood is coming. We readers can imagine such motivation, if we want to bother, but the Middle Dutch author provides none. The only motivation we can imagine is an authorial one: that is, we can understand that the author needed to provide motivation for Willem in the trough above to cut the rope and by doing so bring the plot to its end, so he has the priest loudly predict a flood. But he offers no motivation for the priest himself wanting to offer a post-coital flood prediction.

Chaucer, on the other hand, offers convincing double motivation for Nicholas's pre-coital prediction of the flood: that Nicholas wants to secure Alison as his lover and that he wants to show both Alison and John that a bright young clerk is can outwit a dull old carpenter. But let us consider some of the narrative data of that scene. If we count the lines, we find that in this scene there is far more dialogue than narration. The narrator speaks only 86 of the 236 lines in the scene—slightly more than a third of the lines—while the characters themselves have 150 lines—almost two-thirds. See Chart 5 for the breakdowns by character in this, the longest scene in the tale.

Chart 5 reveals a number of interesting facts. First, it shows that while old John has more individual speeches than the other principles in the scene, his lines are shorter, making up only a fifth of the scene. It is appropriate, after all, for a carpenter, who makes his living with his hands rather than his tongue, to be a man of few words. On the other hand, though Nicholas has fewer individual speeches, his speeches are much longer, averaging sixteen lines per speech in this scene, and make up more than 40 percent cent of the scene. As an Oxford student who reads books, he would naturally tend to go on and on verbally, and he does. Indeed, his longest uninterrupted speech, by far the longest in the tale, is sixty-four lines. The chart does not show it, but while the narrator has more than a third of the lines, many of those lines come at the very start and finish of the scene. In the first twenty-eight lines the narrator

Chart 5. Speeches in the scene where Nicholas tricks John in the *Miller's Tale*.

	Number of speeches	Total number of lines	Average number of lines per speech	Percentage of total length of scene
Narrator	9	86	9.6 lines	36.4%
John	9	48	5.3 lines	20.3%
Nicholas	6	96	16 lines	40.7%
Alison	1	4	4 lines	1.7%
Robyn	1	2	2 lines	0.9%
Totals	26	236		100%

IX. The Pre-Bedroom Sequence

sets up the action and the dialogue of the scene, while in the last twenty-two lines he comments on that action and dialogue. If we set aside his opening twenty-eight lines and his closing twenty-two lines, then the narrator's percentage goes down considerably. Of the remaining 186 lines, the narrator has only thirty-six lines, a mere 19.4 percent of the central part of the scene. He has only seven speeches, and they average only 5.1 lines per speech. In other words, once the action part of the scene begins, the narrator steps aside and lets the characters, very much like actors, carry the weight of the scene.

What actually happens in this dialogue-heavy scene? On Saturday, Nicholas puts his too-too-clever plan into effect by locking himself into a room with food and drink. It is not until Sunday night that old John notices that he has not seen Nicholas about and immediately fears that his boarder may be dead. He sends his knave Robyn up to Nicholas's room to check. Robyn does so, in a scene with sufficient action:

> This knave gooth hym up ful sturdily,
> And at the chambre dore whil that he stood,
> He cride and knokked as that he were wood [343–36].

Robyn then looks through a hole in the wall, sees Nicholas apparently dead, and runs down to tell his master what he has seen. Then he and John run back up again and break into the room. When he sees Nicholas's condition, John suspects necromancy, runs down and blesses the four walls of his house and his door, then comes back up. Nicholas pretends to come to and immediately sends John back down to fetch some ale. John goes down again, and then climbs the stairs again with the ale. All of this action—none of it in *Heile of Beersele*—is downright theatrical: running up and down stairs, banging on and shouting at the door, sneaking peaks through cat-holes, breaking into rooms, shaking the trance-like occupant, running around the house saying charms, fetching ale—all against a backdrop of a foolish old man who does not suspect that his boarder has designs on his wife. John thinks Nicholas spends too much time studying (see lines 3463, 3467), totally missing the truth: that Nicholas has been spending his time not studying but seducing his wife.

Once the action part of the scene is mostly over, the main part of the dialogue comes into play with the "awakening" of Nicholas. I need not here go into the details of Nicholas's verbiage. Well-known are his insistence that John be secretive about what he is about to learn, his revelation that his astrological studies and his trance have indicated that the next night a terrible rain will come and drown the world, his comparing the coming flood to the flood that destroyed the world in Noah's time, his detailed instructions about getting and provisioning the three tubs and about hanging them from the roof beams, separated so that there may be no sin between John and his wife on the night of the flood.

Nicholas's long speech is roughly parallel to the priest's prediction of a coming flood in *Heile of Beersele*, but the differences are far more insistent than the parallels. In Chaucer's tale, Nicholas predicts the flood after faking a trance, not after enjoying an evening of sexual activity. He predicts it in conjunction with the biblical Noah's flood rather than in isolation of that familiar event. He predicts it to the husband of the woman he wants to have sex with, not uselessly to the woman herself. He predicts it in conjunction with directions about preparing the three little arks, not as an isolated event unconnected with the rest of the story, and so on. But my main interest here is that we hear about that prediction at length and in Nicholas's own words, not in summary statement of a few lines by the narrator of the tale. Chaucer, in short, dramatizes the prediction rather than reports it. That makes all the difference.

The scene in which Nicholas tricks John into thinking that a flood is coming and into hanging three tubs from the roof beams closes with Alison's assurance to her husband that "I am thy trewe, verray wedded wyf" (3609) and her sendoff to him: "Go, deere spouse, and help to save oure lyf" (3610). John does go, and in summarized action does rustle up three tubs, then provisions then with bread, cheese, and ale. After that, still following Nicholas's directions, John sends his knave and his wench to London.

As always in this tale, Chaucer lets us "see" his characters. We can visualize Nicholas "evere capyng upright, / As he had kiked on the newe moone" (3444–45). We can visualize Robyn banging on the door and later helping to lift it off its hinge pins. We can visualize John and Nicholas there drinking ale while the clever student lectures the gullible carpenter. And when that scene is over, we can visualize old John:

> This sely carpenter bigynneth quake;
> Hym thynketh verraily that he may see
> Noees flood come walwynge as the see
> To drenchen Alison, his hony deere.
> He wepeth, weyleth, maketh sory cheere;
> He siketh with ful many a sory swogh [3614–19].

Chaucer lets us see John quake and weep, lets us hear him sigh and groan before he swings into exhausting action getting tubs, provisioning them, building ladders, and, near exhaustion, hanging the tubs from the roof beams.

Thus ends the third of the three scenes that Chaucer provides us as preparation for the bedroom sequence. With fully two-thirds of the tale behind us, we are now ready to see where all this talk and action are taking us: straight to the bedroom and its shot-window. In these three new scenes that make up the majority of the *Miller's Tale*, Chaucer describes the three principle characters— Nicholas, Alison, and Absolon—who are to play such important roles in the bedroom sequence. The fourth, and lesser character, John, has a simpler role to play. He needs to be old so that we know why his frisky wife wants to take a younger lover. He needs to be stupid so that he does not see the designs that Absolon and Nicholas have on his wife, does not see what is going on right before his eyes—and ours. And of course he needs to be gullible enough to buy into Nicholas's absurd prediction so that he can work as a kind of set-designer to prepare the elaborate stage for the big scenes to come—and then go to sleep to get out of the way until the plot requires him to wake up and come crashing down onto that stage.

X

The Bedroom Sequence

The bedroom sequences in both *Heile of Beersele* and the *Miller's Tale* are made up of several scenes. In the Middle Dutch tale we find four scenes: **(1) the first window scene**, where the three lovers come to visit Heile and the smith kisses the priest's bottom (eighty-four lines, 47–130); **(2) the smithy scene**, where Hughe runs home to his smithy to heat up an iron (six lines, 131–36); **(3) the second window scene**, where Hughe punishes the priest with his hot iron and Willem cuts himself loose from the roof beams and falls to the floor (thirty-five lines, 137–71); and **(4) the latrine scene**, where the frightened priest runs into the corner, falls into the cesspit, and emerges all covered with excrement (seven lines, 172–78). At the very end of *Heile of Beersele* we have a short expository moral: the story shows that men who associate with prostitutes will be punished for it (twelve lines, 179–90). It will be useful to have before us in table form in Chart 6 the numbers of speeches spoken or thought[1] by the various characters in *Heile of Beersele*.

Chaucer gives us, on the other hand, six scenes in his 217-line bedroom sequence: **(1) the ladder scene**, where John, Alison, and Nicholas climb their ladders and then, while John sleeps, where Nicholas and Alison sneak down their ladders and go to bed (24 lines, 3633–56); **(2) the Oseney scene**, where Absolon makes enquiries about John, then goes home to get some rest before he approaches Alison's window (30 lines, 3657–86); **(3) the first window scene**, starting with Absolon's rise at the first cock's call and ending with his kissing Alison's bottom (73 lines, 3687–3759); **(4) the smithy scene**, where Absolon goes to Gerveys's smithy to fetch a hot coulter (28 lines, 3760–87); **(5) the second window scene**, where Absolon returns and scorches Nicholas's bottom with the hot coulter and John cuts himself loose from the roof beams (36 lines, 3788–3823); and **(6) the**

Chart 6. Lines assigned to speakers in four scenes of *Heile of Beersele*.

	Window Scene 1	Smithy Scene	Window Scene 2	Latrine Scene	Total	Percentage
Narrator	50	6	20	7	83	62.9%
Willem	5	—	8	—	13	9.8%
Priest	2	—	1	—	3	2.3%
Heile	19	—	—	—	19	14.4%
Hughe	8	—	6	—	14	10.6%
Total	84	6	35	7	132	100%

Chart 7. Lines assigned to speakers in six bedroom scenes of *Miller's Tale*.

	Ladder Scene	Oseney Scene	Window Scene 1	Smithy Scene	Window Scene 2	Neighbor Scene	Total	Percentage
Narrator	22	8	34	11	25	25	125	57.6%
John	1	—	—	—	1	—	2	0.9%
Nicholas	1	—	2	—	1	—	4	1.8%
Alison	—	—	12	—	2	—	14	6.5%
Absolon	—	15	25	7	7	—	54	24.9%
Others	—	7	—	10	—	1	18	8.3%
Total	24	30	73	28	36	26	217	100%

neighbor scene, where Nicholas and Alison call in the neighbors to laugh at John and declare him mad because of his nonsensical gibberish about Noah's flood (26 lines, 3824–49). I am aware that there is a window scene in the prebedroom sequence in the *Miller's Tale*, when Absolon serenades Alison. In this chapter, however, I use the term "first window scene" to refer to the first one in the bedroom sequence. I do not include as part of the bedroom sequence the five lines summarizing the punishment that the three men receive for their actions.

It will be useful to have before us in Chart 7 a scene-by-scene allocation of the lines[2] to the various personages in the *Miller's Tale*.

A hasty comparison of the numbers in Charts 6 and 7 shows some interesting similarities in the two tales. For example, in both *Heile of Beersele* and the *Miller's Tale* the two window scenes are the longest and have the most dialogue. In both, the narrator does most of the "talking" in the whole bedroom sequence: in *Heile of Beersele* the narrator speaks 62.9 percent of the lines, while in the *Miller's Tale*, he speaks 57.6 percent. Always, however, it is the differences that are of most interest to Chaucerian scholars who want to see what is new or most original about Chaucer's version. Among the more significant differences are that in the first of the two window scenes in the bedroom sequence Chaucer has the narrator carry a smaller percentage of the burden. The Middle Dutch author lets the narrator speak 50 of the 84 lines, or 59.5 percent. Chaucer reduces that percentage by having the narrator speak only 34 of the 73 lines, or 46.6 percent. He wants to let the characters speak for themselves in most of the all-important scene where Absolon presents himself as a would-be lover to fair Alison. Another difference, to be discussed in more detail below, is that Chaucer increases the dialogue in the whole bedroom sequence by inventing lines assigned to the cloisterer at Oseney, to Gerveys at the smithy, and to John's neighbors. None of those characters appear in the Middle Dutch tale. Perhaps most interesting is that to judge by the apportioning of the dialogue, Chaucer appears to have reduced the importance of Alison in the bedroom sequence. He reduces the percentage of her lines from 14.4 percent in *Heile of Beersele* to less than half, or 6.5 percent in the *Miller's Tale*. On the other hand, Chaucer greatly enhances the importance of Absolon. His counterpart, the smith in *Heile of Beersele*, was given only 10.6 percent of the lines in the bedroom sequence, a percentage that is more than doubled for Absolon, to 24.9 percent. Clearly, then, by devoting nearly a quarter of the lines to Absolon in the bedroom sequence, Chaucer was letting him be the major actor in that scene, just as Nicholas had been the major actor in the long scene where he tricked old John.

We cannot help but notice, right up front, that Chaucer gives us six scenes in the bedroom sequence whereas the Middle Dutch author gave us only four. We will consider why as we analyze each of Chaucer's six scenes, looking back always at the way the Middle Dutch author treated—or did not treat—the materials in that scene.

The Ladder Scene

Chaucer's brief twenty-four-line ladder scene has no counterpart in the Middle Dutch tale. To be sure, the first visitor, Willem, does get himself into the tub in Heile's house, but he does it not to escape a flood but to escape detection by the priest who is Heile's second paying client. At the time he gets into the tub, Willem has no idea that a flood may be coming. He hears that prediction later. Besides, little is made of the tub or Willem's climbing into it. It has no provisions or rope-cutting tools because none are needed. What I am calling the ladder scene, then, can be considered fully original with Chaucer. Chaucer makes it an action sequence. I italicize the verbs. After John shuts the door ("*shette* his dore" [3634]), he, his boarder, and his wife climb up their ladders ("up they *clomben* alle three" [3636]), say their Paternosters and warn each other to be quiet ("*Clom*!" [3639]). Then John sits quietly ("stille he *sit*" [3641]) listening for the sound of the rain, falls asleep, groans ("he *groneth* soore" [3646]) and snores ("eft he *routeth*" [3647]). Although old John plays only a small part in the bedroom sequence, Chaucer wants to make sure that we keep a picture of him in the theater of our minds, sitting there absurdly in his cramped tub, uncomfortably asleep in his private little ark, exhausted after his frenzied day of activity in preparing the "set" for Nicholas's preposterous game. Against that backdrop, Nicholas sneaks down his ladder ("Doun of the laddre *stalketh* Nicholay" [3648]), and Alison rushes down her ladder ("ful softe adoun she *spedde*" [3649]). The Middle Dutch author tells us only that Willem gets into the tub ("es in den bac geuloen" [74, flees into the trough]), but is vague about how he gets there. We find no mention of a ladder or any other means of climbing. It does not matter to the Middle Dutch author that we may wonder how Willem gets into the trough, or whether, if we imagine that he may have stepped on some piece of furniture, that we imagine correctly. For Chaucer it matters. He wants us to see the three tubs hanging far apart. He wants us to see the three ladders. He wants us to see the three principles climb up their ladders, then two of them sneak down their ladders, leaving the third sitting foolishly up there with his food, his drink, and his axe, waiting sleepily for the stormy action of the evening to begin. John has no idea, of course, that the real action is steamy, not stormy, and that it has already begun down in his bedroom.

The Oseney Scene

Leaving old John waiting for the rain and Nicholas having "myrthe" and "solas" (3654) in bed with Alison, Chaucer takes us, in another scene that has no counterpart in the Middle Dutch story, to the nearby town of Oseney. What, we might wonder, is Absolon doing there in the first place? Chaucer tells us in words that help further to characterize the worldly parish clerk:

> This parissh clerk, this amorous Absolon,
> That is for love alwey so wo bigon,
> Upon the Monday was at Oseneye
> With compaignye, hym to disporte and pleye [3657–60].

Instead of attending to the religious duties of a parish clerk, the amorous, lovesick Absolon is at Oseney having fun with his friends.[3] While there, he goes into the abbey and draws one of the cloisterers aside and asks about John. Absolon determines from him that John may be off at a grange getting lumber for his building project there. Ignoring the cloisterer's alternative possibility—"Or elles he is at his hous, certeyn" (3669)—Absolon stupidly assumes that this is his chance to find Alison home alone. The purpose of Chaucer's scene is clear enough. Unlike Hughe in *Heile of Beersele*, Absolon has not made an appointment with the woman he desires, and unlike Hughe, he has every reason to assume, from her past lack of interest in his courting, that she will not welcome him. Chaucer, then, needs to give Absolon some reason to hope that John is out of the way, some motive to come to her house to try his luck with John's wife on that particular night. The new scene, the only one in the tale that does not take place in Oxford, is a logical enough choice. Oseney is not far away, and the cloisterer—who has no counterpart in *Heile of Beersele*—is a logical enough addition. After all, John has been doing carpentry work on the abbey there, and a monk assigned to the abbey might well be expected to have knowledge of the carpenter's whereabouts. Although he is not a developed character in his own right, the cloisterer gives Absolon the appropriate misinformation to get him back to town eager to make his amorous move.

Absolon carefully plans his actions. He will quietly knock at Alison's window and tell her about his love-longing, believing that at the very least he will get a kiss from her. He thinks that all the signs are good:

> "My mouth hath icched al this longe day;
> That is a signe of kissyng, atte leeste.
> Al nyght me mette eek I was at a feeste" [3682–84].

All eager with anticipation, Absolon rushes back to town, grabs a quick nap to refresh himself for the amorous adventures ahead, and at first cock's crow, dresses himself carefully and goes off to John's house for his nocturnal encounter with Alison's bottom.

The First Window Scene

The first window scene in the bedroom sequence is crucial to both stories. In it the hopeful lover is spurned, begs for a kiss, and is punished for his persistence by being tricked into kissing a bottom presented out the bedroom window. We need to begin by reminding ourselves that this scene essentially begins the Middle Dutch tale, for the first window scene there begins in *Heile of Beersele* at line 47—really only the 34th line of the tale proper, if we exclude the thirteen-line prologue. In the *Miller's Tale*, on the other hand, it begins at line 3687, the 501st line of the tale proper. For the Middle Dutch author we are less than a quarter of the way into the tale. For Chaucer, we are fully three-quarters into it.

For the Middle Dutch author the tale has barely begun when we get to the first window scene. For Chaucer, the tale is almost over when we get to the parallel scene. Chaucer, then, has front-loaded his tale with three long scenes (the three in the pre-bedroom scenes discussed in the last chapter) and two short ones (the ladder scene and the Oseney scene) that have virtually no counterpart in the Middle Dutch tale. Those scenes provide such a wealth of description, action, and dialogue that we are ready to understand and enjoy the scene that begins the last quarter of the *Miller's Tale*. In the Middle Dutch tale the four characters are essentially strangers to us, so the ensuing window scenes will be our introduction to their characters. In the English tale we know them very well indeed, so the ensuing window scenes will let us see how characters familiar to us already will act in a new situation. In the Middle Dutch tale, where the characters are cyphers, we concentrate on the plot that is about to open up for us. In the English tale, where the characters are old friends of ours, we concentrate on the people who are to about play their climactic role in the plot that is about to open up for us.

The author of *Heile of Beersele* has to pack into the first window scene much of the information that Chaucer has worked in much earlier. In *Heile of Beersele* Willem comes to Heile's house in the first window scene; his counterpart John in the *Miller's Tale* is already in it because of course it is his house. Willem gets into the tub when the second lover comes, in order to escape detection; in the *Miller's Tale* John is already asleep in the tub into which he has climbed to escape a flood. After Heile has satisfied him sexually three times, the priest predicts the coming flood; Nicholas has already done that the day before. And only then does Hughe the blacksmith come to Heile: "Ay, Heile, dat benic vore waer" (98) ["Oh, Heile, it is I for sure"]; Absolon has already had more than one encounter with Alison. Chaucer takes this bare-bones exchange and expands it with real dialogue. Hughe's "Oh, Heile, it is I for sure" becomes:

>"What do ye, hony-comb, sweete Alison,
>My faire bryd, my sweete cynamome?

> Awaketh, lemman myn, and speketh to me!
> Wel little thynken ye upon my wo,
> That for youre love I swete ther I go.
> No wonder is thogh that I swelte and swete;
> I moorne as dooth a lamb after the tete.
> Ywis, lemman, I have swich love-longynge
> That lik a turtel trewe is my moornynge.
> I may nat ete na moore than a mayde" [3699–3708].

Because we have come to know Absolon well by now, his syrupy speech is very much in character for him.

The brusk Heile responds to Hughe's one-line statement with a simple one-line rejection: "Ghine moget niet inne" (99) ["You may not come in"]. Chaucer lets Alison respond more fully, and in words very much in character for her:

> "Go fro the wyndow, Jakke fool," she sayde.
> "As help me God, it wol nat be 'com pa me.'
> I love another—and elles I were to blame—
> Wel bet than thee, by Jhesu, Absolon.
> Go forth thy wey, or I wol caste a ston,
> And let me slepe, a twenty devel wey!" [3708–13].

In neither of Chaucer's multiline expansions of the single-line speeches from his source does he add materially to the content of the speech. Absolon still says, "I am here," and Alison still says, "You may not come in," but the expansions reveal the character of the speakers far more in Chaucer. Absolon expresses his courtly effusiveness, his mournful self-pity, his saccharine metaphors, and egregious similes. Alison expresses her no-nonsense directness, her honesty, her fearless insistence on her own needs. For the Middle Dutch author the important thing is that Hughe is there and Heile says no. For Chaucer the important thing is that Absolon is a romance-eyed fool who cannot see his own limitations as a suitor, while Alison is a sexy young thing who knows how to get rid of romance-eyed fools and have fun while doing it.

It is worth noting that Hughe has a total of eight lines in the first window scene, while his English counterpart Absolon has a total of twenty-five lines in the parallel scene. Chaucer did not need to triple the number of lines he gives to Absolon to make the plot work out right. The Middle Dutch author had showed him a more economical way to move the plot forward. The point is that Chaucer knew that to bring Absolon alive, he needed to let Absolon reveal his slimy personality and sleazy motives through his own direct speech.

Hughe's actions in the first window scene in *Heile of Beersele* are minimal. He knocks on the door, he speaks, he asks. His central action, of course, is kissing the priest's bottom, thinking it is Heile's mouth:

> Ende Hughe waende da Heile ware
> End custe spapen ers al dare
> Met soe heten sinne
> Dat sine nese vloechder inne [117–20].
>> [And Hughe thought it was Heile and kissed the priest's arse right there with such hot zeal that his nose went right in.]

Chaucer gives Absolon additional actions as well as additional speech. Absolon rises up at the crowing of the first cock, dresses himself handsomely, chews sweet-smelling grain and licorice, combs his hair, places a herb leaf under his tongue, walks to the carpenter's house, stands under the window, and coughs to get Alison's attention. Then, as he prepares for the kiss, Absolon gets down on his knees and wipes his mouth dry. Only after describing all these actions does Chaucer let Absolon kiss Alison's bottom:

> But with his mouth he kiste hir naked ers
> Ful savourly, er he were war of this [3734–35].

It is interesting that Chaucer eliminates the action of the nasal penetration, not because it is gross but because it is unrealistic. He substitutes for that detail another image just as gross, perhaps, but more realistic:

> Abak he stirte, and thoughte it was amys
> For well he wiste a womman hath no berd [3736–37].

I call particular attention to Absolon's actions after the kiss. We see Absolon performing more actions than Hughe before the kiss, but more actions afterwards, also. He jumps back, bites his lips, then rubs them "With dust, with sond, with straw, with clooth, with chippes" (3748). Except for the actually kissing, none of these actions appear in the Middle Dutch story. The Middle Dutch author wants us to see only the action of Hughe's misdirected kiss. Chaucer, on the other hand, wants us to see a whole series of Absolon's actions surrounding the misdirected kiss. Those actions, from the rising to the dressing to the perfuming to the walking to the kneeling to the kissing to the jumping back to the rubbing—all help us to visualize this scene in the theater of our minds.

The role of the pursued woman in the first window scene is crucial to the success of the scene in both tales, though Chaucer has made some interesting changes. For one thing, Chaucer has reduced the role of the woman in his version of the tale. In *Heile of Beersele*, where the narrator has fifty-one of the eighty-four lines, or 60.7 percent, Heile herself has eighteen lines, or 21.4 percent. In the *Miller's Tale*, on the other hand, where the narrator has only thirty-four lines, or 46.6 percent of the seventy-three lines, Alison has only twelve lines, or 16.4 percent. Chaucer, in other words, has reduced her role by giving her fewer lines and Absolon more. Clearly, the first window scene is Absolon's. Whereas in *Heile of Beersele* Hughe has eight lines, or 9.5 percent of the total, Chaucer gives his counterpart twenty-five lines, or 34.3 percent of the total. Chaucer has taken from his source a character who has less than a tenth of the lines in this scene and assigned him more than a third of them. Some of those lines he took from Alison. Even though Chaucer reduces Alison's speaking role in the first window scene, however, she is nevertheless of the utmost dramatic importance.

Heile is a woman of few actions, and those few are strictly sexual. She plays the love-game with Willem, then she plays it three more times with the priest. She talks to all three men, but those are words, not actions. Her words may result in actions, but the actions are not hers. She tells the priest to put his bottom out the window, but the action of doing so is his, not hers. The only actions she herself is said to take are directly related to her profession as a prostitute. Her job in the story is to sell sex to men with money. She has no actions beyond that. Chaucer, on the other hand, describes Alison's actions more fully in the window scene. She has sex with Nicholas, but hers is a lust-for-love action, not a lust-for-money action. Chaucer's most important change, of course, is to have Alison present her own buttocks out the window rather than merely telling someone else to: "And at the wyndow out she putte hir hole" (3732). That is her central action, but she also takes action to open the window ("the wyndow she undoth, and that in haste" [3727]), and then after the kissing she closes it ("and clapte the wyndow to" [3740]). There is no mention of opening or closing the window in the Middle Dutch story. Indeed, so far as we can tell, the window is just an opening in the wall with no glazing or shutter to open or to close. Not only do we know in the *Miller's Tale* what Alison looks like from earlier scenes, but we also get to see her in action in this one. And though her actions may seem to be few and only marginally important, they are important enough that they ignite the angry passions of Absolon and in doing so bring on the next scene.

The Smithy Scene

The smithy scene is scarcely a scene at all in *Heile of Beersele*. It runs to a mere six lines and has no dialogue whatsoever. Indeed, there is no one to have dialogue with, since Hughe the blacksmith goes to his own home to fetch a hot iron:

X. The Bedroom Sequence 117

> Hi liep thuss als die wes erre;
> Hi woende van daer niet verre.
> Een groet yser nam hi gereet
> Ende staect int vier ende maket heet
> Soe dat gloyde wel ter cure,
> Ende lieper mede vore Heilen dure [131–36].
>> [He ran home as if he were mad. He did not live far away. He immediately took a big iron and stuck it into the fire to make it hot, so that it glowed, just the way he wanted, and ran with it to Heile's door.]

Those six lines get the job done. All that the scene really needs to accomplish, after all, is provide the victim of the cruel jest with an instrument for revenge.

For Chaucer the minimal was not enough. For one thing, since the third or outside-lover is a parish clerk, not a blacksmith, Absolon, unlike Hughe, cannot just run home for an iron. Rather, he has to run to the smithy of a friend of his, Gerveys. Chaucer could, of course, have given a brief narrative summary of the action: "Then Absolon ran to a local blacksmith shop, where he borrowed a hot coulter, and came back immediately and knocked at Alison's window." That would have done the job, but it was not the job the Chaucer wanted done. Chaucer wanted further to characterize Absolon by having him interact with a new character. Having already created for us the cloisterer at Oseney for Absolon to talk with, he now balances that creation with a second one for Absolon to talk with. The scene is itself a nice balance to the scene immediately previous. As Absolon had "ful pryvely knokken" at Alison's window a few minutes earlier, here he "knokketh al esily" at Gerveys's door. Gerveys, of course, is far more friendly[4]:

> "What, Absolon! for Cristes sweete tree.
> Why rise ye so rather? Ey, benedicetee!
> What eyleth yow? Some gay gerl, God it woot,
> Hath broght you thus upon the viritoot,
> By Seinte Note, ye woot wel what I mene" [3767–71].

Absolon, we recall, has been "heeled of his maladie" (3757), and "his hoote love was coold and al yqueynt" (3754). Absolon's retort to Gerveys signals the profound change in him. He refuses to pick up the banter that Gerveys initiates:

> This Absolon ne roghte nat a bene
> Of all his pley; no word agayn he yaf;
> He hadde more tow on his distaf
> Than Gerveys knew [3772–75].

Cured of his love-malady, Absolon wants only his revenge against Alison. Instead of responding to Gerveys's question, he asks to borrow the hot coulter in the hearth, "That hoote kultour in the chymenee here, / As lene it me" (3776–77). Gerveys generously agrees to let him have it, but asks, "What wol ye do therwith?" (3782). Again, Absolon refuses to give a direct answer:

> "Therof," quod Absolon, "be as be may,
> I shal wel telle it thee to-morwe day" [3783–84].

This is a new Absolon. Where once he might have bragged to his friend about his exploits with pretty girls, now he has nothing to brag about and wants only revenge for the humiliation he has suffered. He grabs the hot coulter by the cold handle and sneaks back to get that revenge. Chaucer has expanded a six-line transitional scene four-fold into a twenty-six-line dialogue designed to demonstrate the change in Absolon and so to prepare for the second window scene. Here Absolon's lines (seven, or 25 percent of the twenty-eight) are outnumbered by Gerveys's (ten, or 35.7 percent), because in this scene Absolon has become a man of action rather than of words. Absolon's curtness and indirection are a marked contrast to his loquacious verbiage in earlier scenes, and we are ready to accept the more violent madness that we are about to see him engage in.

The Second Window Scene

In both *Heile of Beersele* and the *Miller's Tale* the second window scene in the bedroom sequence is short and sweet—the duration is short and the revenge is sweet. The spurned lover comes back and asks for a second kiss. He strikes with his hot iron and the man whose buttocks are burned cries for water. His cries for water signal to the man in the trough that the predicted flood must have arrived, so he cuts the rope and crashes down to the floor. The scene takes only thirty-five lines in *Heile of Beersele*, though for the Middle Dutch writer that is almost a fifth (19.9 percent of the 176 lines) of the tale proper. At thirty-six lines, the scene is a bit longer in the *Miller's Tale*,[5] but it is a far shorter percentage, only a twentieth (5.4 percent of the 663 lines) of the tale proper. It is almost as if, the tale mostly over, Chaucer wants to rush on to the end.

Like his Middle Dutch counterpart, Chaucer relies more on narration than on dialogue to tell this part of his story. Chaucer does make changes in the actions described, however. Whereas the priest in the Middle Dutch story merely puts his buttocks out for a second kiss, Chaucer tells us that Nicholas had "risen for to pisse" (3898), and that it was his idea to vary the trick by having Absolon kiss not Alison's bottom a second time, but his own. The Middle Dutch author describes the priest's actions in general terms:

> Die pape die sijns niet vergat,
> Hine sette weder zijn achterste gat
> Daer hijt te voren hadde gheset [143–45].
>> [The priest remembered, and once again put his hind-hole where he had put it before.]

There is no mention of a window or of opening it. Chaucer, on the other hand, specifies that Nicholas opens the window and gives details about his action in placing his buttocks there:

> And up the wyndowe dide he hastily,
> And out his ers he putteth pryvely
> Over the buttok, to the haunche-bon [3801–03].

That last detail, of course, nicely balances Nicholas's earlier grabbing Alison "by the haunchebones" (3279). Chaucer adds the humorous touch of Absolon's asking Alison to "speke, sweete bryd" (3805) and adds Nicholas fart in response—an action that has no parallel in the Middle Dutch work. Chaucer eliminates the second anal penetration that he found in the Middle Dutch tale:

> Ende die smet stac ongelet
> Tgheloyende yser in den ers [146–47].
>> [And the smith quickly stuck the red-hot iron in his arse.]

Having changed the generalized "yser" [iron] to a specific piece if farm equipment, the broader, blade-like coulter used to cut the earth ahead of the plowshare, Chaucer replaces a scorched anal canal with a scorched buttocks. It is a more fitting punishment to the "hende" Nicholas that the coulter takes off the "the skyn an hande-brede aboute" (3811). What better punishment could there be to for Nicholas, who uses his hands to grab Alison by the buttocks in the first scene, to exit the story with a hand-sized scar to his own buttocks?

The resulting cries for "Water, water!" are nearly identical in the two versions of the story, and they serve a similar function in the plot: to cause the man in the tub above to cut the rope. Willem, however, never falls asleep in the Middle Dutch tale, while the exhausted old John does. Chaucer's change is an important one, since it helps us to understand why John does not hear any of the business between Absolon and the two lovers inside the bedroom. It is hard to understand why Willem, sitting in his tub awake, is able to hear the priest's little sermonette to Heile, but not the other events at the window when Hughe comes a-knocking. In any case, the wide-awake Willem hears Hughe's call for water and thinks the predicted flood has come:

> Hi peinsde, "nu eest waerheide
> Van dat de pape te nachte seide,
> Dwater es comen sekerlike
> Nu sal verdrinken al erterike;
> Mer eest dat ic henen driue
> Die bac houd mi wel te live" [155–60].
>> [He thought, "now comes what the priest said tonight. The water has surely come now, and all the earth will be drowned, but if I can float away, this trough will keep me alive just fine."]

Chaucer's John, who has just awakened from a deep sleep, seems incapable of such reasoned thought processes. In one of the very few cases where he reduces the number of words assigned to a character, Chaucer wants the sleep-drugged John to jump to a quick conclusion:

> [He] thoughte, "Allas, now comth Nowelis flood!" [3818].

The cutting of the ropes and the crashing down to the floor are similar enough in both tales, and in both bring on the brief denouement.

The Neighbor Scene

In *Heile of Beersele* the brief denouement involves the priest, who is so alarmed and frightened when Willem comes tumbling down that for some reason he assumes that Willem is the devil. In a panic he dashes into the corner where there is a cesspit of some sort—one not described earlier, and not described now, either—and falls in. He then goes home in humiliation:

> Quam hi thuus al besceten
> Ende sinen ers all verbrant,
> Te sceerne gedreuen ende ghescant [174–78].
>> [He went home all beshitten, with his ars all burned, all shamed and scorned.]

Chaucer cuts that entirely. Instead, the priest's counterpart in the *Miller's Tale*, Nicholas, emerges victorious rather than being further humiliated. Chaucer transfers humiliation and scorn to a different character, foolish old John. Nicholas and Alison run out into the street to arouse their neighbors with cries of "Out" and "Harrow" (3825). These neighbors enlarge the number of characters that Chaucer invents for the story (we have already seen him add the servants Robyn and Gille, the cloisterer at Oseney, and the blacksmith Gerveys). They serve the sole purpose of humiliating John. They "laughen" at him and his foolish fantasy (3840, 3849). They refuse to take seriously John's side of the story:

> It was for noght; no man his reson herde.
> With othes grete he was so sworn adoun
> That he was holde wood in all the toun [3844–46].

Chaucer even assigns a spoken line to the collective neighbors:

> For every clerk anonright heeld with oother.
> They seyde, "The man is wood, my leeve brother" [3847–48].

And thus ends both the action and the dialogue in the *Miller's Tale*. Perhaps no one would have missed the final scene if it were not there, but it does serve two important functions. First, it lets us know that Nicholas and Alison will not be punished for their adulterous acts by the foolish John, whom no one will take seriously. In the Middle Dutch tale there was no question of husbandly recriminations since Heile has no husband, but the question might arise in the *Miller's Tale*. Would old John, made painfully aware that there was no flood after all, figure out the truth and get his revenge? Chaucer seemed to want to assure us that that would not be the case, or at least that no tribunal of his neighbors would blame anyone but him for the foolishness of that long Monday night. Second, and more important for my purposes, Chaucer seemed to feel the need of an audience for the final part of the "game" of the *Miller's Tale*. John is humiliated for his foolishness in the tale, and that humiliation is made more poignant if there is a group in the tale to observe and comment on that foolishness. The neighbors, then, can be said to be a dramatic chorus in its function as commentator on the action. Certainly they serve as a closing reminder that the *Miller's Tale* is in some ways a kind of play, with a kind of audience. That audience, of course, blends in directly with the other audience of the story, the pilgrimage "folk" who, picking up their cue from the neighbors of Nicholas and Alison, laugh at what they have seen and heard performed:

> Whan folk had laughen at this nyce cas
> Of Absolon and hende Nicholas,
> Diverse folk diversely they seyde,
> But for the moore part they loughe and pleyde [3855–58].

The laughter of the neighbors at the end of the tale spills over into the laughter of the pilgrims in the link. Both audiences clearly have fun with the playfulness of the game.

An Overview of the Dialogue in the Two Tales

Earlier in this chapter we looked at the dialogue in the various scenes in *Heile of Beersele* and the *Miller's Tale*, but it is useful to combine the data and

Chart 8. Dialogue in *Heile of Beersele* and the *Miller's Tale*.

	Heile of Beersele		*Miller's Tale*	
	Lines	Percentages	Lines	Percentages
Narrator	116	70.3%	Narrator 400	60.4%
Willem	13	7.9%	John 52	7.9%
Priest	3	1.8%	Nicholas 107	16.1%
Heile	9	11.5%	Alison 28	4.2%
Hughe	14	8.5%	Absolon 56	8.4%
Others	0	0.0%	Others 20	3.0%
Totals	165	100%	Totals 663	100%

look at the dialogue in the two whole tales. In Chart 8 I present the composite data in chart form.

Let us consider the raw numbers first. I noted early in this chapter that the Chaucerian narrative is, at 663 lines, five times as long as the Middle Dutch narrative. Chaucer not only increases the number of lines given to the narrator, but he also increases the number assigned to all four of the major characters. He also invents and gives speaking parts to what I call in the chart "Others" not even mentioned in *Heile of Beersele*: John's knave Robyn, the cloisterer at Oseney, Gerveys the smith, and John's neighbors. Chaucer's tale is bigger than its Middle Dutch counterpart in virtually every way. I noted earlier that the bigness comes mostly at the start of the tale, with Chaucer adding three major pre-bedroom scenes to what he found in his probable source. These scenes are Nicholas's direct sexual approach to Alison, Absolon's subtler courtship of Alison, and Nicholas's successful effort to convince John that a second Noah's flood is coming. Although it is one of the shorter tales told on the road to Canterbury, the *Miller's Tale* is far longer than *Heile of Beersele*.

A look at the percentages, however, shows a somewhat different and more important trend. We see, first that Chaucer reduced by nearly 10 percent the percentage of the lines that he assigns to the narrator. Whereas the Middle Dutch author had given fully 70 percent of the lines to the narrator, Chaucer gives only 60 percent. Instead of having the characters speak in their own voices almost 30 percent of the lines, Chaucer has them speak almost 40 percent. Clearly, then, Chaucer is more interested in letting his characters speak for themselves than the Middle Dutch author was. But we also see that Chaucer is more interested in letting some of the characters speak than others. He does not change the percentage of the total number of lines that John and Absolon speak, but he dramatically changes the percentages that Nicholas and Alison speak. While the priest speaks less than 2 percent of the lines in *Heile of Beersele*, Chaucer gives Nicholas, his counterpart, more than 16 percent, making his voice by far the most-heard speaking voice in the tale. Most of those lines come in the scene where he convinced the gullible John that a second flood is coming. Since he is the director of much of the action in the tale, he is the one who needs to do most of the actual talking elsewhere, also.

Perhaps the most surprising change that Chaucer made is that he reduced the percentage of the lines given to Alison. Whereas Heile speaks more than 11 percent of the lines in *Heile of Beersele*, Alison speaks only slightly more than 4 percent. It is not so much that Chaucer de-emphasized the importance of Alison as that he changes the nature of her role. Alison is still a commanding figure in the *Miller's Tale*, but her role is more visual than spoken. She is less to be heard than to be seen on "stage," looking pretty and performing crude actions. It is worth noting that Heile was much more the director of the action in the Middle Dutch tale. She arranges the visits of her three clients and when they come to see her, she tells them what to do, where to hide, and so on. One of the most dramatic changes that Chaucer made in the *Miller's Tale* was to take the role of director away from the young woman and give it to Nicholas. In doing so, of course, he took away much of Alison's need to be a speaker. Nicholas picks up the role of director and speaker.

In sum, then, Chaucer gives us in the *Miller's Tale* a story that is more like a play than is the simple narrative he found. He takes what is essentially a bedroom sequence in *Heile of Beersele* and adds three substantial scenes in front of it. Then he adds to the bedroom sequence with its four scenes from his source two important scenes. In addition to letting us "see" the staging of these scenes, Chaucer also shows us more theater-like action than he found in his source. And, perhaps most important, Chaucer lets his characters, particularly Nicholas, talk, lets us "hear" their words, their songs, and even their farts. To be sure, there is still plenty of narrative description of character, scene, and action in Chaucer's tale, but even those descriptions, in conjunction with the increased use of dialogue, help us to visualize the "game" of the *Miller's Tale* in the theater of our minds.

PART TWO

Modern Transformations of the *Miller's Tale*

XI

Early Retellings for Adults: Cobb (1712), Smith (1713), Anonymous (1791)

An anonymous reteller of the *Canterbury Tales* published in 1791 a lengthy introduction in which he explained why Chaucer's tales—the *Miller's Tale* in particular— needed to be retold for eighteenth-century readers. The coarse stuff, he said, that Chaucer put into his tale was simply unsuitable for the refined readership of a more modern England. This anonymous reteller felt that he needed to make excuses for Chaucer, who "had every difficulty of a barbarous language, a cramped education, and a taste vitiated by bad examples or obscur'd by ignorance." Even so, he went on to say, Chaucer's sentiments "are often more indelicate than the lowest vulgarity, the most boorish rusticity will now be found to authorize."[1] Chaucer was a fine writer, the commentator goes on, but "the gross indecency of Chaucer's humour, as originally written, is so great a drawback from his sterling merit, that his warmest admirers must confess it to be an insurmountable objection to his being a general favourite in this age of refinement" (Anon. 169).

Speaking specifically of the *Miller's Tale*, the anonymous modernizer went on to say that while a paraphrase can "soften" the "gross as well as the obsolete phrases" in Chaucer's language, "so interwoven is the tenor of his stories with indecency, that no subterfuge can be devised, by which that blot may be absolutely obliterated. This is the case with that tale, which I have endeavored to paraphrase: the point of the whole turns on a circumstance, which no circumlocution or guarded expression can convey delicately to the reader's mind, since it is the idea itself that is indecent" (Anon. 168–69). I shall return to this anonymous critic and his "paraphrase" of the *Miller's Tale* at the end of this chapter, but first let us consider the way two earlier eighteenth-century retellers presented four sets of lines: the opening lines of the tale, the lines where Nicholas first grabs Alison's crotch, the lines where Absolon kisses Alison's bottom, and the lines announcing Nicholas's fart.

Samuel Cobb (1712)

Samuel Cobb (1671–1713) was a London school teacher who felt called to rewrite the *Miller's Tale*, which he renamed *The Carpenter of Oxford*. At the start of the *Miller's Tale* Chaucer wrote:

> Whilom ther was dwellynge at Oxenford
> A riche gnof, that gestes heeld to bord,
> And of his craft he was a carpenter.
> With hym ther was dwellynge a poure scoler [3187–90].

Cobb opened his 1712 retelling thus:

> Whilom in Oxford an old Chuff did dwell,
> A Carpenter by Trade, as Stories tell,
> Who by his Craft had heap'd up many a Hoard,
> And furnished Strangers both with Bed and Board.
> With him a Scholar lodg'd, of slender Means [Cobb 1–5].

Two features of Cobb's revision of Chaucer bear mentioning. First, he wanted his readers to know that the tale was not his own, but one he learned from old "Stories." In doing so, of course, he was doing what Chaucer himself had done by pretending that the *Miller's Tale* was the Miller's, not his own:

> Blameth nat me, if that ye chese amys.
> The Miller is a cherl; ye knowe wel this [3181–82].

Second, Cobb emphasizes old John's greed. Chaucer had said merely that he was rich. Cobb expands that word into five—"heap'd up many a Hoard"—and indicates that John takes in not "guests" but "strangers," as if he did so only for the money.

Chaucer had described Nicholas's sudden grabbing of Alison in straightforward language:

> And prively he caughte hire by the queynte,
> And seyde, "Ywis, but if ich have my wille,

> For deerne love of the, lemman, I spille."
> And heeld hire harde by the haunchebones,
> And seyde, "Lemman, love me al atones,
> Or I wol dyen also God me save!" [3276–81].

Cobb is confusingly vague about what Nicholas grabs—he gives no clue what *That same* refers to—and what part of Alison's body Nicholas then holds her by or what he wants her to "let me" do:

> And prively he caught her by *That same*.
> "My Lemman Dear" (quoth he) "I'm all on Fire,
> And perish, if you grant not my Desire."
> He clasp her round, and held her fast, and cry'd,
> "O let me, let me—never be deny'd" [Cobb 92–96].

It is pitch dark on that Monday night when Chaucer's Absolon gives his famous kiss:

> Derk was the nyght as pich, or as the cole,
> And at the wyndow out she putte hir hole,
> And Absolon, hym fil no bet ne wers,
> But with his mouth he kiste hir naked ers
> Ful savourly, er he were war of this.
> Abak he stirte, and thoughte it was amys,
> For wel he wiste a womman hath no berd.
> He felte a thyng al rough and long yherd,
> And seyde, "Fy! allas! what have I do?"
> "Tehee!" quod she, and clapte the wyndow to [3731–40].

Samuel Cobb's eighteenth-century retelling of that scene is somewhat different:

> Dark was the Night, as any Coal or Pitch,
> When at the Window she clapt out her Breech.
> The *Parish Clerk* ne'er doubted what to do,
> But ask'd no Questions, and in haste fell to;
> On her blind Side full savoury he prest
> A loving Kiss, e'er he smelt out the Jest.
> Aback he starts, for he knew well enough,
> That Women's Lips are smooth, but these were rough.
> *What have I done,* quoth he? and rav'd and star'd,
> *Ah me! I've kist a Woman with a Beard.*
> He curst the Hour, and rail'd against the Stars,
> That he was born to kiss my Lady's _____
> *Tehea,* she cry'd, and clapt the Window close [Cobb 588–600].

Cobb has changed Chaucer's tale in several ways. Where Chaucer had mentioned the rough "thyng" (3738) that Absolon kisses, Cobb specifies the rough

"Lips" of the vulva. Where Chaucer's Absolon knows "a womman hath no berd" (3737), Cobb's Absolon says that he has "kist a Woman with a Beard." Cobb cuts the reference to Alison's "hole" and invents entirely the incomplete couplet about Absolon's cursing the hour he was born, his railing against the stars that predestined him to kiss his "Lady's _____." It is curious that while he is comfortable referring to Alison's "breech," he leaves it to his readers to supply as a rhyme for "Stars" the word "arse."

John Smith (1713)

A contemporary of Cobb's named John Smith (1662–1717) spent most of his life in Oxford, where he worked at Magdalen College. He opened his modernization of the *Miller's Tale* thus:

> In Days of Old, if Story does not err,
> In *Oxford* dwelt an aged *Carpenter*;
> But tho' with Riches he was amply stor'd,
> Greedy of Pelf, he *Scholars* kept at Board;
> Daily he thriv'd, and thriving learn'd to Save;
> A Jealous Dotard, and a Purse-proud Knave.
> It so befel, a Youngster of the Gown,
> For his Diversion, took a Room in Town
> And at this old *Carpenter's* good Mansion-House;
> He let the Room—the *Scholar* paid his *Spouse* [Smith 1–10].

Like Cobb, Smith wanted it known that he was telling an old story, not one of his own. And even more than Cobb, he wanted to portray old John not merely as rich, but also as greedy and miserly, a "Purse-proud Knave." It is not clear why Smith added the information that the scholar pays his rent to John's wife. It was probably a veiled sexual joke about paying the marriage debt.

Smith was far more graphic than Cobb in his description of Nicholas's "attack" on Alison—whom he called "the Fair." Smith's Nicholas got to feel and explore her pretty much as he pleased:

> And with outrageous Love attack'd the Fair;
> He kiss'd—he ogl'd her—with Ardor press't
> Her balmy Hand, and squeez'd her heaving Breast;
> Then wantonly he stole down by degrees,
> First strok'd her swelling Thigh, then grasp'd her Knees,
> Till his impatient Hand like Lightning flew
> To a strange Place—which scarce her Husband knew;
> (There had he been indeed, but had been in vain,
> Gave her small Pleasure, and Himself much Pain.)

> One Arm in strictest Folds the Fair embrac'd,
> Clinging like *Ivy* round her slender *Waste*.
> "For Love of You" (says he) "I truly mourn,
> All Night I languish, and all Day I burn.
> Permit me then—or I will ne'er remove,
> O grant me—or I perish for your Love;
> Thus on your panting Bosom will I lie,
> Here conquer, or—upon this Spot will die" [Smith 132–47].

Smith seemed to enjoy writing that scene, to enjoy adding the business of Alison's "heaving Breast" and "panting Bosom" that Chaucer never mentioned, and the business of the "strange Place" that Nicholas's impatient hand flew to. To make explicit to adult readers while leaving youthful readers pretty much in the dark about what that "strange Place" is, Smith parenthetically invented details about John's geriatric sexual ineptitude.

In his presentation of Absolon's kiss, Smith, like Cobb, specifically avoided mentioning Alison's "hole." For him it was not her "ers" or her "breech" that Alison stuck out the window, but her *"Nether Countenance"*:

> Blind was the Night, and black as *Pitch* or *Cole*
> When fair and soft She to the Window stole,
> And thro' the Casement jutted out behind
> Her *Nether Countenance* with *Cheeks* as blind;
> Where Absolon close buckling to the Matter,
> Kiss'd her full sav'rily—'twixt *Wind* and *Water*.
> At first he started back, surpriz'd with Fear,
> Something he felt bush'd o're with curling Hair,
> Monstrously rough, and shaggy as a Bear;
> On second Thoughts his error soon appear'd,
> He well consider'd Woman wore no beard;
> [...]
> "Te-He" (quoth She) and clapt the Window too [Smith 677–87, 693].

Though Smith did not mention Alison's rectum directly, he referred to it with scatological indirectness by saying that Absolon kissed her in that region between the rectum and the vagina, for so I take his "'twixt Wind and Water." And unlike either Chaucer or Cobb, who mention the length of Alison's pubic hair, Smith found it to be not long but curly and both monstrous and animalistic.

Anonymous (1791)

The anonymous author of the third eighteenth-century version of the *Miller's Tale* began his "paraphrase" thus:

> There dwelt at Oxford, in the times of old,
> A carpenter, whose coffers teem'd with gold;
> Yet miserable still, to eke his hoard,
> He furnish'd clerks with lodging and with board.
> A scholar with this miser slept and din'd;
> Scant was his purse, but learning grac'd his mind [Anon. 1–6].

Like Cobb and Smith, this later eighteenth-century writer wanted his readers to know that he was retelling an old story. It was a way of blaming the indecency of the story on the coarseness of an earlier age. And like Cobb and Smith, this anonymous later writer emphasized, in ways that Chaucer did not, the old carpenter's great wealth and greed. His coffers were stuffed with gold, yet he sought to augment his "hoard" by renting rooms out to poor students. For all his gold he was a *miser*able miser.

The anonymous author of the 1791 retelling felt the need to embellish Nicholas's grab into something that he called "wanton dalliance" (Anon. 84):

> They kiss'd, caress'd—the mounting blood grew warm—
> Beneath her stays he thrust his letcherous arm—
> Fast round her supple loins one hand he prest,
> And with the other grasp'd her heaving breast—
> And "bless me now," he cried, "with all your charms,
> Meet all my wishes with luxurious arms—
> Or kill me with your frown" [Anon. 85–91].

Chaucer made no mention of Alison's stays or breasts. He did mention her "haunchebones," but in the eighteenth-century retellings these were transformed into her "swelling thigh," "supple loins," and "Knees."

Like Cobb and Smith, this later reteller avoided referring to Alison's "hole" and "ers," but he felt comfortable with "buttocks" and "bum." He avoided direct mention of Alison's pubic hair, but referred instead to "something" that was "rougher than the down" on a woman's cheeks. He kept Chaucer's line about Absolon's realization that a woman "has no beard." In anticipation of criticism that he followed Chaucer too closely in mentioning a woman's "beard" at all, he had in his introduction said that he was not telling women in his audience anything they did not already know about their bodies: "The most mincing prude is not only herself conscious that the structure of her body differs in some particulars from that of her brother's body, and that Nature has not restrained the growth of hair to the scalp alone, but she knows that every reasonable creature, past the age of puberty, in the room where she sits, is as thoroughly possessed of those circumstances as herself" (Anon. 169).

I close this chapter with a quick comparison of the various treatments of Nicholas's fart, beginning with Chaucer's:

> This Nicholas anon leet fle a fart
> As greet as it had been a thonder-dent [3806–07].
>
> At this the Scholar let a rouzing Fart;
> So loud the Noise, as frightful was the Stroke,
> As Thunder, when it splits the sturdy Oak [Cobb 672–74].
>
> *Nich'las* full-charged, in loud Return let fly
> A *Bomb,* that burst like Thunder from the Sky;
> The Sulph'rous Exhalation from behind [Smith 765–67].
>
> But Nicholas, who wish'd the joke to share,
> Of wind a treasure in his bowels bare,
> And (straining, lest too soon the storm should burst)
> His brawny buttocks thro' the window thrust
> [...]
> Nicholas at once discharg'd the load,
> Like peals of thunder from a bursting cloud [Anon. 564–67, 573–74].

The *Miller's Tale* held a particular fascination for educated British men and women of the eighteenth century. They felt that they were more refined than Chaucer had been many years earlier, but they wanted to read and retell what they considered to be his most unrefined story. They sometimes used different words for scatological actions, and they sometimes brought into prominence body parts—breasts and bosoms, for example—that Chaucer had not mentioned. By and large, however, the parts, actors, and actions stayed much the same. These writers were, after all, writing for adults. When writers of a later generation thought they should retell the *Miller's Tale* for younger readers—well, that was a different story.

XII
Early Retellings for Young Readers: Johnstone (1895), Darton (1904), Farjeon (1930)

The *Miller's Tale* has always been an unlikely candidate for adaptation as a story for children. It is about an old man who brings home a teenaged bride; a teenaged bride who is easily persuaded to be unfaithful to him with a college student; a college student who grabs her by the crotch. Its plot turns on crotch-grabbing, haunch-holding, loin-patting, ass-kissing, pubic-roughening, piss-rising, fart-letting, and butt-burning. While there is much in that story that children would enjoy, there is little in the story that most adults would want children to enjoy. It is not surprising that the earliest attempts to retell the *Canterbury Tales* for children quietly passed over the *Miller's Tale*: Charles Cowden Clarke's *Tales from Chaucer, in Prose* (1833); H. R. Haweis's *Chaucer for Children: A Golden Key* (1877); Clara L. Thompson's *Tales from Chaucer* (1903); Janet Harvey Kelman's *Stories from Chaucer Told to the Children* (1905); J. Walker McSpadden's *Stories from Chaucer* (1907), and Ada Hales's *Stories from Chaucer* (1911). In their preface to *Canterbury Chimes*, Storr and Turner put it this way: "the occasional coarseness of the *Canterbury Tales* makes it an unfit book to be placed in the hands of children. A translation or paraphrase of selected tales is then the only way of making Chaucer at all accessible to children."[1] The *Miller's Tale* is not one of those they choose to make accessible to children. Not all early retellers, however, totally avoided the *Miller's Tale*. Three early attempts to retell the *Miller's Tale* for children bear mention.

Edith Johnstone (1895)

One of the earliest retellings of the *Miller's Tale* for young readers appeared in 1895 in one of William T. Stead's sixty-four-page Penny Poets volumes. I quote in full the summary of the tale as retold by one of Stead's employees, Edith Johnstone:

> There was once a carpenter who had a very pretty wife a good deal younger than himself. He was so careful of her, and so jealous, that not one of her admirers could get [away with] exchanging a word with her. A certain clerk, named Nicholas, decided at last to manage, by stratagem, to have a little time with the wife Alison, whom he very much admired. So he locked himself up, and after some days John the carpenter, in whose house he lodged, sent to know what the matter was, and as he received no satisfactory answer, he went himself. To him Nicholas said that he had learned by divination that a great flood was about to visit the earth, and that only they three, John, Alison, and Nicholas, might escape, and then only on condition that John should get three huge kneading tubs, and fill them with provisions, and hang them to the roof, so that when the flood came they might be saved, but each must get into his own tub, and when they heard the cry of "water," cut the ropes and the tub would float. And the most absolute secrecy must be observed in the matter. Poor foolish John, desirous, above all things, to save his beloved Alison from the flood, did everything as Nicholas suggested, and on the night arranged, at the appointed time, according to directions, he climbed up into his tub, and sat there waiting for the rain and water, from which he was to be saved. Meantime, Nicholas and Alison were downstairs, laughing over the poor, silly carpenter, and enjoying themselves as they pleased. Now it happened that Alison had yet another lover, and that night, while she and Nicholas were together, this man Absolon came tapping at her window, and begging that she would give him a kiss; instead, she opened the window and gave him a dreadful slap. Absolon went away in a great rage, and got a large stick, with which he returned, and again tapping, begged for one kind word. This time Nicholas decided to give him a slap, so, going to the window, he prepared to give the blow, when Absolon came down on his head with a terrific whack. At that Nicholas roared with pain, and the carpenter, hearing the cry, awoke, and fancying in the dark that it was the flood come, he promptly cut the ropes that bound him to the roof, and in a moment he and his tub came bump on the floor. Then there was a great uproar; the carpenter roared, Absolon roared, Nicholas roared, and the neighbours came pouring in to them. Alison said it was all right, her husband was a little mad, that was all. Everybody believed her, and that was the end. It was not a very long story, but then the miller was drunk.[2]

That inaccurate little summary is almost totally undramatic. There are no descriptions of the house, no scene changes, no dialogue. There is perhaps a certain slapstick drama to the slaps and whacks and bumps and roars, but those were not in the *Miller's Tale*. Several key dramatic features of the *Miller's Tale*—

the kissing, the pissing, the farting, the burning—were not included in the Penny Poets version.

F. J. Harvey Darton (1904).

Another early version considered to be suitable to children appeared in 1904 in F. J. Harvey Darton's *Tales of the Canterbury Pilgrims*. The story entitled "The Miller is a Churl" is given only the briefest of summaries:

> The Miller would not be silent or orderly.
> "Listen to me, all of you," he shouted. "I will tell you a tale about a carpenter who was tricked and made to look a fool by a clerk."
> "Stop your noise," said Oswald the Reeve, who did not like a carpenter being thus laughed at. "It is wrong and foolish to slander other men."
> The Miller, however, heeded neither him nor anyone else, but told a rude and churlish tale about a carpenter of Oxford.
> This carpenter, so the story said, was persuaded by a clerk that there would be second great flood, and that if he wished to be safe from drowning he must make himself an ark. So he used his kneading-trough as a sort of boat, and was hoisted in it up to the ceiling of the kitchen. When the water began to rise, the clerk told him he was to cut the cords that held the ark, and drop into the flood and sail safely away. He did exactly as he was told, and for a little while hung quietly up in the air, close to the roof, waiting for the deluge in a state of great fear and wonder. Suddenly he heard someone crying "Water!" He cut the cords, thinking that the flood had come, and down he fell to the hard floor, breaking his arm, and getting nothing but laughter for his folly.
> When the tale was ended, the pilgrims were not sure whether to be angry with the Miller for his rudeness or to laugh.[3]

In thus reducing the *Miller's Tale* to a brief anecdote, Darton eliminates entirely two of Chaucer's major characters, Alison and Absolon; two of the three tubs; the motivation for Nicholas's desire to trick old John; the bedroom window; and of course all of the sexual and scatological actions. Darton tells us the Miller's story was "rude and churlish," but there is in the tale as he reports it nothing either rude or churlish.

Eleanor Farjeon (1930)

Rather than leave it out altogether, Johnstone and Darton settled for much-abbreviated plot summaries of the *Miller's Tale*. Eleanor Farjeon wanted to give more than that in her retelling aimed especially at young readers. In the preface to her 1930 *Tales from Chaucer*, she explains why she wrote her book and the choices she made:

> The one excuse for presenting Chaucer in any words but his own, is that he *may* be read, and a taste for him be got by people (especially young people) who would never try to read the foreign language of his English, and so would miss forever something of the fun, the beauty, the wisdom, the humanity, and the romance, in which he stands among our poets second only to Shakespeare. [...] I have had to decide between the complete omission of certain tales in which particular incidents would prevent their being given to young people —and the suppression, or alteration of the incidents.[4]

Farjeon opted for both suppression and alteration of the incidents in Chaucer's *Miller's Tale*. She all but eliminated from her prose retelling Nicholas's lusting for Alison. In her version Nicholas never touches Alison, but is merely "friendly" with her: "So this scholar, his name was Nicholas, who was friendly to the young wife Alison, thought he would play a trick on the jealous old man, and make him look a fool before everybody" (Farjeon 46). In Chaucer's *Miller's Tale* Nicholas devises the elaborate ruse because he wants to show Alison how much cleverer a young college lad is than an unschooled old carpenter and because he wants to get rid of John so that he can spend the night in bed with his wife. In Farjeon's retelling Nicholas wants to play a trick simply because he wants to play a trick. The trick works well enough: Nicholas pretends to be in a trance. John believes his nonsense about a second Noah's flood, acquires the tubs and provisions, builds the three ladders, and, exhausted, falls immediately asleep on Monday night. Then the storyline departs from Chaucer's.

In Chaucer's tale, while John snores, Nicholas and Alison climb down their ladders and together go

> to bedde,
> Ther as the carpenter is wont to lye.
> Ther was the revel and the melodye;
> And thus lith Alison and Nicholas,
> In bisynesse of myrthe and of solas,
> Til that the belle of laudes gan to rynge,
> And freres in the chauncel gonne synge [3650–56].

For Farjeon there is no bed and no sex, just merry laughter at the trick they have played on John: "Then down their ladders crept Nicholas and Alison, and laughed and made merry till the bells began to ring, and the friars to sing in the chancel" (Farjeon 49). Then Absolon comes a-calling. In Chaucer, Absolon had been introduced before and had visited before—

see lines 3307–96. Farjeon cuts those ninety lines and introduces Absolon only on that Monday night while Nicholas and Alison enjoy their little joke:

> Now you must know that the Parish Clerk, whose name was Absolon, had taken a fancy to young Alison, the Carpenter's wife, and happening to pass through Osney had been told that the Carpenter was from home, getting timber for the Abbot. So thinking he might have a word with Alison while the Carpenter was away, he rose at cockcrow on this very morn, dressed himself at point device, combed his hair, chewed licorice to sweeten his breath, and sped away to the Carpenter's house. There he stood under the window and sang:
> "What are you doing, Alison, my honeycomb? My pretty bird, my cinnamon stick, wake, sweetheart, and speak to me! I shall mourn like a turtle-dove till you give me a kiss" [Farjeon 49–50].

Absolon gets his kiss, but it is not Alison's bottom he kisses. Indeed, it is not anyone's bottom:

> The night was black as pitch, and instead of Alison, Nicholas put out his head, and Absolon kissed him.
> "What's this, what's this?" cried Absolon. "A woman with a beard!" And Alison laughed "Te-he!" and Nicholas laughed "Ho-ho!" and Absolon knew they had played him a trick [Farjeon 50].

The angry Absolon then goes to the blacksmith and borrows a hot iron. He brings it back and knocks on the window, begging for another kiss:

> So once more, for mischief, Nicholas put his face out of [the] window, and smack! he got the hot iron on his cheek [Farjeon 51].

The rest of the story follows Chaucer—sort of. When Nicholas hollers "Water!" old John wakes up and cuts the rope. He does not break his arm, though, but lies there after his fall, stunned. The neighbors come in and, guided by Nicholas and Alison, declare him mad. Here is the closing summation in Chaucer:

> Thus swyved was this carpenteris wyf,
> For al his kepyng and his jalousye,
> And Absolon hath kist hir nether ye,
> And Nicholas is scalded in the towte.
> This tale is doon, and God save al the rowte! [3850–54].

None of that appears in Farjeon's retelling: no jealousy, no swiving, no ass-kissing, no burned butt. Here is the new closing summation:

> And so the Carpenter was held for a madman, and Nicholas was burned, and Absolon went home without his kiss, and the Carpenter's wife was merry. And that's the end of 'em, and God bless you all [Farjeon 51].

In making her version of the *Miller's Tale* more accessible than the Chaucerian originals were, Farjeon may or may not have succeeded in her goal of introducing young people to "the fun, the beauty, the wisdom, the humanity, and the romance" (Farjeon v) of Chaucer. She seems not to have been concerned that in her "suppression, or alteration of the incidents" of the *Miller's Tale*, she replaced Absolon's heterosexual horror at kissing a woman's buttocks with his homophobic horror at kissing another man's face.

XIII
Later Retellings for Adults: Clarke (1870), Haweis (1887), Raffel (2008), Ackroyd (2009)

Many translations and retellings of the *Canterbury Tales* for adults have appeared over the years. I select for inclusion here only four. The authors of the first two were, like the earlier translators, motivated in part by a desire to tell the *Miller's Tale* in such a way that it was less crudely explicit. The second two, on the other hand, seem to have been motivated by a desire to enhance its crude explicitness.

Frederick R. Clarke (1870)

Eighty years after the anonymous reteller of 1791 published his version, a British printer and bookseller named Frederick R. Clarke published the first volume of what was to be an eight-volume edition and facing-page translation of the *Canterbury Tales*. His stated reason for his effort was that because "Chaucer in his original dress is a sealed book to almost all readers of the present day," he wanted to "make Chaucer readable by a large number of persons."[1] By changing the language Clarke showed that he was in sympathy with Chaucer's eighteenth-century retellers who wanted to protect the refined ears of his countrymen from the most potentially embarrassing passages in the *Miller's Tale*.

In the grab scene, for example, Clarke's Nicholas catches Alison not by the queynte but "below the waist." Are we to suppose that he grabs her kneecaps or ankles perhaps? Then, instead of holding her hard by the haunches, he "gripped her harder than before" (Clarke 187). And here is Clarke's rendition of Chaucer's kiss scene:

> Dark was the night as pitch or coal, and at
> The window with stern outermost she stood;
> And Absolon knew neither more nor less,
> But kissed her as she stood full savoury [Clarke 211].

Clarke does not mention Alison's bending to put her hole out the window, but has her standing "stern outermost." Clarke does not mention Absolon's kissing Alison's naked arse, but merely his kissing her "as she stood." And the sentence is constructed such that Clarke's "full savoury" may describe not the way he kisses her but to the way she stands. Instead of feeling something all rough and long-haired, Clarke has Absolon kiss something "roughly hirsute" (Clarke 211).

Then, when Absolon comes back with the hot coulter and asks his sweet bird to speak, Chaucer's Nicholas famously lets fly a fart as loud as a thunderclap. Clarke never mentions a fart, but rather has Nicholas "let backwards flee / What seemed like thunder unto Absolon" (Clarke 215).

To his credit, Clarke presents his euphemistic translation on facing pages directly across from the Chaucerian original. His goal was to conceal what Chaucer really said only from those who were too young to make much sense of expressions like "stern outermost" and "roughly hirsute," and too lazy to glance across the page to find the words that Chaucer' actually used, words like queynte, ers, hole, hairy, and fart.

Mrs. [Mary Eliza] Haweis (1887)

In her earlier retelling of the *Canterbury Tales* for children,[2] Mrs. Haweis had quietly skipped over the *Miller's Tale*. A decade later in her "adaptation" of some of Chaucer's stories for adults,[3] she included it—or a prose tale close to it. Apparently convinced that the tale was improper even for adults, Haweis both made excuses for it and altered it. In her brief afterword to the *Miller's Tale*, Haweis says that "the amusing story related by the Miller is one of those which Chaucer excuses quaintly, because the scene is laid among common people whose standard of life has always varied and must vary from that of the classes refined by education. [...] I have made a very slight alteration in this tale" (Haweis 65). Actually, she has made several alterations, not all of them "slight."

She cuts entirely toe scene in which Nicholas grabs Alison. Instead, we have this bit of narration: "Now Nicholas being very young too, was great friends with this little wife, and they were both annoyed by the old carpenter's treating every look and action with suspicion, till, in their silly spirits, they thought it would be fine fun to play a trick on the carpenter which might teach him a lesson" (Haweis 55). Their goal, then, is not, as in Chaucer, to become lovers but to teach the jealous old John a lesson. To do so, Nicholas sets in motion his elaborate plan to convince old John that he is to be a second Noah. John obediently prepares the tubs and ladders, then on Monday night quickly falls asleep in his tub: "Then down the ladder creeps Nicholas, down creeps Alison too, and shifted the ladders, and in high spirits made ready for a real good time—it was the first time they had ever had a moment's freedom" (Haweis 60). Haweis makes no mention of the carpenter's bed or what the "real good time" involves, but shifts immediately to Absolon's visit and his presenting himself at the shot window to request a kiss.

Instead of having Alison present her buttocks for Absolon to kiss, Haweis tells us that she "rushed at him with a broom of no great purity, which he received on his face with considerable force" (Haweis 62). To get his revenge for the assault-by-broom, the angry Absolon goes to his friend Gerveys, returns with the hot coulter, and asks Alison for a second kiss:

> Nicholas, who was still pranking about the house with Alison, thought it was his turn to play Absolon a trick, and ran forward and hastily put up the window with a view to repeating the former successful feat. But this is always a mistake; the instant the window opened Absolon was ready with his hot coulter, and attacked him with so much vigour that whole patches of skin flew off, so that Nicholas, much sobered, and half killed by burns and blows, shouted wildly in terrific pain, "Help, water, water, help for heaven's sake!" [Haweis 63].

Haweis does not tell us what Nicholas's "pranking about the house with Alison" involved, says nothing of his getting up to take a piss, nothing of his sticking his buttocks out the window, nothing of his farting in Absolon's face, nothing about what part of his body receives the "burns and blows."

Haweis's admission that she made "a very slight alteration," then, greatly understates the number and extent of the changes she made in adapting the *Miller's Tale* for her readership. We must credit her, nonetheless, with being one of the first to see in the tale evidence of Chaucer's skill as a dramatist. In her short afterword she uses theatrical terminology when speaking of the *Miller's Tale*:

> Whether this tale be founded on some current *fabliau* or on private incident, it is one or the most completely funny tales ever conceived, and written with

admirable skill and comic power. The incongruities beneath the surface in each of the *dramatis personae*, the contrast of the characters, all drawn from nature, and the pictorial power which makes us almost see pretty Alison, foolish Absolon, and the reckless handy Nicholas as they wind their toils about the slow-brained, self-satisfied old carpenter, stamp Chaucer as a great dramatic master [Haweis 64–65].

Verily.

Burton Raffel (2008)

Burton Raffel's name is well-known to those who read medieval literature in translation. He explains in the "Translator's Preface" to his 2008 *Canterbury Tales* that his sole reason for offering the translation is that Chaucer's language is no longer accessible to native speakers of English: "Time has, however, continued to move on, and our language has moved with it. As is always the case, what was is now no more. And that is why I have translated *The Canterbury Tales*."[4] Here is his translation of the scene in which Nicholas grabs Alison:

> Now, my lords, and then it came to pass
> That once upon a day, this Handy Nicholas
> Happened to flirt and fool about with this pretty
> Wife, when her husband was working in another city.
> Clerics are smooth, and sly, carefully taught,
> And suddenly he caught her by the crotch
> And said: "By God, unless I take you to bed,
> Sweetheart, I want you so badly I'll end up dead."
> He gripped her thigh-bones hard, and pressed against her,
> And said: "Sweetheart, let me love you this minute
> Or I really will die, may God preserve me!" [Raffel 81–91].

Raffel's translation works well enough, and I have no objection to his translating Alison's "queynte" (3276) as her "crotch," but the "carefully taught" puzzles me, since Chaucer said nothing about Nicholas's teachers at Oxford. Are we to assume that Raffel thinks that at least one them had taught Nicholas to grab girls by the crotch?

I also wonder why he translates "yonge wyf" (3273) as "pretty wife"; "rage and pleye" (3273) as "flirt and fool about"; the specific town "Oseneye" (3274) as the more general "another city"; "prively" (3276) as "suddenly"; the more general "but if ich have my wille" (3277) as the more specific "unless I take you to bed"; "haunchebones" (3279) as "thigh-bones"; and "love me" (3280) as "let me love you."

Raffel's translation of the first Monday night kiss scene works well enough also:

>Absolon carefully set himself down on his knees,
>Saying, "I am noble, in every way,
>So after this, let there be more, I pray.
>Oh sweetheart, your grace! O lovebird, your mercy, this day!"
>She undid the window, and opened it very swiftly.
>"All right," she said, "come on, and do it quickly,
>Or else our neighbors, alas, might see you there."
>Absolon hurriedly wiped his lips all clear.
>The night was dark as pitch, as dark as coal,
>And out of the window she stuck her bare asshole,
>And Absolon, who could have done much worse,
>Put forth his mouth and lovingly kissed her ass,
>Licking his lips, as it were, before he'd grasped it.
>He jumped right back, knowing something was wrong.
>He knew no woman was bearded—and this was a long one!
>The skin was coarse and rough, the smell was strong.
>"O God, alas," he said, "What have I done?"
>"Tee hee," she said, and slammed the window down,
>As Absolon went walking slowly off [Raffel 524–42].

We may wonder where Raffel picked up the adverb "carefully" in the first line quoted above and "slowly" in the last, and where he got the idea that Alison's asshole was "bare" (can an asshole be clothed?). We may wonder where Raffel got the idea that Absolon wiped his mouth "all clear" rather than "ful drie" (3730), kissed "lovingly" rather than "savourly" (3735), and licked his lips after the kiss. We may wonder where Raffel got the idea that Alison's smell was strong. In his introduction Raffel says, "I am myself a poet—but Chaucer is far better than I am. I have no desire to compete with him, or to rewrite his poem" (Raffel xxxi–xxxii). It is inevitable that a translator, especially a translator of rhymed Middle English verse into rhymed Modern English verse would to some extent rewrite the poem. We would expect a mostly-unrhymed prose translation like Raffel's to be more faithful to its original.

Peter Ackroyd (2009)

Peter Ackroyd was even less encumbered by the need to worry about meter and rhyme. Here is his translation of the grab scene:

>Now it so happened that one fine day, while the old carpenter was working at Osney Abbey, sweet Nicholas began to flirt and play with her. He was, like many

students, a crafty and resourceful young man. What does he do? He begins to caress her cunt, saying to her, "You know if I don't have you then I will die for love of you." Then his hand wandered further down, and he began to stroke her thighs. "Sweetheart," he says, "make love to me now or, God help me, I will lie down and die. Fuck me or I am finished."[5]

The modern word "cunt" sounds nastier than the Middle English "queynte" (3276), just as "fuck me" sounds nastier than "love me" (3280). I am more concerned, however, about Ackroyd's substituting the word "caress" for "caught." It is a far different thing for Nicholas to "catch" or grab Alison's genitals than for him to caress them. The second implies some level of consent or acquiescence, but Alison's reaction in neither version is that of a willing victim. Her reply in Chaucer is:

> "I wol nat kisse thee, by my fey!
> Why, lat be!" quod she. "Lat be, Nicholas,
> Or I wol crie 'out, harrow,' and 'allas!'" [3284–86].

Ackroyd renders Alison's response somewhat differently, but with equal conviction:

> "Sod you, Nicholas!" she screamed at him. "Do you really think I'm going to kiss you? Sod off. Take your hands off me, too. Or else I'll cry 'rape!'" [Ackroyd 84].

Did Chaucer's Alison threaten to cry "rape"? Here is Ackroyd's rendering of the kiss scene:

> Meanwhile Absolon had got down on his knees in front of the window. "I have scored," he said. "I don't think she will stop at a kiss. Oh my sweetheart, be kind to me. Give me more."
> Then Alison opened the window in all haste. "Hurry up," she told him. "Come on. I don't want the neighbours to see you."
> So Absolon wiped his mouth in preparation. It was very dark. It was still night, after all.
> "Here I am," said Alison. Then she put her naked arse out of the window. Absolon could see nothing at all, of course, and so he put out his tongue and gave her a French kiss. He was eagerly slurping her bum. But then he knew that something was wrong. He had never known a woman with a beard before. But he knew this much—he had licked on something rough and hairy. "Fuck me," he said. "This isn't right." Alison laughed out loud, and shut the window. Absolon shook his head, and began to walk away [Ackroyd 94].

In his introduction Ackroyd speaks of older literature as if it were a near-dead slave or prisoner unfairly locked away in jail. The translator, then, plays the hero's role by freeing him:

> Translation can be a form of liberation, releasing an older work into the contemporary world and thereby infusing it with new life. [...] I thought it best to

approach my own task in the manner of Chaucer himself, whose translation of part of the *Roman de la Rose* (to give one of many examples) was faithful to the spirit if not always to the letter of the great original. He seems to have worked on the principle of inspired improvisation, guided by no other criterion than his own good sense. [...]

The *Canterbury Tales* is perhaps best known for its bawdy and sometimes scatological humour. The modern translator can maintain the salacious energy of the original simply by translating Chaucer's words accurately. The language of sex, unlike the language of prayer, has not changed materially over the centuries. [...]

I believed that my task was essentially to facilitate the experience of the poem—to remove obstacles to the understanding and enjoyment of the tales, and by various means to intimate or express the true nature of the original. I hope that I have not failed in my purpose [Ackroyd xix, xxi–xxii].

Judging from Ackroyd's retelling of the kiss scene, has he succeeded or failed? More specifically, by talking about Absolon's French kissing and "eagerly slurping" of Alison's bottom and then having him say, "Fuck me," is Peter Ackroyd engaging in "inspired improvisation" that has expressed "the true nature of the original"? Has he succeed in "releasing" the *Miller's Tale* "into the contemporary world and thereby infusing it with new life"?

XIV
Later Retellings for Young Readers: McCaughrean (1984), Hastings (1988)

Late adapters of the *Miller's Tale* for young people, like the earlier ones mentioned in Chapter XII, continued to think it necessary to make substantial changes in the characters and the plot of the tale.

Geraldine McCaughrean (1984)

In her *Canterbury Tales*, Geraldine McCaughrean recreated for children thirteen of Chaucer's tales. The name "Chaucer" is mentioned nowhere on the cover or title page of the book, perhaps because the stories McCaughrean tells bear but slender similarity to those that Chaucer told. She even renamed the tales. The tale of the Knight she called *Chivalry and Rivalry*. The tale told by the pilgrim whom she renamed Matt the Miller is entitled "A Barrel of Laughs." The tale comes with this warning by the frame-tale narrator, who is named Geoffrey Chaucer:

> I'm not sure I ought to relay the story with which Matt the Miller regaled us. It wasn't—how shall I say—it wasn't the kind of story you hear in church or recount to your mother when you get home. Still, it fetched a lot of laughter from some of the pilgrims, so I had best not keep it from you. If you find it a little *rude,* you had better cover your eyes while you read.[1]

The reference to telling the story "to your mother when you get home" reflects the audience of children that McCaughrean was writing for.

Figure 16. Cover of Geraldine McCaughrean's *The Canterbury Tales* (1984).

In Chaucer's *Miller's Tale* we find these memorably rude lines:

> And prively he caughte hire by the queynte,
> And seyde, "Ywis, but if ich have my wille,
> For deerne love of thee, lemman, I spille."
> And heeld hire harde by the haunchebones,

XIV. Later Retellings for Young Readers

> And seyde, "Lemman, love me al atones,
> Or I wol dyen, also God me save!"
> And she sproong as a colt doth in the trave,
> And with hir heed she wryed faste awey,
> And seyde, "I wol nat kisse thee, by my fey!" [3276–84].

Here is what McCaughrean does with that scene:

> She was as pert and as pretty as a squirrel up a tree, though to tell the truth, she should not have flirted so much with the men. [...] Nicholas was a lodger in the Carpenter's house. And Alison just could not take her eyes off him. He was allowed to steal a kiss in the dark of the larder and while he helped her hang out the washing [McGaughrean 19].

Most of the plot is familiar enough. Alison goes along with Nicholas's plan to trick old Oswald (as McCaughrean renames John) by pretending to go into a trance. When Oswald breaks down Nicholas's door (without the help of a servant), Nicholas describes his vision of a coming flood. He directs Oswald to fetch three barrels, provision them, and hang them from the rafters. As soon as Oswald falls asleep, Nicholas and Alison climb down. They do not go to bed or make love, however: "Nicholas and Alison fell into each other's arms in fits of helpless, silent laughter. They sat on the settle and held hands and kissed and carried on until the darkest hours of the night, when the whole town was asleep" (McCaughrean 22). They are still "carrying on" when Absolon comes and asks for a kiss. After that, the storyline departs widely from Chaucer's.

Absolon's request for a kiss wakes old Oswald up. He sleepily asks if the flood has come:

> "No, dear. Go back to sleep," called Alison, and soon snores were rending the rafters like a bow saw. But still Absolon was at the window. "What shall I do?" hissed Alison.
> "I suppose he must have his kiss," said Nicholas rising from the settle. The window was high up, higher than a man's head. In a voice as high as a filleted cod, Nicholas whispered through the shutter: "Dearest boy. How I've longed for this moment! But close your eyes. It is not fitting that a woman should be seen in her nightclothes, even on the darkest of nights, and even by one she loves so dearly!" And he leaned out of the window to plant a kiss on Absolon's waiting lips [McCaughrean 23].

Feeling Nicholas's beard and hearing Alison and Nicholas giggling, Absolon figures out that he has been tricked and vows to have his revenge. He goes to the blacksmith's forge and heats up a branding iron, then rushes back and asks for a second kiss. Nicholas is eager enough to comply, but this time, "edging to the window sill, he proffered Absolon the seat of his pants." Then, "as

Nicholas's trousers came through the window, Absolon lunged!" Nicholas's cries for water "as he galloped round the room and fell over the settle" (McCaughrean 24) wake Oswald up. The old man thinks the flood has come and cuts the rope: "He dropped like a stone—right on top of the settle, his wife, and the lodger" (McCaughrean 25). The tale ends with the neighbors coming in to find "Oswald, Nicholas, and Alison, the settle, a barrel, and a plentiful supply of bread and cheese, all squandered in a heap. The carpenter was shrieking, 'It's the end of the world! Swim for your lives!' A trickle of smoke was still rising from the seat of the lodger's trousers" (McCaughrean 25).

The inventive storyline of "A Barrelful of Laughs" speaks for itself, but I offer four comments. First, McCaughrean apparently felt it to be inappropriate for children to read about a woman's bottom. A man's bottom could be referred to only indirectly by the clothing covering it—"the seat of his pants" and "his trousers." Second, McCaughrean invents a new piece of furniture for her story, the settle, and places it directly under Oswald's barrel, thus setting up the closing crash in which Oswald, his wife, and his lodger are all three punished. Third, it was apparently important for McCaughrean that, innocent though their "carrying on" was, they be punished for their sins. And fourth, Absolon never kisses Alison's bottom and is never the facial recipient of a fart. His only punishment is to kiss a man. For a man's inadvertent kissing of another man to be taken as sufficient punishment for a parish clerk who lusts after a married woman in his parish suggests a homophobia that McCaughrean, like Farjeon before her, may not have been fully aware of. If she was aware of it, I wonder, did she think that homophobia an appropriate theme for "A Barrel of Laughs"?

Selina Hastings (1988)

As a lead-in to her 1988 retelling of the *Miller's Tale*, Selina Hastings announces that the Miller "was a bit of a buffoon [and] had a fund of dirty stories to tell."[2] Although she does not specify on the cover or in the introduction that her retellings of seven of the Canterbury stories were designed for a young audience, the large-page format and the colorful illustrations have caused it to be placed in the children's literature room of most libraries. Perhaps reflecting her having read Anglo-Saxon and Middle English literature at Oxford, Hastings's retelling of the *Miller's Tale* is less altered than most retellings for young people. Still, she felt that it was necessary to clean up some parts of the Miller's "dirty" story. Here is the grab scene:

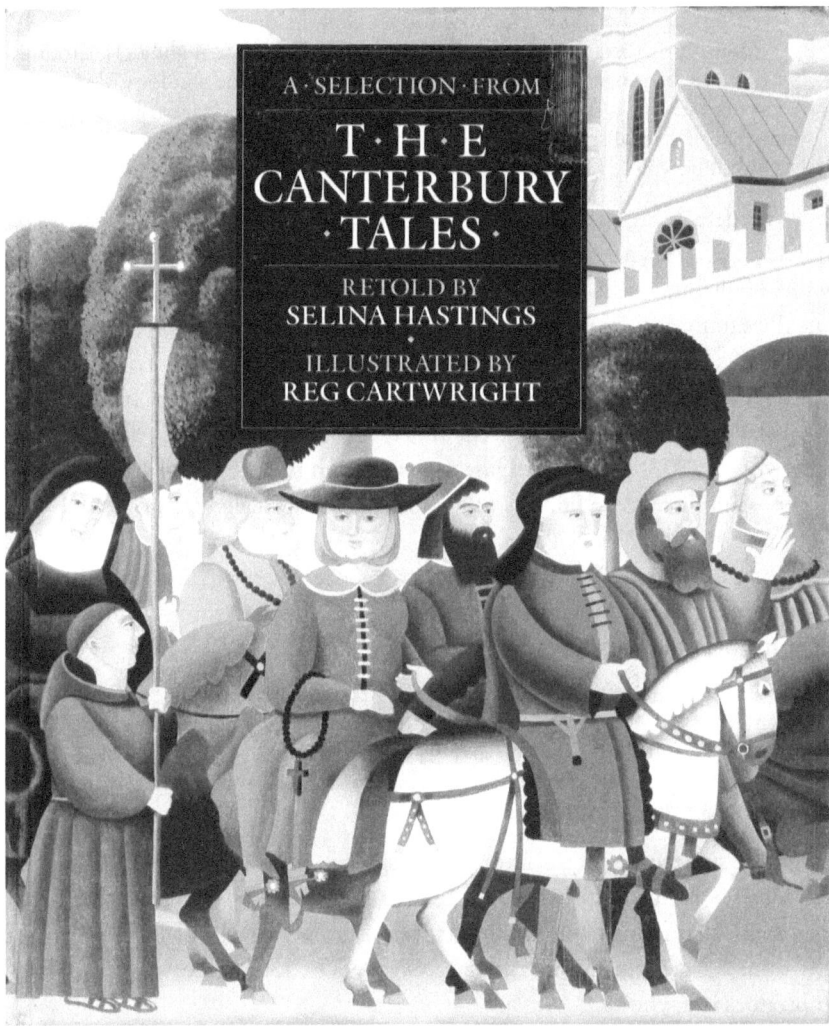

Figure 17. Cover of Selina Hastings's *A Selection from The Canterbury Tales* (1988).

Nicholas began to flirt with Alison. At first she was skittish, giving a little shriek when he tiptoed up behind her and put his hands round her waist. "Don't do that, Nicholas!" she cried. "No, I won't kiss you! Take you hands away" [Hastings 28].

Chaucer's Nicholas was doing more than flirting, his hands went lower than her waist, and he wanted far more than a kiss. Chaucer's Alison did not give a little shriek, but merely threatened to scream.

Hastings renders somewhat more faithfully the general sense of Absolon's kissing of Alison at her bedroom window:

> Getting out of bed she crossed the room and flung the window wide.
> "Come here, Absolon, and kiss me quickly. It's cold in the night air!" Turning her back she bent over and stuck her bare bottom out of the window. Absolon heard her but it was far too dark to see anything at all. He closed his eyes and pursed his lips in blissful expectation—but what was this! Not Alison's lips but her naked bottom! [Hastings 33].

But the details are different. Chaucer had had Alison unlatch the window quickly ("The wyndow she undoth, and that in haste" [3727]), not fling it wide. He had her tell Absolon to hurry up not because it is cold, but because she does not want the neighbors to see. He had not had Absolon close his eyes for the kiss. Hastings cuts entirely some of the most vivid features of the kissing scene, Absolon's wiping his mouth "ful drie" (3730), his kissing "ful savourly" (3735), and his shock when he encounters Alison's pubic hair, "al rough and long yherd" (3738). Because Hastings makes no mention of that hair, she of course cannot use the famous line where Absolon realizes that "a womman hath no berd" (3737).

Just as she removes from the story all reference to Alison's genitals, so Hastings removes all reference, in the next window scene, to Nicholas's need to urinate and his desire to fart:

> "It's Absolon again!" said Nicholas. "This is too much! This time it's my turn to teach him a lesson!" An striding across the room he flung open the window and he too stuck out his bottom.
> Absolon was ready with his iron and stuck it fair and square in the middle of the scholar's rump [Hastings 34].

The subtraction of the fart requires also the subtraction of such Chaucerian niceties as Absolon's hilarious "'Spek, sweete bryd'" (3805) and the "thonder-dent" that helps to signal to old John, slumbering above in his tub, that the rains have come and it is time to chop his little ark free of her mooring. John does it anyhow:

> "The flood has come!" he cried. And taking up his axe he cut the ropes holding the barrel to the ceiling, and down he crashed, barrel and all.
> The noise brought Nicholas and Alison tumbling down the stairs shouting, "Help! Murder" [Hastings 34].

In Chaucer's *Miller's Tale*, of course, they say nothing about murder, and they do not come tumbling down any stairs because they are already downstairs in the bedroom that has a shot-window so low that Absolon must kneel to receive the unsavory kiss and the blinding fart.

XV

In the Modern Missouri Ozarks: Milburn (1956)

Absolon, who had begun drooling at the thought of kissing her, wiped his mouth dry on the back of his hand. The night was still dark as a tar barrel.

She turned, and over the window sill, instead of her face, she popped out her plump bare bottom.

Absolon, none the wiser, met it with his lips and kept his mouth pasted there, savoring this moment he had so often dreamed about.

Then, suddenly, his inflamed mind was pierced by an awful thought. Something was wrong!

"Oh, my God," he breathed, backing away. "What have I done? Are you sure that's you, Julie?"

He heard a little giggle. And the window was clapped shut.

Absolon just stood there in bewilderment for a moment, still unable to get a grasp of the awful disgrace that actually had befallen him.

Then he overheard within the bedroom low laughter and whispers.

He heard Dexter Nichols' gurgling laughter. "Oh, my God! What a joke that was to pull on the poor bastard."

Only then did Absolon fully understand what had happened to him.[1]

That passage will sound familiar to anyone who knows Chaucer's *Miller's Tale*, but few will recognize the actual text. The quotation is taken from chapter 22 of George Milburn's 24-chapter novel *Julie*. This 188-page novel had a sexy cover somewhat in the style and tradition of an Erskine Caldwell paperback. Its plot, however, is clearly built on Chaucer's *Miller's Tale*. Milburn's version is some fifteen times as long as Chaucer's. Most of the new material Milburn has placed up front, before the specific events of the *Miller's Tale* begin to show up in the second half of the novel.

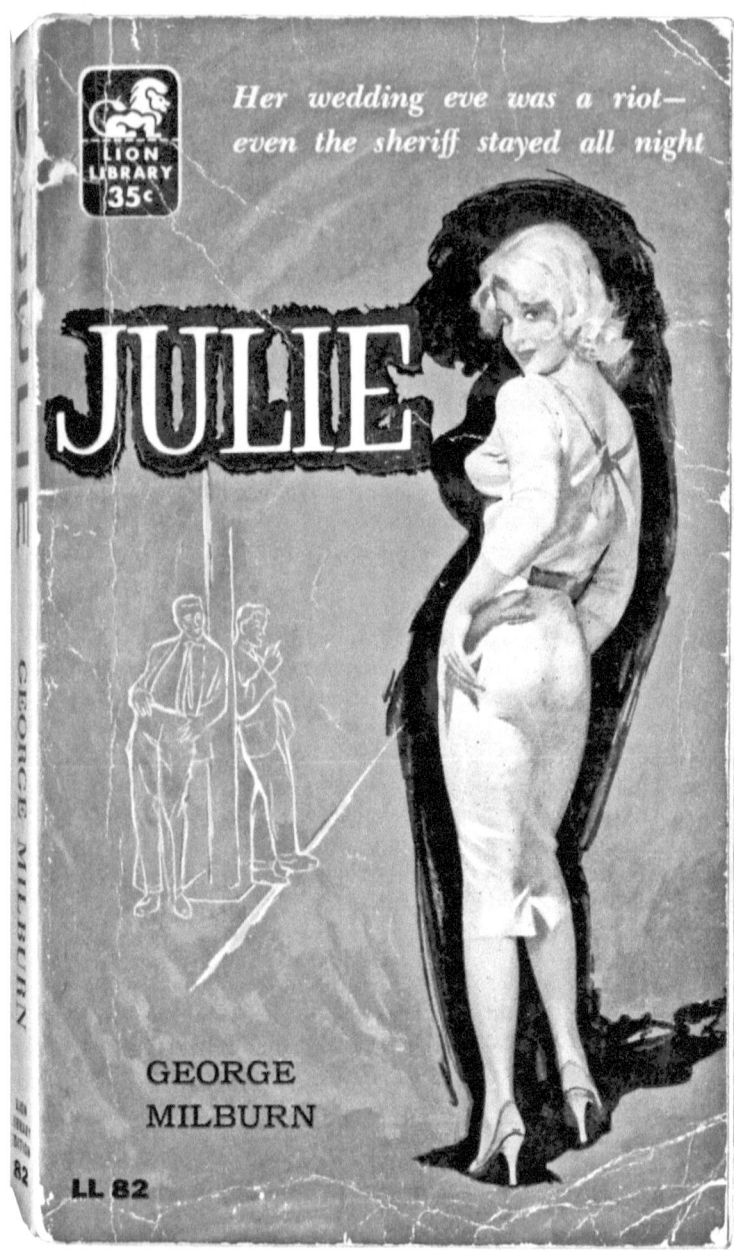

Figure 18. The cover of the 1956 Lion Library paperback of George Milburn's *Julie*, emphasizing Julie in a seductive pose. In faint outline to the left, leaning on the lamp post, are two lazy gawkers. Old John Bundix is nowhere to be seen. The words at the top read, "Her wedding eve was a riot—even the sheriff stayed all night."

Chapter-by-Chapter Summary

Because Milburn's *Julie* is unfamiliar to most Chaucerians and because it has long been out of print and almost impossible to come by, readers will be well-served by a chapter-by-chapter plot summary of the novel. It is interesting that the first fourteen chapters, which deal with the pre-marriage negotiations, the wedding, and the post-wedding partying, have no counterpart in the *Miller's Tale*. John and Alison have been married for some time at the start of Chaucer's tale. There are no chapter titles for the twenty-four chapters in *Julie*. In my summary I give at the start of each summary the setting for that chapter.

1. Outside courthouse. Various hangers on—particularly Jewel and Pearly Pruitt—get all excited when they see John Bundix take the lovely Julie into the courthouse.
2. Inside courthouse. John tries to get Judge Throgmorten to marry them, but the judge sends them to Absolon Kendall across the hall for a license.
3. Inside courthouse. Absolom Kendall is busy dealing with Dexter Nichols, who claims not to be selling books and so not to need a peddler's license.
4. Inside courthouse. John comes in to get his marriage license from Absolon Kendall.
5. Inside courthouse. John gets the marriage license and takes it back to Judge Throgmorten.
6. Inside courthouse. The ceremony is completed despite Dexter Nichols's efforts to delay it, on astrological grounds, until October.
7. John's house. The townspeople come, uninvited, to a wild wedding-night shivaree.
8. John's house. The shivareers break into the house and find Julie hiding in the closet. Granny Gosnell breaks up a knife fight between Pearly and Jewel Pruitt, cousins.
9. Outside John's house. The shivareers find John hiding in a laundry tub and are about to throw him into the creek, but Dexter Nichols "saves" him from drowning. The grateful John takes Dexter home.
10. In town. The community reacts to Julie in different ways. The women are jealous of her clothes and the men want her clothes off.
11. Holiness Church. Virgil Pruitt preaches a sermon on sin and says that John should leave the church because he has fornicated before the church ceremony has sanctified the wedding.
12. Holiness Church and thereabouts. There is much increased attendance at church because men are eager to see and get to know Julie.
13. John's house. Dexter Nichols pretends not to be interested in either food or Julie, and Julie wonders whether he is gay.
14. Around town. Robin Goodkind, John's servant-helper, is courted as a go-between to carry letters and gifts to Julie. Although a "half-wit," he seems clever at making use of his station.

15. Outside and inside John's house. Robin Goodkind tells Absolon Kendall that Julie is enamored of him. Absolon makes a long confessional prayer. Then, having heard that John is a heavy sleeper he goes and serenades Julie at John's bedroom window.
16. John's house. When John and Robin go off to the sawmill, Dexter Nicholas makes his play by grabbing Julie. She agrees to be his if he can come up with a sure plan for deceiving John.
17. John's house. Dexter Nichols pretends to be in a trance. John sends Robin Goodkind up to check. They batter the door down.
18. John's house. Dexter Nichols reveals God's plan to drown the world and tells John Bundix to get three tubs and hang them high. John has a laundry tub and a rain barrel, but needs one more.
19. John's house and baker's shop. After telling Julie about the terrible flood coming, John goes to Adolphus Schultz's bakery shop to buy back the kneading trough he had earlier sold him.
20. John's house. John prepares the tubs, ropes, ladders, and provisions, then climbs up into his kneading trough and falls asleep.
21. John's house. Dexter Nichols and Julie climb down and make love.
22. John's house. Absolon learns that John is away and visits Julie at the window. After kissing her bottom, he realizes what he has done and vows revenge.
23. John's house and the blacksmith shop. Absolon goes to see Jarvis Gerveys, returns with a hot colter, and scorches Dexter. When Dexter cries "Water, Water!," John cuts the rope, tumbles down, and breaks his arm.
24. Around town. The women punish Julie with whips, and Doc Sinclair sends her off on a bus.

It is instructive to compare the percentages devoted to the buildup to the climactic window scene in three of the kiss-and-burn narratives—the anonymous fourteenth-century Middle-Dutch *Heile of Beersele*, Chaucer's late-fourteenth-century adaptation of it as the *Miller's Tale*, and Milburn's twentieth-century adaption of that as *Julie*. In *Heile of Beersele*, 20.0 percent of the tale is pre-bedroom, 80.0 percent bedroom. In Chaucer's *Miller's Tale*, 67.3 percent is pre-bedroom, 32.7 percent bedroom. In Milburn's *Julie*, 91.5 percent is pre-bedroom, 8.5 percent bedroom. Clearly, the author of the Middle Dutch story wanted to minimize the pre-bedroom descriptions—only a fifth of the tale—and take us straight to the window-action in Heile's bedroom. Chaucer significantly altered that by shifting the emphasis—more than two-thirds of the tale—to the pre-bedroom descriptions. Milburn moved even further in that direction by devoting more than nine-tenths of *Julie* to the events preceding the climactic bedroom scene. The result is that *Julie* is so front-loaded that it is not until well into the novel that readers begin to feel that the story they are reading is really an imaginative retelling of Chaucer's wonderful tale of lust, jealousy, foolishness, adultery, deception, humiliation, revenge, and punishment.

Once they get to the bedroom scenes, readers will find that the story sounds familiar indeed. I quote at the start of this chapter the scene in which Julie presents her buttocks to Absolon Kendall. Once he realizes what he has kissed, Absolon Kendall is horrified. He rubs his lips with dust and clumps of grass, then rushes off to Jarvis Gerveys's blacksmith shop and borrows a hot coulter. He rushes back to John's house and asks for another kiss, saying that he has brought Julie a solid gold ring that his mother had left to him:

> Now Dexter Nichols had got out of bed a moment before to make water and he thought it was too good a chance to miss.
> He whispered low to Julie, "Just lay quiet there, sweetheart! Let me do this up right!"
> Barefooted, he stole across the bedroom, jerked the window open wide and stuck his naked haunches out over the sill.
> Absolon had the iron colter all set. It had turned black by now, but it was still sizzling hot.
> "Speak to me, my pretty little bird," Absolon wheedled. "I can't see where you are."
> Dexter Nichols answered with a noise as loud as a thunderclap. It struck Absolon full in the face.
> He staggered back, but in the same motion he made a stab with the hot iron.
> It struck Dexter full in the middle of the rump, burning off a patch of skin as big as a flapjack.
> Stricken with pain, Dexter leaped away from the window screaming, "Help! Help! Water! Water! For God's sake, help!" [Milburn 182–83].

These window scenes clearly derive from Chaucer. Milburn makes no effort to conceal his indebtedness to Chaucer. On the contrary, he celebrates it by dedicating the novel "To Chaucer, my master" and by giving as an epigraph to the novel Chaucer's famous five-line warning in the prologue to the *Miller's Tale* stating that he does not want to "falsen" his material:

> And therfore every gentil wight I preye,
> For Goddes love, demeth nat that I seye
> Of yvel entente, but that I moot reherce
> Hir tales alle, be they bettre or werse,
> Or elles falsen som of my mateere [3171–75].

In fact, just as his master Chaucer did before him, Milburn "falsened" his material in some productive ways. The first half of *Julie* is about characters in a story barely recognizable as Chaucerian. Just as we should resist being annoyed at Chaucer's bastardization of a clever little Middle Dutch tale, so we should resist being annoyed at George Milburn's bastardization of Chaucer's clever little Middle English one.

Who Was George Milburn?

Few now have heard of the author of *Julie*. Born and raised in Coweta, Oklahoma, George Milburn was the son of the town lawyer, postmaster, and justice of the peace. Milburn became a significant enough writer that at his death in late 1966, at age sixty, he was given an eighty-line obituary in the *New York Times* (for September 23). As a writer, Milburn drew heavily on his experiences with the people and landscapes of Oklahoma and neighboring states. His most enduring writing involves the people of the Ozarks—that mountainous region west of the Mississippi River where Kansas, Arkansas, Oklahoma, and Missouri come together. Milburn published many short stories and several novels. He spent almost a year (1926–27) traveling with tramps and hobos, and in 1930 published *The Hobo's Hornbook*. In 1934 he won a Guggenheim fellowship that permitted him to travel in Europe. Milburn's fiction came to the attention of H. L. Mencken, who praised it.[2]

Julie, Milburn's last novel, was reissued under a different title, *Old John's Woman*, by Pyramid Books in 1960. It had a different cover but the text and pagination were unchanged. It still sold for 35 cents.

Alison and Julie

Milburn knew the *Miller's Tale* well and incorporated many of its details into his novelistic version of it. His description of Julie herself, for example, has many conscious parallels with Chaucer's description of Alison. In the paired quotations below, I give Chaucer's lines first, then Milburn's corresponding phrasing immediately following:

> Whit was hir smok, and broyden al bifoore
> And eek bihynde, on hir coler aboute,
> Of col-blak silk, withinne and eek withoute.
> The tapes of hir white voluper
> Were of the same suyte of hir coler [3238–42].

[T]hose white blouses she wore were thin. [...] And then she had a way of wearing hair ribbons, the like of which had not been seen in our town. [...] And she would have ribbons at the collar of her blouse to match the ones on her head [Milburn 90–91].

> Ful small ypulled were hire browes two,
> And tho were bent and blake as any sloo [3245–46].

[S]he had plucked her eyebrows into thin little arches, and it took another woman to surmise that these were so black only because she had carefully pencilled them [Milburn 90].

Figure 19. The cover of the 1960 Pyramid Books reissued paperback of George Milburn's *Julie*, under the new title *Old John's Woman*. Julie is still shown in a seductive pose, but here in a room with her puzzled-looking husband, John Bundix. The words across at the top read, "Every man in town was hot after Julie."

> And by hir girdel heeng a purs of lether,
> Tasseled with silk and perled with latoun [3250–51].
> She used to carry a fancy leather purse at her side. [...] It shone with brass ornaments and was tasseled with bright-colored silk [Milburn 91].
>
> Ful brighter was the shynyng of hir hewe
> Than in the Tour the noble yforged newe [3255–56].
> But the girl from Joplin was as bright as a new-minted dollar [Milburn 100].
>
> Hir mouth was sweete as bragot or the meeth,
> Or hoord of apples leyd in hey or heeth [3261–62].
> [T]he faint smile that quirked her moist, parted lips (red as apples lying in the hay) held a promise of forbidden delights [Milburn 21].

Both Alison and Julie marry at age eighteen rich and jealous old carpenters, and both become the love-objects of two young men, one more direct in his approach to her than the other. One serenades her at night, the other grabs her by the crotch. To demonstrate again just how well Milburn knew the details of *Miller's Tale*, I give here some of the parallels between the two grab-scenes:

> And prively he caughte hire by the queynte [3276].
> Suddenly, the handsome young stranger reached out his hand and grabbed her by the quaint part [Milburn 137].
>
> And heeld hire harde by the haunchebones [3279].
> Then he ran his hands down her back and gripped her low, holding her tight against him [Milburn 137].
>
> "Lemman, love me al atones,
> Or I wol dyen, also God me save!" [3280–81].
> "Oh, my God, baby, don't you see I love you! Don't you know that if I can't get you now I'm just going to die!" [Milburn 137].
>
> And she sproong as a colt dooth in the trave,
> And with her heed she wryed faste awey [3282–83].
> Just then she shoved him away with both arms and gave a leap like a colt when it has been put in a trave to be shod the first time. She jerked her head away [Milburn 137].
>
> "Why, lat be!" quod she. "Lat be, Nicholas,
> Or I wol crie 'out, harrow,' and 'allas'!
> Do wey youre handes, for youre curteisye!" [3285–87].
> "Stop this! Mr. Nichols!" she said, without raising her husky voice. "Take your hands off of me! [...] Let go of me, or else I'm going to scream" [Milburn 137].

Although the description of Julie's body, dress, and actions are remarkably similar to those of Alison in these passages, *Julie* is a vastly different narrative from the *Miller's Tale*. When he wrote *Julie* Milburn changed the plot about a married woman, a lovesick parish clerk, and a clever college boy in fourteenth-century Oxford, to one about a not-yet-married woman, a one-legged lovesick courthouse clerk, and a clever itinerant astrologer-bookmonger in the twentieth-century American Ozarks. To continue focusing on Milburn's portrayal of Julie herself, let us consider three changes: he explained why Julie married John, he gave Julie breasts, and he made Julie less animalistic.

Chaucer never quite tells us the circumstances that led to Alison's marriage to John the carpenter. We can suppose that she marries him because he is rich, but we are not told that directly. As for Milburn's story, why in the world would Julie marry old John Bundix, a man thrice her age who refers to her, in her presence, as "this here pretty little play-doll" (Milburn 34). She has known him only a day when they show up at the courthouse to get married. How can she not be insulted that her husband-to-be cannot even remember her name for the marriage license application: "*Her* name? Odd dang if I don't disremember it myself!" (Milburn 34). It turns out that she had no choice about marrying him. John Bundix puts it this way: "I just taken one look at her last night while I was attending the protracted meeting up to Joplin, and I found out her pappy was the preacher, so after services I went up to him, and he claims he's got a whole retinue of good-looking daughters he's anxious to get shut of, so if I want this one—come to think of it, my little ewe lamb, what *is* your name?" (34). John Bundix apparently never even asked Julie to marry him. Rather, he just negotiated with her father "before I consented to tote her away in my truck!" (Milburn 35).

Chaucer makes no reference to Alison's breasts. Milburn, on the other hand, makes Julie's breasts a prominent feature of her anatomy. On the first page of *Julie*, one of the town loafers, on seeing Julie walk into the courthouse, says: "Did ary one of you get a look at her just a-bobbing and a-bouncing?" (Milburn 9). When one of the riotous partygoers finds Julie on her wedding night hiding in a wardrobe "clad only in her pink rayon slip," she has her hands "crossed against her mounting bosom" (Milburn 69). Later she walks "with her shoulders back, her breasts out" (Milburn 91). There are lots of ways to say that John Bundix is shorter than his wife, but Milburn's narrator tells us that John "pranced along bosom-high beside her" (Milburn 89). He even gets grossly specific about Julie's breasts: "it did not take a pair of x-ray eyes to see where the cleft between her breasts began. These were not the least of her beauties, but they did not seem too large. She could have skipped rope without blacking her eyes. However, while she had the decency to keep them covered in public, she actually showed more than a nursing woman" (Milburn 90–91).

The focus on Julie's breasts is not entirely gratuitous. Early in the novel, shortly after Julie bobs and bounces into town, Virgil Pruitt classifies men according to the way they look at a pretty woman: "Now hit's been my personal observation that there air three different classifercations of men in this world: There's the type of man that looks at a woman's bosom first. Well, sich a man ain't never been weaned proper" (Milburn 13). Surely it is no accident that, a few pages later, when Absolon Kendall first meets Julie, he "ventured a quick stare at her bosom" (Milburn 34). Given Virgil's classification, that stare leads naturally to Absolon's naively impassioned statement later to Julie at her window, "I mourn after you like a little lamb does after its mama's tit" (Milburn 177). Apparently Virgil Pruitt was right about unweaned boy-men being drawn to a woman's breasts.

Chaucer repeatedly emphasizes Alison's "wylde" (3225) and animalistic nature. Within just thirty lines she is compared to six different animals: her body is like that of a "wezele" (3234); she is softer than the wool on a "wether" (3249); she sings like a "swalwe" (3258); she skips like a "kyde or calf" (3260); and she is as skittish as a "colt" (3263). Julie is described by the narrator in some mildly animalistic terms—he says that she has a form "like a mink's" (Milburn 90)—but usually it is other characters who use animal epithets of her. John calls her "my little ewe lamb" (Milburn 34, 117) and later, in anger, a "bitch dog in heat" (Milburn 118); Absolon calls her "my pretty little bird" (Milburn 177, 183) and, later, in anger, a "little bitch" (Milburn 179) and a "whore bitch" (Milburn 179; see also 187, where another man uses the same term of her). In making such comparisons, however, these men say more about themselves than about Julie. The narrator himself rarely uses such epithets.

Julie's Animal-Men

Indeed, Julie seems for Milburn less an animal herself than the Circe who turns men into beasts. As the narrator puts it, Julie had "a kind of come-hither look in her eyes that seemed to tease men's animal appetites" (Milburn 90). Unlike Alison of the *Miller's Tale*, who is not obviously surrounded by man-beasts, Julie is surrounded by just such men.

Her husband John is "built on the lines of an ape, his knuckles hanging on a level with his knees" (Milburn 17), has a "lower lip pooched out like a bull dog's" (Milburn 42), and is described as "prancing about like a quarter-horse" (Milburn 56), "snorting like a stable-horse" (Milburn 36), and "stepping as high as a bantam rooster" (Milburn 90). This ape-man brags that "I am apt to fight like a swinjed bobcat!" (Milburn 78). On that fateful Monday night, "dog-tired after his exertions" (Milburn 171), John snores "like a hog in a bog" (172) as he waits for the rain that will make a second Noah of him.

Absolon Kendall's chin is "wimpled like a rabbit's but his eyes were as intent as a bird dog's" (Milburn 30). When he first looks at Julie, he is said to act like "a pointer pup froze on a quail" (Milburn 31). Although his nickname is "Caterpillar," the presence of Julie in town makes him act "more like a butterfly" (Milburn 107) than a caterpillar. Later, outside her bedroom window, not only does he mourn for her "like a little lamb," but he imagines himself cooing "like a turtle dove" (Milburn 177).

Dexter Nichols is not described with many animal images, but his actions in grabbing Julie and, later, in farting on Absolon are sufficiently gross that they could stand in for animal behavior. Perhaps it is not coincidental that the last we see of Dexter Nichols in the novel he is lying on the ground with a scorched butt, "naked as a jaybird" (Milburn 184).

Even the minor characters are compared to animals. As he watches Julie, Judge Throgmorton's eyes "move along her curves with all the hypnotic intensity of a chicken's beak following a chalk line" (Milburn 21). Sheriff Speck arrives at the shivaree—the after-dark party interrupting John and Julie's wedding night[3]—"sweating like a Hereford bull" (Milburn 71). A few minutes later, when Troy finds John hiding in a laundry tub, he brags to his fellow townsmen, "Well, I'll be a suck-egg pup! Hey, fellers, come look at what I smelt out with my little old foxy nose!" (Milburn 76). Robin Goodkind is kept as "busy as a bird dog" (Milburn 120), and is fed so well he grows "as pursy-gutted as a poisoned pup" (Milburn 120). Is it any wonder that the narrator says that Julie drives "the whole town hog-wild" (Milburn 89; see his use of "hog-wild" again on 185)?

The Narrator

Milburn greatly admired Chaucer's *Miller's Tale*, but in adapting it to a modern American setting and audience, he changed the narrator. Whereas the *Miller's Tale* is part of a larger narrative sequence involving many narrators, *Julie* stands alone. This novel is part of no pilgrimage, no tale-telling competition. It has no irate Miller[4] in drunken competition with a gentle knight. The story of John and Julie is in no sense a reaction to an earlier tale. The closest we come to an actual narrator of *Julie* is the reference to "in our town" in the second sentence of the novel: "One hot Saturday afternoon Old Man John Bundix parked his truck on the east side of the courthouse square. He climbed out of the rusted cab and hauled forth one of the prettiest things anybody in our town had ever laid eyes on" (Milburn 9). Similar expressions showing that the narrator lives in the town are dropped in elsewhere: "Anyone who was not there at the time might find it hard to believe how much sentiment that girl from Joplin aroused in our community" (Milburn 89); "most of the stories seemed to develop out of thin air, the way gossip in our town has a way of doing" (Milburn 174). These identify the narrator as a local person, probably a man, to judge by his interest in pretty women. He never refers to himself as "I," however, and he plays no direct role in the action of the story. His only apparent motivation for telling the story is that it had not yet been told and that it really did happen: "So the story about the girl from Joplin never has been told, and several people around town like to let on that nothing of the kind ever happened" (Milburn 186).

That phrasing—"the story about the girl from Joplin"—brings up another obvious change: *Julie* is indeed very much Julie's story. Whereas Alison plays an important but relatively small role in the *Miller's Tale*, her counterpart in *Julie* becomes much more the focal character. The story begins when John Bundix drives her into town and she is "hauled forth" (Milburn 9) by him from his truck; it ends when the women of that same town "haul her forth" (Milburn 186) from John's house and drive her off. In the twenty-two chapters between the two haulings, Julie's comings and goings dominate the narrative. Even when she is not *in* the scene, the scene is usually *about* her.

The Setting

When Milburn relocated the tale from fourteenth-century Oxford to an unnamed twentieth-century Ozark town, that relocation called for a host of other changes. Most of Chaucer's original audiences for the *Miller's Tale* would have known more or less what a fourteenth-century English town looked like and how it was laid out. Milburn, writing in the prosperous East-coast postwar 1950s about an unnamed Missouri hick-town in the late 1940s,[5] had to provide details of the setting.

There is at the center of Milburn's Missouri town[6] not a university but a county courthouse presided over by Judge Throgmorten. In that courthouse most of the action of the first half-dozen chapters takes place. In front of the courthouse is a lawn from which some lazy hangers-on, including several members of the Pruitt family, gawk at old John Bundix dragging into that courthouse his luscious young fiancee. That they are impressed that she is wearing "[s]tore boughten clothes and all" (Milburn 9) tells us something about the rural, backwoods, nature of the town.

In the course of the novel Milburn mentions several places that also give us a sense of the cultural ambience of the town: the McKenzie County Bank, Doc Sinclair's Sanitary Pharmacy and Soda Fountain, the Luckenbill Funeral Home, Kidd's Sawmill, Schultz's Warehouse, the Purity Bakery, Pritchet's Pool Parlor, the Palace Barber Shop, Lulu's Dew Drop Inn Café, the Odd Fellows Cemetery, and several churches—all Christian, of course. Just east of town on Honeybucket Creek are Jarvis Gerveys's blacksmith forge and the abandoned Fox and Finn watermill, now temporary home to the Holiness Church that John Bundix attends.

A little further east of those, on the other side of the Little Honeybucket Creek, accessed by a swinging bridge, is old John Bundix's unfinished house. Though John takes his new bride to live in the part of the house that he has finished, its roof beams are still clearly visible up through the second floor: "The big, main room of his residence did not have any ceiling to it. A person could look right up through the two-by-four scantlings to the rafters and see the underside of the shingle roof, thirty feet high" (Milburn 59). In their unfinished state, the rafters provide a place from which John can later suspend the three tubs. Milburn, then, gives his readers not only a sense of the place and of the various occupations of the men and women who live in this lazy Ozark town, but also of the house containing the window that plays so prominent a role in the climax to *Julie*. As for that window, in preparation for its role later in the novel, we are told that it "was not an ordinary sash-window to be raised and lowered in the way most windows are made nowadays. It was a double swing-out window with a catch in the middle. John Bundix was old–fashioned about such things, and those were the kind of windows he put in when he built his house" (Milburn 130–31).

Names and Neighbors

In Chaucer's time people generally had only one name, like "John" or "Robin." Appropriately enough for a novelist telling a story set in twentieth-century America, Milburn gives most of his characters last names and at least minimal personal histories appropriate to their roles in the novel. Chaucer's old John, by trade a carpenter in the *Miller's Tale*, becomes for Milburn old John Bundix, a carpenter who is active in an evangelical Christian church called the Holiness Church. Eighteen-year-old Alison, of indeterminate ori-

164   Part Two: Modern Transformations

gins, becomes eighteen-year-old Julie Armbruster, the daughter of a Joplin, Missouri, preacher. The church clerk Absolon becomes a courthouse clerk named Absolon Kendall, nicknamed "Caterpillar" because he has lost a leg and hobbles around on a chrome crutch. The Oxford scholar "hende" Nicholas becomes an itinerant astrologer and book pedlar named Dexter (suggesting "dexterous") Nichols.

Even the minor characters generally get two names and their own histories. Robin becomes Robin Goodkind, a half-witted apprentice to old John, and Gille becomes Jilladeen Mapes, the maidservant in the house. Robin and Jilladeen do not live in the Bundix household, but they come in for day-work. The blacksmith Gerveys becomes blacksmith Jarvis Gerveys, John Bundix's deaf-and-dumb neighbor[7] who has a deaf-and-dumb wife and two deaf-and-dumb children.

Whereas Chaucer had named only seven characters, Milburn names many more. In addition to those mentioned above, we have Addie Bushager, the local gossip-writer; Nadine Jones, clerk-typist; Granny Gosnell, "witch-woman"; the Widow Quimsby, Absolon Kendall's landlady; Sheriff Speck and Buford Hayes, his deputy sheriff; J. Rutherford Cook, lawyer, and his son Reston; Jasper B. Glasscock, banker; Orpheus Clark, barber; Doc Sinclair, medical doctor and soda fountain owner; August Schultz, baker; Dr. Heflin, itinerant dentist; the Reverend Higgenbotham, the Baptist minister; Virgil Pruitt, preacher at the Holiness Church, and his two quarrelsome nephews Pearly and Jewell Pruitt; Verna Sears, daytime telephone operator; and assorted other characters with names like Freddy Openshaw, Harvey Womack, Gifford Collins, LeRoy Jenkins, and Sam Crawford; not to mention John's five former wives—the first named Cally, the third Clarice, and the last Maybelle—now all dead or run off. Milburn, then, is far more specific than Chaucer, who had grouped such people as "men" (3195), "the wyves" (3341), "the neighebores" (3729, 3826), and "the folk" (3840).

John Bundix's neighbors play a vastly larger role in *Julie* than the neighbors do in the *Miller's Tale*. In Chaucer's tale their role is tiny: they appear mostly in a dozen lines at the end, and then merely to laugh at the fallen and humiliated John, whom they (wrongly) declare mad:

> The neighebores, bothe smale and grete,
> In ronnen for to gauren on this man.
> [...]
> The folk gan laughen at his fantasye;
> Into the roof they kiken and they cape,
> And turned al his harm unto a jape.

> For what so that this carpenter answerde,
> It was for noght; no man his reson herde.
> With othes grete he was so sworn adoun
> That he was holde wood in al the toun;
> For every clerk anonright heeld with oother.
> They seyde, "The man is wood, my leeve brother";
> And every wight gan laughen at this stryf [3826-27, 3840-49].

None of these neighbors is named or made specific in any way. They show up at the last minute, accept without question the explanation of Nicholas and Alison that John is mad, laugh at the broken-armed old carpenter, and disappear from the story.

The importance of the neighbors in *Julie* can be measured in part by the amount of dialogue they contribute. The neighbors in *Heile of Beersele* say not a peep. They say only three percent in the *Miller's Tale*. But the neighbors[8] contribute more than twelve percent of the words—some 685 of them—in *Julie*. The neighbors in *Julie* are not only talkative, but collectively they play a huge role. They appear not only in the last few pages, but throughout the novel. At the very start they drool at the arrival of Julie, listen as she and John apply for a marriage license, fill the courtroom in which Judge Throgmorton performs the civil ceremony, listen to Dexter Nichols's astrological objections to the wedding, and then watch John Bundix seize his new wife "in a bear hug" and begin "smothering her face with hungry kisses" (Milburn 57). This "curious mob" (Milburn 38), which comprises "half the voting population of McKenzie County" (50), dominates the first six chapters—that is, the first fifty pages—of *Julie*.

That same mob, augmented by others, take part in the shivaree the night of the wedding: "Nearly everyone who lived in McKenzie County was there, and then some" (Milburn 58). The events of chapters 7 through 9—thirty more pages—also involve the neighbors as important characters. After all, there would have been no shivaree if the neighbors had not decided to interrupt John's wedding night by closing in on his house, "creeping up on it like wild Indians, about an hour after sundown" and making "shotgun blasts, whoops and hollers and bitch-kitty caterwauls [...] banging on old tin tubs and pans" (Milburn 61). These neighbors pass the jug around, fight amongst themselves, throw rocks to break John Bundix's windows, listen to his demands that they leave, and then surge into the house to look for Julie. After finding her they discover John Bundix hiding in a tub of sour laundry, drag him out and threaten to throw him into Honeybucket Creek, listen when Dexter Nichols preaches at them and tries to sell them books, and finally scatter when a lightning storm hits. Their departure leaves John Bundix and Dexter Nichols alone together, to work out the details of Dexter's becoming a resident in John's house. In the first eighty pages of the novel, then, pages that recount the events of the first day, the neighbors play such key roles in the story line that it is difficult to imagine *Julie* without them.

The neighbors also play an important role at the end. Many readers of Chaucer have commented on the fact that the three men are punished for their transgressions—Absolon with a nasty kiss and a fart in the face, Nicholas with a scorched buttocks, and John with a broken arm—but they wonder why Alison, who is no less guilty than they, escapes unpunished. There are ways, of course, of answering that question, but Milburn fills the gap by adding an episode in his last chapter in which Julie is punished by the jealous women of the community:

> The women folks broke right in and dragged that pretty little thing out of the house, kicking and screaming.
> They lifted up her skirts and stripped off her lacy little underpants and then they took safety pins out of their mouth to fasten up her dress so that her trim little bottom was bare.
> The girl from Joplin began running toward the swinging bridge across Big Honeybucket Creek. The women kept right after her, slashing at her bare buttocks with hickory whips. The men followed along, yowling all the dirty things they could think of.
> The women whipped her all the way across the swinging bridge and up the creek path past the Holiness church, and along the streets, until they reached the courthouse square.
> The pretty little thing fell sobbing on the concrete curb before the Sanitary Pharmacy with her bleeding buttocks turned up to the cruel sticks the women kept laying on her [Milburn 186].

For Milburn it is not enough that only one of the adulterous pair has his buttocks punished. The townsfolk apparently think it is fitting that Dexter Nichols is punished for putting his bare buttocks out the window, but they want Julie, who has also stuck her buttocks out the window, to be punished in the buttocks as well. It is significant that Julie is punished in front of the very courthouse in which, at the start of the novel, she had married John Bundix and made to him her vows of fidelity. The agents of her punishment are the neighbors.

It is interesting that just as the fifteenth-century Henryson rewrote the end of Chaucer's *Troilus and Criseyde* in such a way as to punish an unfaithful woman by giving her leprosy, so the twentieth-century Milburn rewrote the end of Chaucer's *Miller's Tale* to punish an unfaithful woman with a bloody whipping and banishment, a more severe punishment than any of the men suffer. Milburn, it seems, wanted to make sure that his readers knew that a woman who betrays her husband, no matter how delightful she is or what the circumstances of the betrayal, is punished for her infidelity.

Filling Gaps

I have focused mostly on Milburn's changes involving his central character Julie, but readers of the novel will notice many other changes and expansions. For example, why does the jealous John take in a handsome young man as a boarder? Many readers of Chaucer's *Miller's Tale* have wondered about the apparent inconsistency in old John's behavior. If he is, indeed, "jealous" and wanting to keep Alison "narwe in cage" (3224), why would he allow a college kid to live in that very cage with her? Chaucer never says, but Milburn fills that gap by letting us know that John Bundix gives Dexter Nichols a place to stay because he becomes convinced that the young man had saved his life the night of the wedding when the rowdy shivareers tried to drown him. John tells the shivareers that he is *"afeerd of water"* and *"I caint swim a stroke"* (Milburn 80). He is so grateful to Dexter Nichols for appearing to frighten off the men who want to drown him that John Bundix allows the itinerant astrologer to stay with him.

But why in the *Miller's Tale*, having taken in Nicholas, does the jealous John of Oxford never seem jealous of his handsome young boarder? Specifically, why does he go off on his business trips with never a suspicious thought about leaving Alison back home alone with him? Chaucer does not answer that question, but Milburn fills the gap in part by having Dexter Nichols pretend to be so uninterested in Julie that John Bundix is convinced that his boarder could have no interest in sex. He is taken in by Dexter Nichols's acting like a prophet. Steeped in the Bible, John tells Julie, "I'm a-telling you, that feller's a prophet and prophets don't have no intrust in the female flesh" (Milburn 118). Julie herself feeds John's belief that Dexter Nichols has no interest in her: "he acts like a queer" she tells her husband. "He just treats me like I wasn't here or something. There's something *queer* about him. He just don't act like an ordinary man" (Milburn 117). Whether or not Julie is playacting with John, Dexter Nichols surely is playacting. As soon as John goes off and leaves Julie alone with him, the bold boarder, encouraged by Julie, grabs her "by the quaint part" (Milburn 137).

Milburn fills other gaps, as well. He tells us, for example, where Absolon lived and how he found out that John Bundix was out of town. He tells us where John Bundix got the three tubs—one a rain barrel, one a wine cask, and one an old kneading trough that he bargains with the baker August Shultz with for two pages. He tells us what Julie and Dexter Nichols said to each other in bed. Readers will find other gaps that Milburn, justifiably or not, filled. I want, however, to mention one last gap that Milburn felt he needed to fill. We never do find out from Chaucer what happens to Alison next. Does she run off with Nicholas? Stay married to John? Become a successful businesswoman like her namesake of beside Bath? Unlike Chaucer, Milburn felt called upon to answer such questions about Julie's fate. He tells us that Julie goes back home to Joplin. He lets us know that she has been seen there in a fancy hotel bar where she is "wearing diamonds as big as buckeyes" and that "she was hooked up with a man who owned a big lead and zinc mine" (Milburn 188). Cast out by her father and then banished by the women of McKenzie County, Julie is a survivor.

After reading the *Miller's Tale*, we feel that we know Alison well enough to be pretty sure she will survive, though we don't know how or where. Nor do we feel any need to know what happens next. Chaucer's tale ends when it is over. Milburn, writing for a modern audience, felt the need to tell us more, to fill a gap that did not bother Chaucer. I do not, of course, hold *Julie* up as superior to the *Miller's Tale* or to defend Chaucer against Milburn's implied criticism of his master for what he saw as gaps in Chaucer's narrative. The *Miller's Tale* needs no defense.

XVI
In Coloring Books and Cartoons: Adkins (1973), Lorenz (1981), Williams (2007), Chwast (2011)

In Part One of this book I showed that Chaucer rewrote the barebones narrative he found in *Heile of Beersele* so that we can "see" the story, almost as if we are watching a performance on a stage. Several graphic versions of the *Miller's Tale* let us more literally see what is going on in the tale.

Lieuen Adkins and Gilbert Shelton (1973)

A coloring book of the *Miller's Tale*. Who in the world would think of such a thing? What publisher in the world would publish such a thing? Who in the world would buy such a thing? The answer to the first question is Lieuen Adkins, writer, and Gilbert Shelton, illustrator. The answer to the second is Bellerophon Books.[1] The answer to the third is me.

Gilbert Shelton's drawings are delightful, but my chief interest here is in the text of the *Miller's Tale* as it is "rendered new" in a facing-column format. In the left column is the Middle English. In the right is the Atkins modern English rendition. For example, in the Miller's prologue we find these six lines in the left column paired with what follows in the right:

> Our Hoste saugh that he was dronke of ale,
> And seyde: "abyd, Robyn, my leve brother,

> Som bettre man shall telle us first another:
> Abyd, and lat us werken thriftily."
> "By goddes soul," quod he, "that wol nat I,
> For I wol speke, or elles go my wey" [3128–33].
>> Our Host saw he'd been dipping in the sauce
>> And said, "Whoa, Robin. Get in line, old hoss.
>> You cool your heels and let some other guy
>> Go first. We'll hear your tall tale by and by."
>> The Miller said, "Damned if I'll take hind tit!
>> I'll tell my story now, or else I'll split" [Adkins (3)].

Adkins's approach is clear enough. Instead of attempting a literal translation he gives a nonliteral, colloquial, "rendition" of the passage. Instead of drinking ale, Robyn has been dipping into the sauce. Instead of being addressed as a dear brother, Robyn is called an old hoss. Instead of saying that he won't wait, Robyn says he won't take hind tit. Instead of threatening to go his own way, Robyn threatens to split.

Let's compare a few other passages. Here is Nicholas making his famous grab for Alison:

> Now sire, and eft sire, so bifel the cas
> That on a day this hende Nicholas
> Fil with this yonge wyf to rage and pleye,
> Whyl that hir housbond was at Oseneye,
> As clerkes ben ful subtile and ful queynte;
> And prively he caughte hir by the queynte,
> And seyde, "y-wis, but if ich have my wille,
> For derne love of thee, lemman, I spille" [3271–78].
>> One day our old friend Nicholas got the itch
>> While hubby was away far from the house,
>> To get into the pants of his young spouse.
>> These students being sly, he made a catch
>> Between her legs and snatched her by the snatch
>> And said, "Sweet thing, I've got the hots for you.
>> If you don't give me some, I'll die for true" [Adkins (13)].

The Adkins rendition gives Nicholas an itch to get into Alison's pants that Chaucer's Nicholas had not had—at least not in that language. The itch comes not when her husband is at Oseneye but when her hubby is away from the house, wherever. Instead of catching her by her pretty little thing, Nicholas more specifically snatches her by the snatch between her legs. Instead of telling Alison that he feels a secret love for her, he tells her that he has the hots for her and wants her to give him some. Chaucer's Nicholas at least pretends to be in love with Alison. Adkins's Nicholas pretends to nothing but raw lust for her.

Figure 20. The cover of Lieuen Adkins's coloring book *The Miller's Tale* (1973). It depicts the Miller playing his bagpipes.

What does Adkins do with the first Monday night window scene? We recall that Nicholas and Alison have been frolicking in bed together while old John, exhausted, slumbers fitfully in his kneading trough up in the roof beams. Absolon comes up and, thinking that John is out of town, gives a little cough to get Alison's attention. She tells him to go away, but he asks for at least a kiss. She tells him to get ready and she will give him what he wants:

> This Absolon doun sette him on his knees,
> And seyde, "I am a lord at alle degrees;
> For after this I hope ther cometh more!

> Lemman, thy grace, and swete brid, thyn ore!"
> The window she undoth, and that in haste,
> "Have do," quod she, "com of, and speed thee faste,
> Lest that our neighebores thee espye."
> This Absolon gan wype his mouth ful drye;
> Derk was the night as pich, or as the cole,
> And at the window out she putte hir hole,
> And Absolon, him fil no bet ne wers,
> But with his mouth he kiste hir naked ers
> Ful savourly, er he was war of this.
> Abak he sterte, and thoghte it was amis,
> For wel he wiste a womman hath no berd;
> He felte a thing al rough and long y-herd,
> And seyde, "fy, allas! What have I do?"
> "Tehee!" quod she, and clapte the window to.
> And Absolon goth forth a sory pas [3723–41].
>> Down to his knees this Absolon did bow
>> And said, "Oh, I'm in seventh Heaven now.
>> The feast may follow once I've had this snack.
>> Bless me, my precious, with a big wet smack!"
>> She threw the window open hastily.
>> "Don't drag your feet. Hop to it, now," said she.
>> "You know how nosy neighbors like to spy."
>> This Absolon, he wiped his kisser dry.
>> The night showed not a star, but pretty soon
>> Fair Alison gave Absolon the moon.
>> He was so eager that he gave a jump
>> And made a hicky on her naked rump
>> Before he flashed that there was something weird.
>> He knew a woman doesn't have a beard,
>> But what he'd kissed was whiskery as one.
>> And when he tumbled to what he had done,
>> He cried out, "Yuk!" and started bellowing,
>> "I can't believe that I kissed the hole thing!"
>> She laughed and shut the window in his face,
>> And Absolon was left there in disgrace [Adkins (38, 42)].

In keeping with his practice in the rest of his rendition, Adkins goes for the physical, the crass. Absolon asks not for Alison's mercy or her grace, but for a big wet smack. Alison gives Absolon the moon and he gives her a hicky on her naked rump. When he begins to understand what he has kissed, Absolon says not "Alas" but "Yuk!" And Adkins invents a line that has no counterpart in Chaucer: "I can't believe that I kissed the hole thing!" That line derives not from Chaucer but from the famous 1972 ad for Alka-Seltzer, "I can't believe I ate the whole thing." It apparently did not occur to Adkins that while it might make sense for Absolon to think such a line, it makes no sense whatever for him to "bellow" it out. For the next window scene to be believable at all, Nicholas cannot be permitted to hear such a line. If Nicholas knew that Absolon realized what he had kissed, he would surely not have stuck his bottom out the window to receive the second kiss. Had he heard such a line bellowed out, Nicholas would surely have suspected that an angry Absolon would be seeking revenge.

Adkin's rendition of the *Miller's Tale* has many virtues. It modernizes the language so that a twentieth-century audience can easily figure who is who and why they do what they do. The fast-paced, realistic language no doubt appeals to younger readers for whom Chaucer's Middle English or a more sedate translation would be impediments both to understanding and to enjoyment. Adkins is especially to be praised for providing side-by-side versions of the *Miller's Tale*. That seems to be his way of saying, "Look, I know that what I have written here is not a Chaucerian text. But I give you what Chaucer really wrote in a facing column so that you can see just how far my rendition strays from Chaucer's tale. Both versions are here for you to enjoy."

Lee Lorenz (1981)

Lee Lorenz was already famous as a regular *New Yorker* cartoonist when he decided to try his hand at retelling two of Chaucer's fabliaux in cartoon-books for children. A year before his retelling of the *Miller's Tale* was published, Lorenz's retelling of the *Reeve's Tale* appeared. To give some notion of how Lorenz worked, we should have a quick look at his version of the *Reeve's Tale*.

Lee Lorenz's *Scornful Simkin* identifies itself on the title page as having been "Adapted from Chaucer's *Reeve's Tale*."[2] Can we imagine the *Reeve's Tale* without the miller's daughter, without any sexual contact at all, without horses set loose, without the miller's farting, without the miller's wife's getting up in the night to urinate, without the cocky Aleyn slipping into the wrong bed and bragging about his exploits to the angry miller? It is easy enough to criticize Lorenz for abandoning a perfectly good Chaucerian tale, but *Scornful Simkin* is actually a pretty good tale on its own terms. It makes the miller Simkin a thoroughly despicable man who cheats his friends and his customers. He prepares for his two paying student guests a fine meal and then, with his greedy wife, eats it all up and leaves them only the crumbs. It makes the miller's wife alert enough to hear the students' footsteps and notice the new location of the cradle, foolish enough to think that her husband is in the other bed, and

Part Two: Modern Transformations

PINCHPENNY JOHN

LEE LORENZ

Figure 21: The cover of Lee Lorenz's *Pinchpenny John* (1981).

strong enough to give her husband the beating he so sorely deserves. In recasting *Scornful Simkin* for a youthful audience, Lorenz places our sympathies with the two students. They are good, clever, resourceful, smiling, kind. They are drawn as young boys bullied by a man twice their size. They are not lustful rapists or adulterers. They are clever enough to find their stolen flour where the miller has hidden it under the baby's cradle. They move the cradle not to trick anyone, but merely to get the bag of stolen flour that the miller had hidden under it. Our sympathies are clearly with them.

If at first it is difficult to imagine a retelling of the *Reeve's Tale* without the miller's daughter, so it is at first difficult to imagine the *Miller's Tale* without the carpenter's wife. That is what we have, however, in Lorenz's *Pinchpenny*

John.[3] Identified on the title page as "Suggested by incidents in Chaucer's *Miller's Tale*," *Pinchpenny John* eliminates not only old John's wife, but also but also her suitor Absolon. There is no window scene, no buttocks-kissing, no blacksmith, no branding iron. There is an Alison in the story, but she is John's orphan granddaughter, not his wife.

Like his Chaucerian counterpart, Lorenz's John is a rich carpenter, but he is a miser. He hides his money away and spares not a penny for beggars. To make even more money, Pinchpenny John rents a room out to an Oxford scholar named Nicholas. Nicholas studies astrology by night, but by day he

Figure 22: Alison and Nicholas climb down their ladders, from page [21] of Lee Lorenz's *Pinchpenny John*.

tries to figure out a way to find and steal old John's money. Nicholas has no interest in Alison except as a possible accomplice in finding where John hides his money.

One day John leaves to do business at Olney. He locks his granddaughter in the garden, apparently because he does not want her to go out and spend money. From his window Nicholas sees her crying there in the garden. He climbs down to ask her why she is upset: "Grandfather won't let me go to the fair in Oxford. He says I'm too young, and besides it costs too much. He never lets me go anywhere" (Lorenz [4]). Sensing an opportunity, Nicholas convinces Alison to show him where her grandfather hides the money. If we "could borrow a few coins," he tells her, "we could both go" (Lorenz [5]). Alison is tempted, but sees an impediment: "Even if we *did* take some money, I could never get out. Grandfather watches me every minute" (Lorenz [8]).

Nicholas has a reply ready: "Show me where the money is and I'll see to it that your grandfather doesn't stop us. When he returns, tell him I'm sick. Bring him up to my room and I'll do the rest" (Lorenz [8]). When John goes to see him, Nicholas tells him of his vision about the coming flood. John is distraught: "Lord help us all. Everything is lost—my granddaughter and my gold. Is there no way to be saved?" (Lorenz [14]).

Nicholas then tells John to make three tubs, provision them, and hang them by ropes from the roof beams. John sets to work immediately. He makes one tub from a rain barrel, another from a wine barrel, a third from two pig troughs strapped together. Alison puts in the provisions. Then John and Nicholas pull them up under the rafters and place the three ladders. That night, while the exhausted John snores, Nicholas and Alison climb down. Alison shows Nicholas the loose stone in the fireplace behind which the bag of gold is hidden. When she sees that the greedy Nicholas wants to take not only a few coins, but the whole bag of gold, she objects. Nicholas is derisive: "Ha! You're a bigger fool than your grandfather. Why should I take you to the fair when I can take all this gold and go to London?" (Lorenz [22]).

Alison angrily grabs a stick of wood from the hearth and takes a swing at Nicholas, not realizing that the other end of the stick is on fire. When she strikes Nicholas, she accidentally sets his coat on fire. Panicking, Nicholas shouts, "Help! I'm on fire! Water! Water!" (Lorenz [23]). John, of course, wakes up and cuts the rope with his axe, and down he falls. His tub lands right on top of Nicholas.

Alison confesses to her part in the scheme and apologizes to her grandfather. She just wanted, she said, to go to the fair with Nicholas, never dreaming that he would try to steal the whole bag of gold. Old John is moved: "My dear,

I see now that it is I who must ask to be forgiven. For I have selfishly kept you locked away here, making you an easy prey for such a villain. But things will be different from now on" (Lorenz [27]). John sends Nicholas away and the story ends happily: "The carpenter was as good as his word. From that day forward, his house rang with the laughter of Alison and her friends. And although he was still called Pinchpenny John, he never again turned a beggar away from his door empty-handed" (Lorenz [30]).

Lorenz's little narrative is not without its problems. It is never clear, for example, why Nicholas feels that he has to devise that elaborate tale about a flood or why he needs to send John on his quest to build and dangle the three barrels. He had already convinced Alison to tell him where John hid his gold, so nothing is gained by the elaborate ruse. There are problems with the details, also. We are specifically told that John makes Nicholas's tub "from two pig troughs strapped together" (Lorenz [17]), but the drawings do not reflect such a tub. And we are specifically told that before he went to bed, John had doused the fire. That was necessary so that Alison and Nicholas could gain access to the loose stone in the fireplace that concealed John's hoard of money. But if the fire is dead, how can it provide Alison with the burning frond with which she soon after sets Nicholas's coat on fire? Still, Lorenz has successfully steered clear of topics he thought inappropriate for children: fornication, farting, and butt-burning. *Pinchpenny John* is far more about money than about lust. John is a miser, Nicholas a thief, Alison an accomplice. Alison helps Nicholas deceive John, not out of desire for him but out of desire to go to the fair. All three learn their lessons. Alison learns not to trust greedy men like Nicholas. Nicholas learns that thieves are punished and banished. And John learns that money is useless if it is hoarded, useful if it is spent to help the poor and to bring joy to members of his own family. Those are not Chaucer's lessons, but they are important lessons. As for Absolon, he had no role to play in such economic lessons, so Lorenz jettisoned him.

Marcia Williams (2007)

Lee Lorenz's cartoon drawings are delightful. Marcia Williams's are too, though in a very different way. Whereas Lorenz wrote a 1400-word, 30-page story with some big illustrations, Williams wrote a 500-word, four-page-story with some small illustrations. Her *Miller's Tale* is actually a twenty-three-panel cartoon strip with the narrative, presented in captions beneath the cartoons. Her storyline is much closer to Chaucer's *Miller's Tale* than Lorenz's.

Figure 23. The cover of Marcia Williams's *Chaucer's Canterbury Tales* (2007).

Even so, the narrative is little more than a plot summary: "In Oxford there lived an elderly carpenter named John. He had recently married a young and beautiful girl named Alison, whom he adored. He guarded her with a jealous eye, because she was only eighteen and very flirtatious."[4] The summary itself is colorless. It gives no detail, no dialogue, no humor. The drama of this version is in the drawings. The first four cartoon-strip frames—the four just above those three sentences—show Alison attempting to kiss other men while her husband tries to restrain her. Those scenes are not in the Chaucerian

XVI. In Coloring Books and Cartoons

Miller's Tale, but they dramatize John's helpless jealousy in the face of Alison's eager flirtatiousness.

The next four panels show Alison flirting with Nicholas and Absolon, and again old John in all four panels tries to restrain her. The caption summary under those four panels reads thus: "Their tenant, Nicholas, a penniless student and astrologer, was smitten by Alison's youthful charms and longed to kiss her. The parish clerk, Absolon, a rather prim but very stylish youth who fancied himself a musician, had also fallen for Alison's charms. Absolon tried to win Alison's love by offering her valuable gifts, but she always met his adoration with mocking indifference. Nicholas was too poor to offer gifts; he just offered his heart, over and over again, until Alison could resist him no longer" (Williams 16). That takes us up to about line 3396 of Chaucer's *Miller's Tale*—about 210 lines. Those 210 lines Williams covers in seven sentences, 125 words. What has she left out? Just about everything, it seems: the detailed description of Nicholas's room, of Alison's clothing, beauty, and spriteliness, of Absolon's hair, clothes, singing and playacting, his putting the make on several parish wives, his serenading of Alison, his squeamishness about farting, and so on. She leaves out, in other words, most of the details of personal appearance and individualizing characterization.

Though she leaves out of her summarizing captions what most readers admire most in Chaucer's *Miller's Tale*, Williams emphasizes in her drawings several features that Chaucer had at best only hinted at: John's jealousy, Alison's flirtatiousness, and Nicholas's heartfelt love for Alison. Chaucer had said, almost in passing, that John was "jalous" and held his young wife "narwe in cage" (3224). Alison complains to Nicholas that her husband is "ful of jalousie" (3294). In fact, however, there is little evidence of that jealousy in Chaucer. On the contrary, John frequently goes off to work and leaves her in the house with Nicholas, and he seems the opposite of jealous when he hears Absolon serenade his wife. Nor does he seem to keep Alison caged. He makes no objection, for example, when she goes off alone to the parish church. Williams, on the other hand shows John in all of the first eight frames attempting to pull his wife away from men she is talking to. As for Alison's flirtatiousness, Chaucer never says she is flirtatious. Indeed, she firmly resists the initial flirtations of both Nicholas—"Lat be, Nicholas / Or I wol crie 'out, harrow' and 'allas'!" (3285–86)—and Absolon—"Go fro the wyndow, Jakke fool" (3708). As for Nicholas's offering Alison his heart, most readers of Chaucer would emphasize more his offering her another part of his anatomy. His opening courtship ritual—to grab her crotch—is about as unromantic as a man can get. In that context, as he holds her by the haunches, his request that she "love me al atones"

(3280), means for her to make love to him. Nicholas never says that he loves her, never offers his heart. Williams's illustrations, however, show him once on his knee to her, apparently singing her a love song, and another time sending seven hearts her way as the jealous John attempts to pull her away with a chain. These illustrations do not show him grabbing her genitals and hips.

Those eight frames are all on the first page of Marcia Williams's *Miller's Tale*. On the fourth (and last page) we find three larger frames. In the first of those Absolon is standing beside the ladder below the bedroom with a branding iron. The caption reads, "Absolon dashed to the local forge and returned with a red-hot iron. He then begged Alison for one last kiss, in return for a precious ring" (Williams 19). The next frame shows him atop the ladder receiving Nicholas's fart and simultaneously branding Nicholas's bottom. The caption reads, "This time, Nicholas stuck his bottom out the window, while letting fly a fart! Absolon almost fainted, but still branded the proffered backside!" (Williams 19). The final frame shows John crashing to the floor, Alison smirking at him, Nicholas cooling his bottom in a barrel of water, Absolon wiping his face outside the window, and a half-dozen neighbors pouring into the room to make fun of John.

Seymour Chwast (2011)

In the short General Prologue to his graphic novel adaptation of the *Canterbury Tales*, Seymour Chwast has Chaucer say that the red-headed Miller was "not very bright" and that the Miller and Chaucer "seemed to have a mutual distrust of one another."[5] I see no justification for either statement in my reading of Chaucer's General Prologue.

Chwast's pen-and-ink drawings portray the various pilgrims not on horseback but on motorcycles. Except for that, his *Miller's Tale* seems to have a generally medieval setting. The storyline follows Chaucer closely enough most of the way, though he leaves a lot out to make way for his illustrations. For example, Chwast reduces the opening 120 lines of the *Miller's Tale* to one half-page drawing showing head-shots of John, Alison, and Nicholas, and three short sentences (totaling thirty-three words). One sentence states that John was possessive of his wife Alison, one states that an astrology student named Nicholas lived upstairs, and one states that Nicholas and Alison were lovers but "had yet to consummate their love" (Chwast 25). Chwast drops the descriptions and the grab scene altogether. He moves directly from that half-page drawing to a whole page (three frames) devoted to Absolon's

XVI. In Coloing Books and Cartoons   181

Figure 24. The cover of Seymour Chwast's adaptation of Geoffrey Chaucer's *The Canterbury Tales* (2011).

doings. Then Chwast presents two pages (four frames) on Nicholas's elaborate plan to trick John with a fabricated prediction of a flood, then devoting a full page (three frames) to the events on the night of the supposed flood. The first of those frames shows John asleep in his tub, the second shows Nicholas and Alison sneaking away from the ladders, and the third shows them in bed, mostly under the covers. The captioning in the last of those three frames reports that the two lovers spent the night in bed where they "suffered carnal pleasure." It shows also a bubble in which Alison says, "Do it again, Nicholas" (Chwast 29).

The next page contains seven frames devoted to the window scenes: (1) Absolon asking for a kiss; (2) Absolon kissing Alison's bottom; (3) Absolon saying "Argh" and Alison from inside saying, "Ha! Ha! Ha!"; (4) Absolon asking the blacksmith for a hot poker; (5) Absolon back at the window asking for a second kiss; (6) Nicholas blowing a fart in Absolon's face; and (7) Absolon burning Nicholas's bottom and Nicholas hollering, "Ow! Water! Water!" (Chwast 30). The last page has three frames: (1) John cutting the rope holding up his tub; (2) John sitting in his tub on the floor being laughed at by the neighbors, one of whom says, "What a fool"; (3) the Miller, with a bottle of booze in his hand, falling off his motorcycle. The caption says "the Miller fell off his steed" (Chwast 31).

It all goes by very fast. I wonder if readers who were not already familiar with the plot would make much sense of the cartoon sequences. The drawings no doubt help readers visualize the events in the story, but some of the drawings are inaccurate. Chwast draws the tubs to look more like sardine cans than kneeding troughs, and he has them hanging not from the beams in the carpenter's house but from horizontal poles sticking out of the eaves of a barn. He then shows Nicholas and Alison sneaking away from the barn and running to the house. What readers, we might wonder, are well served by a graphic novel with misleading graphics?

XVII

In Musical Performance: Starkie (1968), Pickering (1988), Brinkman (2006)

The Miller and his tale have long been associated with music. The Miller leads his fellow pilgrims out of town with his bagpipes. Nicholas in the tale is well equipped musically:

> And al above ther lay a gay sautrie
> On which he made a-nyghtes melodie
> So swetely that all the chambre rong;
> And *Angelus ad virginem* he song;
> And after that he song the Kynges Noote.
> Ful often blessed was his myrie throte [3213–18].

After he kisses Alison, Nicholas takes up his "sawtrie, / And pleyeth faste, and maketh melodie" (3305–06). Alison is also musically inclined:

> But of hir song, it was as loude and yerne
> As any swalwe sittynge on berne [3257–58].

Absolon is especially musical:

> [He] pleyen songes on a smal rubible;
> Therto he song som tyme a loud quynyble;
> And as wel koude he pleye on a giterne [3331–33].

He takes his guitar with him when he visits Alison and as he plays it, "syngeth in his voys gentil and smal [...] / Ful wel acordaunt to his gyternynge" (3360, 3363). With all that sweet music, contrasted with the gaseous thunderclap at the end and the cries of "Water!," it seems only natural that some adapters would seek to bring out the musical possibilities of the tale.

Martin Starkie and Nevill Coghill (1968)

On March 21, 1968, a new musical called *Canterbury Tales* opened at the Phoenix Theatre in London's West End.[1] Conceived and directed by Martin Starkie, who worked in close cooperation with his former Oxford professor Nevill Coghill, *Canterbury Tales* offered performances of five of the tales: the *Miller's Tale*, the *Steward's [Reeve's] Tale*, the *Merchant's Tale*, the *Nun's Priest's Tale*, and the *Wife of Bath's Tale*. The show did very well indeed. It ran for almost five years and closed only after 2080 performances. The show opened on Broadway in 1969, with four of those tales (leaving off the *Nun's Priest's Tale*). It got encouraging reviews, but closed after a disappointing 121 performances. So far as I have been able to determine, neither the British nor the American version of the musical was filmed or taped, and the script was never published.

I saw the Broadway production in 1969. I remember only a few of the details, but Alison did stick her bottom out the window, Absolon did kiss it, and Nicholas did fart in Absolon's face. The sound of the fart was portrayed by a very bass trumpet. An audio sound-track was made. It contains the three songs from the *Miller's Tale*: Nicholas singing "I Have a Noble Cock," Absolon singing to Alison "Darling, Let Me Teach You How to Kiss," and Nicholas and Alison together singing "There's the Moon." Here is a sample of the lyrics of Absolon's song to Alison:

> Darling, let me kiss you in the dark.
> [...]
> Take your chances now we got 'em
> And there's no one here to spot 'em,
> Oh, I'd love you top to bottom for a kiss [Starkie 6–7].

Perhaps the Starkie-Coghill musical will someday be resurrected, but for now it stands as the first of a series of modern musical and dramatic performances of the *Miller's Tale*.

Ken Pickering and Derek Hyde (1988)

A decade after the Starkie-Coghill musical was first performed in London and New York, another dramatic version written by Ken Picker-

XVII. In Musical Performance   185

Figure 25. The cover of the playbill for the Martin Starkie and Nevill Coghill musical *Canterbury Tales* (1969) depicting the scene in which Nicholas makes a grab for Alison.

ing with music by Derek Hyde was performed in Tunbridge Wells in southeastern England. The fluid setting of this new musical version, called *Some Canterbury Tales*, is the road from London to Canterbury. *Some Canterbury Tales* is less a musical than a play with several interspersed dances and songs.

The central character in the play is the Miller. He comes on stage singing the opening six lines of the General Prologue, then proceeds to tell about the last time he went on pilgrimage to Canterbury. That time, he says, Chaucer came along and later wrote a book about the experience. The Miller happens to have a copy with him:

> MILLER: In faith, this is the old road to Canterbury and when I last passed this way Master Chaucer himself was with me. You don't believe me? Then you shall hear how Master Chaucer wrote of me, Robyn the Miller [*He produces a book of* "The Canterbury Tales."] Now here it is, listen.
>
>> The Miller was a stout carl—stop your groans—
>> Full big he was of brawn, also of bones.
>> [...]
>
> Now you believe I was with him, don't you? In faith, what a merry company we were![2]

Then the other pilgrims come on stage riding hobby horses, singing the opening dozen lines of the General Prologue. They enter an inn, where two wenches, Moll and Kit, wait on them. The wenches eventually join the pilgrimage and engage in verbal byplay with the other pilgrims along the way. The Miller then describes the Wife of Bath and Pardoner. The Knight tells the first tale, in which Emily sings a ten-line song and Arcite sings a seven-line song. When the Knight has finished, the Miller, by now quite drunk, offers to tell the next tale, but the Host refuses him and calls on the Wife of Bath to speak next. Her tale is followed by the Pardoner's, the Franklin's, and the Nun's Priest's. Finally, just as the pilgrims come to the gates of Canterbury, the Miller says it is his turn to tell a tale. There is strong objection to having the Miller do so, but he insists. Moll and Kit disagree about whether he should be permitted to speak, and finally the Host decides to let him. One of the women on the pilgrimage then turns directly to the audience and tells them that if they are "sensitive" they should "leave your seat and come back later!" (Pickering 40).

Presumably no one left his or her seat. Those who stayed would not have been very shocked. In the grab scene, for example, Nicholas does not grab Alison by the "queynte" but aims higher, as described in a stage direction:

> NICHOLAS [*putting his arms around Alison and cupping her bosom*]:
>> O Alison, unless of you I have my fill,
>> Sweetheart I'll die, I surely will! [*holding her hips*].
>> Darling, love me right away
>> Or I'll certainly die today [Pickering 41].

Pickering introduces Absolon here by having him come at night to serenade Alison as she lies in bed with John. The serenade is only two lines, but those lines are set to music:

> ABSOLON: Now dear lady, if thy will it be,
>   I pray you now take pity on me! [Pickering 42].

Then we have the scene in which Nicholas pretends to be in a trance and tells John about the coming flood. On the night of the predicted deluge we see this stage direction: *Three tubs are brought and placed on a high level and fixed with rope. By candlelight Nicholas, Alison, and the Carpenter creep in and each sit in a tub. They all say "hush" and the Carpenter says his prayers. The Carpenter falls asleep and Nicholas and Alison steal away to bed. There is much energetic love-making* (Pickering 44). The director would presumably have indicated to the actors what "much energetic love-making" would look like.

Absolon arrives, asks for, and receives his kiss:

> ABSOLON: Fie, alas, what is this?
>   A cheek with a beard is what I kiss! [Pickering 45].

Absolon goes to Gerveys's smithy and returns with a hot iron. Nicholas this time sticks his bum out the window:

> ABSOLON: Speak, sweet bird, I know not where thou art.
>   MILLER: At this Nicholas let forth a (*noise of a huge fart*) [Pickering 46].

The Miller gets the last word in the play:

> MILLER: We had such sport when Master Chaucer was with us, and he wrote in his book many more of the tales we heard upon that journey! [...] But you must read Master Chaucer's book! [Pickering 47].

Baba Brinkman (2006)

A young Canadian named Baba Brinkman in the first decade of the twenty-first century gave many one-man rap performances of the *Miller's Tale*. In the preface to his *Rap Canterbury Tales* Brinkman describes how the idea of putting some of the Canterbury stories into rap verses came to him on summer vacation from his pursuit of an undergraduate degree in English from the University of Victoria. Needing to come up with an honors thesis, he thought about the fact that so few people could or would read Chaucer because of its archaic language. He wanted to do a translation:

> What I needed was a new medium that would capture the same ethos as Chaucer did for his age: a live performance mode rich in wordplay and lyrical nuance,

with a technique that could grab a live audience's attention and hold it long enough to tell a complex story. At the same time, I saw this translation project as the solution to another problem. I have been involved with hip-hop culture and rap music (hip-hop's oral expression), either as an avid listener or as an artist, since the age of eleven. [...] The humble ambition that inspired me to write *The Rap Canterbury Tales* was a desire to resurrect Chaucer's brilliant stories from their vellum mausoleum by giving them a new form that would once again delight and edify live listening audiences.[3]

Brinkman clearly enjoyed reciting his version the *Miller's Tale*. Members of Brinkman's audiences who knew Chaucer's *Miller's Tale* enjoyed it too, but some found themselves listening to a tale in which somewhat familiar characters took part in a somewhat unfamiliar sequence of events. Some elements that such an audience expected to be there were missing, and others that they did not expect to be there were there. The most unusual feature of the performance was that it was in rap, sometimes called hip-hop, poetry.

Brinkman sees Chaucer and hip-hop "as bookends representing the earliest and latest expressions of rhymed narrative verse in the English language" (Brinkman 13). He sees a connection between Chaucer and modern hip-hop in that the competitive, contestive, and sometimes combative, spirit of Chaucer's multiple tellers who are motivated by a desire to win a poetry contest is also present in the hip-hop contest known as the "freestyle battle." Brinkman puts it this way in the long "general prologue" to *The Rap Canterbury Tales*:

Figure 26. Cover of Baba Brinkman's *The Rap Canterbury Tales* (2006).

XVII. In Musical Performance

By definition, a freestyle is a rap that is unwritten and unrehearsed, composed by the rapper in the moment of performance, with rhymes that are improvised on beat and, when required, on topic. A freestyle battle is when two or more rappers compete in this way head to head, using punch lines, boasts, and insults to out-rhyme and outwit their opponents [Brinkman 13–14].

Brinkman says that the hip-hop freestyle battle is very like the poetic "quiting" or "getting even" that we find in the *Canterbury Tales*. Indeed, he says, "Chaucer seems to have designed his pilgrim storytelling contest around the exact same principles and guidelines that govern hip-hop's underground" (Brinkman 22).

Rap poetry relies more on vowel sounds, usually referred to as assonance, than on consonants. For example, we find *listen, this, it, rich, licking, silver, lived, in, kid* in the first three lines of the Brinkman *Miller's Tale*. In those three lines we also find a few more traditional rhymes—*tune, spoon, room*— but they are placed almost perversely in the middle of the lines, not at the ends where Chaucerians might have expected them. Multisyllabic rhymes and slant rhymes are especially appreciated in rap. In lines 4–12 of his *Miller's Tale*, Brinkman rhymes *colleges, scholarships, preposterous, astrologist, Nicholas, limitless, libidinous, lick his lips,* and *licorice*. There is ample alliteration in rap— note the many "l" and "s" sounds in the first dozen lines of Brinkman's rap *Miller's Tale* (underlines added):

> Listen to this tune: it's about a rich man
> Licking a silver spoon, who lived in a mansion,
> And rented a room to this young scholar kid.
> Who'd been to the two most respected colleges
> For logic and philosophy; he got scholarships,
> But he still lived in poverty due to the preposterous
> Cost of living; without a dollar he lived as an astrologist
> And followed his dreams; his name was Nicholas,
> And when it came to women his game was limitless.
> The ladies he visited became libidinous
> When he played his instruments; he'd just lick his lips
> And sing a melody as sweet as licorice [Brinkman 193].

If Brinkman's listeners expected a piece of poetry that calls itself the *Miller's Tale* to be a word-for-word, line-for-line, or even event-for-event replica of the story that Chaucer's drunken Miller told, they were disappointed. To be sure, in broad outline the Brinkman story is the same: old John is still foolish, Nicholas still makes lustful grabs at Alison, Absolon still kisses Alison's bottom and still scorches Nicholas's, and Nicholas's cries of "Water, Water!" still cause John to cut the tub-rope and fall down and break his arm—well, his elbow.

But there are many, many differences. Lots of what Chaucer put in—such as the minor characters Robyn, Gille, and Gerveys—Brinkman leaves out. It will be useful have before us the first thirty-four lines of Chaucer's *Miller's Tale*, the lines corresponding—very roughly indeed—to the twelve opening lines I quote above from Brinkman's version:

> Whilom ther was dwellynge at Oxenford
> A riche gnof, that gestes heeld to bord,
> And of his craft he was a carpenter.
> With hym ther was dwellynge a poure scoler,
> Hadde lerned art, but al his fantasye
> Was turned for to lerne astrologye,
> And koude a certeyn of conclusiouns,
> To demen by interrogaciouns,
> If that men asked hym in certain houres
> Whan that men sholde have droghte or elles shoures,
> Or if men asked hym what sholde bifalle
> Of every thyng; I may nat rekene hem alle.
> This clerk was cleped hende Nicholas.
> Of deerne love he koude and of solas;
> And therto he was sleigh and ful privee
> And lyk a mayden meke for to see.
> A chambre hadde he in that hostelrye
> Allone, withouten any compaignye,
> Ful fetisly ydight with herbes swoote;
> And he hymself as sweete as is the roote
> Of lycorys, or any cetewale.
> His Almageste, and bookes grete and smale,
> His astrelabie, longynge for his art,
> His augrym stones layen faire apart,
> On shelves couched at his beddes heed;
> His presse ycovered with a faldyng reed;
> And al above ther lay a gay sautrie,
> On which he made a-nyghtes melodie
> So swetely that all the chambre rong;
> And *Angelus ad virginem* he song;
> And after that he song the Kynges Noote.
> Ful often blessed was his myrie throte.
> And thus this sweete clerk his tyme spente
> After his freends fyndyng and his rente [3187–3220].

In his version of the *Miller's Tale* Brinkman leaves out much that Chaucer put into those first thirty-four lines. For example, Brinkman does not tell us that John lives in Oxford, or that he is a carpenter who boards guests in his hostelry, or that he is a "gnof"—a churl or commoner. Brinkman does not tell us that people ask Nicholas about what will happen in the future, that he is as meek as a maiden, that his room is made aromatic by his use of sweet-smelling herbs, that Nicholas himself is sweet (Brinkman lines 20, 32), or that he plays his psaltery sweetly (line 29). Brinkman says nothing of what astrological equipment and books are on the shelves at the head of Nicholas's bed, of what specific songs Nicholas sings, or of how he supplements his income by getting support from his friends.

Brinkman's *Miller's Tale* is not said to be set in any specific town, city, or even country. We might have assumed that it is set somewhere in England, but the mention of "dollar" in Brinkman's seventh line would seem to rule that out. The setting is apparently not even medieval. While there is a blacksmith shop nearby for Absolon to visit, several suggestions make it seem out of place in this tale. For example, we are told that Nicholas went to college on "scholarships" (Brinkman 193)—did they have scholarships in the middle ages?—and his fart makes a thunderous sound "like a motor revving" (Brinkman 241). There were no revving motors until the twentieth century.

Brinkman transforms John from a commoner who runs a hostelry into a member of the upper class who eats with a silver spoon and lives in a mansion. Brinkman makes Nicholas not a current student at Oxford but a man who *had been* at two respected colleges—not otherwise identified. Brinkman's Nicholas is poorer than his Chaucerian counterpart: rather than living on his income and his friends' donations, he has not even a dollar. He struggles to live on scholarships at a time when the cost of living is preposterously high. Brinkman's Nicholas follows his dreams, whatever that means, and is quite a favorite with women, who grow libidinous when he plays his unspecified instruments. Brinkman repeats the licorice simile, but instead of having Nicholas *be* as sweet as licorice, Brinkman has him *sing a melody* as sweet as licorice.

Moving beyond the opening lines of the *Miller's Tale*, we find many additional changes. John is still foolish and old for Brinkman, but he does not go off to Oseney to work on the church there. Later he builds a tub in his workshop, causing us to wonder why so rich and bejeweled a man would have a workshop, let alone know what to do in it. Of course, Chaucer mentions no workshop, and Nicholas orders three tubs, not one. Chaucer's John does not build any of the three tubs, but just acquires them. He does build the three ladders, but Brinkman makes no reference in his version of the story to any ladders, let alone who builds them. Brinkman spends several lines emphasizing old John's sexual disability, which is strongly contrasted with Nicholas's virility in dealing with their shared filly Alison. Chaucer does no more than hint at these contrasts. Even when he is closely following his Chaucerian source,

Brinkman changes it. Chaucer's Nicholas is bold with Alison. "And prively he caughte hire by the queynte" (3276) becomes in Brinkman "And he reached beneath her skirt with perverted intentions" (Brinkman 199).[4]

The hip-hop Alison is still young and sexy, though Brinkman describes her less in barnyard images than in bordello images: she paints herself a "slutty pink," has a "naughty stink," and has a mouth as sweet, not as a hoard of apples, but as "bubbly drink" (Brinkman 195). Unlike Chaucer's Alison, Brinkman's likes having, displaying, and spending money. She enjoys going into the village because she "liked to shop wearing her husband's ring" (Brinkman 195). Chaucer makes no mention of Alison's shopping or of a wedding ring. Later, when Absolon famously asks for a kiss, Chaucer's Alison calls him "Jakke fool" (3708) and threatens to throw a stone at him, but she is not said to be angry. In Brinkman's retelling of the *Miller's Tale*, however, Alison is "raging mad" at Absolon, laughs at him with "distainful wrath," and in her anger calls him a "disgraceful rat" (Brinkman 233).

Brinkman's Absolon will be familiar to those who know Chaucer's *Miller's Tale*: he is less aggressive than the bold Nicholas in his courtship of Alison, more the stylized serenading romantic who puts Alison on a pedestal. Brinkman makes explicit, however, what Chaucer merely hinted at regarding Absolon's sexuality: he becomes an "emasculate man" (Brinkman 203) who chants "pansy songs" (Brinkman 205) to Alison. Brinkman also makes up some unChaucerian information about Absolon, such as telling us that he had a propensity for "dancing drunk at taverns 'til his cash was gone" (Brinkman 203). Chaucer tells us that Absolon liked to dance (3328) and that he often visited taverns (3334–36), but says nothing of drunkenness or spending all his cash.

Brinkman's treatment of the first kiss scene is familiar enough:

> The night was slate-black as she raised the glass,
> And displayed her backside and waited, relaxed,
> As Absolon reached out his lips and gave it his best,
> And proudly kissed the middle of her naked ass.
> But something was weird; it tasted bad,
> And had a beard of long, rough hairs.
> Absolon's fears were given a nudge
> When Alison giggled and slammed the window shut.
> [Brinkman, 235–37].

And so is the second:

> But Absolon couldn't guess where to strike, so instead he
> Cried, "Say something, Miss!" and Nicholas broke wind heavy
> The sound thunderous, like a motor revving.

> For Absolon there was no forgetting; he knew this joke already,
> But this time he had his red-hot poker ready.
> And he reached overhead and scalded his ass badly.
> With the hole in his flesh expanding, Nicholas ran
> Through the house, cauterized, screaming "Water! Water!"
> [Brinkman 241–43].

I could go on about the way Brinkman has broken, then recast and reset, Chaucer's *Miller's Tale*. I could show all the little things he wrongly left out or wrongly put in. But I have no desire to do that. In his book Brinkman presents his own rap text on the right-hand pages, with the Chaucerian original, complete with ample glosses of the Middle English, on the facing left-hand pages. Far from being embarrassed for not being entirely faithful to what Chaucer actually wrote, Brinkman wants us to notice how fresh and original his own version is. While we might wish that he would not refer to his version as a "translation" in the passage below, his deviations from his Chaucerian source can most productively be viewed not as mistakes but as conscious alterations. He aims, he tells us in his introduction,

> to offer an *interpretation* of the *Tales* for the general reader, with Chaucer's words accompanied by both the modern rap translations and the illustrations[5] for the sake of accessibility and enjoyment, abandoning any pretence of perfect fidelity to the elusive original. As an interpretation, this book presents ideas and methods that will be and should be debated, but my intention has always been to follow the spirit of Chaucer's poetry, rather than the letter of any single historical text. [...] Chaucer was always mindful of the *experience* of a story, and this has been my guiding principle in the editing, adapting, and presentation of the *Tales* in this book [Brinkman 57, 59].

It is interesting that in recasting the *Miller's Tale* for a twenty-first-century audience Brinkman actually, and apparently quite unwittingly, took the tale back in some ways closer to Chaucer's own source. The Middle Dutch *Heile of Beersele* is about the same length as Brinkman's *Miller's Tale*. Like his version, *Heile of Beersele* has no counterparts to Robyn, Gille, or Gerveys (though one of Heile's visitors is a smith), has a prostitute as its female lead, and has only one tub and no ladders. And the poker in both is said to be red-hot. The coulter in Chaucer's tale is never described as being red.

Here are the last fifteen lines of Chaucer's *Miller's Tale*. John has just crashed to the floor and the neighbors, summoned by Alison and Nicholas, rush in to see what all the excitement is about. They hear from Alison and Nicholas that the old man had crazily imagined that a second Noah's flood had come:

> The folk gan laughen at his fantasye;
> Into the roof they kiken and they cape,

> And turned al his harm unto a jape.
> For what so that this carpenter answerde,
> It was for noght; no man his reson herde.
> With othes grete he was so sworn adoun
> That he was holde wood in al the toun;
> For every clerk anonright heeld with oother.
> They seyde, "The man is wood, my leeve brother";
> And every wight gan laughen at this stryf.
> Thus swyved was this carpenteris wyf,
> For al his kepyng and his jalousye,
> And Absolon hath kist hir nether ye,
> And Nicholas is scalded in the towte.
> This tale is doon, and God save al the rowte! [3840–54].

In his abbreviated version of this closing, Brinkman cuts the lines about how everyone thought John was mad and laughed at his foolish fantasies; he has the neighbors laugh not just at John but at all three men; he leaves out the reminder that the jealous John has been cuckolded but adds the reminder that John has broken his arm; and he adds the two lines in which the smug Alison laughs in enjoyment at the men's misery. We can criticize Brinkman for misrepresenting Chaucer, if we want to, but was he really so unwise to shorten the part about John's supposed madness, which had already been mentioned in the previous section? Is it so bad to replace the reminder of the cuckolding of John with a reminder of his broken arm, thus introducing a nice symmetry with the physicality of the other two men's punishments? Is it so bad for Brinkman to have the neighbors laugh not just at John, but at Nicholas and Absolon also? And is it such a bad idea for Brinkman to show us that Alison, who has been physically accosted by all three men, is the real winner in this story by giving her the last laugh at their physical punishments? In his seven-line closing, Brinkman writes no fewer than thirty-three [æ]-sounds—an average of more than four per line (underlines added). To be sure, Chaucer did not write his ending that way, but so what? Chaucer showed us that it is legitimate poetic brinkmanship to take gross liberties with one's literary sources, so let's not leap too fast to give this poet a bum rap for doing so:

> They all had a good laugh at these three sad saps;
> John with his fractured arm, flat on his back;
> And Absolon's kiss, smack dab in the crack;
> And Nicholas with the flesh of his ass scabbed black;
> And Alison sat back, relaxed, and laughed,
> The only one left with her rep intact;
> And that's the end of that, as a matter of fact! [Brinkman 245].

XVIII

In Theatrical Performance: Woods (1974), Wengrow (1983), Riley (1998), O'Connor (2001), Price (2002), Poulton (2005)

In the first half of this book I demonstrated that Chaucer transformed the *Miller's Tale* into something very like a play, that he constructed the tale in such a way that with minimal changes a playwright could take it from the page to the stage. The past half-century has proved that, indeed, the *Miller's Tale* is a natural performance piece. In this chapter I describe six modern stage versions of the *Miller's Tale*. All six of them reduce the role of the Miller as the narrator of the tale so that the four characters can speak directly to the audience. There is, however, wide variety in the approaches and emphases.

Phil Woods and Michael Bogdanov (1974)

Not long after Starkie's musical *Canterbury Tales* closed in London, a quite different version of the *Canterbury Tales* was presented at the Phoenix Theatre in Leicester, a city northwest of London. Written by Phil Woods and directed by Michael Bogdanov, it opened on December 19, 1974. This new play made the Miller the dramatic centerpiece of the performance. Although his tale comes last, the Miller is a commanding presence in the prologue and in the tales told by the other pilgrims. The Phil Woods *Miller's Tale*

Figure 27. Cover of Phil Woods's *Canterbury Tales: Chaucer Made Modern* (1974).

is embedded in a fictional contest known as the annual Geoffrey Chaucer Canterbury Tale-Telling Competition. The Master of Ceremonies (usually called "M.C.") introduces the current year's finalists: the Knight, the Reeve, the Cook, the Wife of Bath, the Franklin, the Nun's Priest, the Pardoner, and the Merchant. Each of these is to tell a tale with the various other tellers performing roles in the tales. The raucous Miller, who is sitting out in the audience, loudly insists that he deserves to be a finalist also, but M.C. tells him that he has been disqualified because his tale is "lacking in common decency and taste."[1] The Miller insists that his tale is "good clean muck" (Woods 7). If he does not get a chance to tell his tale, he says, he will refuse to act his roles in any of the other tellers' tales. So that the tale-telling can proceed, M.C. finally relents.

At the end of the book when the others have told their tales, M.C. tries again to bypass the Miller, but when the Miller insists, M.C. lets the audience decide. Naturally they all want to hear the Miller's raunchy tale. M.C. finally lets the Miller proceed, but not before one last warning:

> M.C.: He told his tale in his own vulgar way,
>   I apologise for repeating it here today [Woods 63].

Then the Miller sets up the basic narrative with a few lines of exposition. For example:

> MILLER: There was this rich geezer called John,
>   Quite old, well, he was getting on.
>   By trade he was a carpenter;
>   He took a young wench and he married her [Woods 63].

After twenty lines of that kind of exposition, the rest of the tale is conducted in dialogue, virtually all of it invented by Phil Woods. There would, of course, have been blocking action and arranged by the director. The published script gives us almost nothing but the dialogue and an occasional parenthetical italicized stage direction.

The basic plot of Phil Woods's *Miller's Tale* is familiar: Nicholas develops an elaborate plan to pretend to go into a trance; John falls for his absurd prediction of a coming flood, hastily prepares three vessels, and hangs them from the rafters; Absolon comes and demands a kiss; Alison has him kiss her buttocks; Absolon returns with a hot iron and burns Nicholas's bottom with it; when he hears Nicholas's cry for water, John cuts his rope and comes crashing down. But within that familiar plot outline, Woods has made many changes. These changes are evident even in the opening dozen lines. Apparently the director of the little play has put Alison on her hands and knees scrubbing the floor, while Nicholas, behind her, lustfully observes her attractive fanny. Their opening speeches are heard by the audience, but not by each other:

> NICHOLAS: By all the sun and moon and stars,
>   Look at Alison's shapely hips.
>   I'd like to touch her back and front,
>   I wouldn't half like to kiss her lips.

> ALISON: I'm so fed up it's disconcerting,
> To think that I could be out flirting.
> I don't enjoy these household chores,
> Washing stairs and scrubbing floors.
> My John's too old to be my lover,
> All I am's his full time scrubber.
> NICHOLAS: *[Creeps up behind her]*
> Oh what a face! What a figure!
> Part of me is getting bigger [Woods 64].

Even in that short opening we can see that Woods has altered the storyline. Chaucer's Alison had done no household chores because her rich husband had hired a servant girl named Gille to do them. Chaucer's Alison had not complained about her husband's sexual incompetence. Woods's changes are logical enough. He needs to establish a motive for Alison's eager acquiescence in Nicholas's desire for sex, and her life as a chore-girl in a sexless marriage provides that. Of course, Nicholas's "getting bigger" not only draws a laugh from the audience, but also, in providing an implied contrast to old John's sexual smallness, further motivates Alison's acceptance of Nicholas.

Woods seems to have imposed on himself several limitations. First, after the Miller's opening twenty lines, the narrator can make no further direct comment, so the actions and words of the characters must carry the story line. Second, there can be only four characters, half as many as in the Chaucerian version: no Robyn, no Gille, no cloisterer, no Gerveys, no neighbors. Third, the action must take place entirely at John's house: no scene at the parish church, no journey to Oseney, no visit to a blacksmith's forge. And fourth, coming at the end of a tale-telling competition with eight earlier performances, the *Miller's Tale* must be short. In fact, it is only a third as long as Chaucer's.

Admirers of Chaucer's *Miller's Tale* will be disappointed at some of what is lost in transition to the stage. Gone are the rich descriptions of Absolon and Alison. Gone are memorable lines like Nicholas's that a clerk can easily "a carpenter bigyle" (3300), John's "Allas, myn Alison!" (3523), Alison's "Tehee," (3740), and Absolon's "Spek, sweete bryd" (3805).

The character whose part seems most to have challenged Woods was Absolon. In Chaucer's version, Absolon first encounters Alison in or near the parish church while he is at work with his censer. With that option not open to Woods, he has Absolon ring the doorbell to John's house, thus interrupting Nicholas's attempt to seduce Alison:

> NICHOLAS: I tell the truth it's not a lie,
> I must have you or I'll die.

XVIII. In Theatrical Performance

ALISON: Oh, Nicholas, you poor dear thing!
Not now, I heard the doorbell ring [Woods 64].

The doorbell is of course anachronistic, but Woods knows that: "In performing this version of the *Canterbury Tales*," he says in his preface, "it should be stressed that we do not for one moment pretend that we are in medieval England. The time is the present" (Woods v). The ringer of the doorbell is Absolon, who has come ostensibly to offer to hear Alison's confession. She tells him to come back when her husband is in. Encouraged, Absolon goes off to fetch his guitar.

As soon as Absolon leaves, Nicholas devises his plan to go into a trance and then goes up and locks himself into his room to put the plan into effect. John comes home a few minutes later and, learning from Alison that Nicholas is sick, goes up to his room. With no knave Robyn to help him break in the door, John asks his wife to help him. Once inside, John hears Nicholas's prediction of a terrible flood. Taking seriously Nicholas's instructions, John sneaks out to fetch three large baskets and provisions for them. Because of the modern setting, he cannot fetch kneading troughs, and he is perhaps too foolish to ask how a woven basket will keep out the flood waters.

As John sets out to acquire the baskets, he bumps into Absolon, who now has his guitar with him. In response to Absolon's question about where he is going, John replies vaguely, "Tonight's the night" (Woods 67). Absolon takes that to mean that John is leaving town and decides to make his move that night. To kill time until nightfall, Absolon practices his guitar. It is an awkward scene, but successful enough as a substitute for Absolon's going to Oseney and happening to talk to the cloisterer there about John's comings and goings.

That night, just as John is about to fall asleep in his basket, Absolon comes back to play his guitar outside her window. The song bothers John, who throws a boot at Absolon. Absolon decides to come back later. As soon as John falls asleep, Nicholas and Alison climb out of their baskets and head to bed. Absolon comes back and, on one knee, asks for a kiss. Alison finally agrees and sticks her bottom out the window. What follows Chaucer had accomplished with narration:

> And Absolon, hym fil no bet ne wers,
> But with his mouth he kiste hir naked ers
> Ful savourly, ere he were war of this.
> Abak he stirte, and thoughte it was amys,
> For wel he wiste a womman hath no berd.
> He felte a thyng al rough and long yherd [3733–38].

Woods, on the other hand, has to accomplish it with stage action and dialogue:

> ABSOLON: I feel your cheeks though I cannot see,
> Your sweet breath is like perfume to me.
> My tongue it tingles, you taste so lovely.
> Funny, though, your chin feels stubbly.
> I've kissed her bum, the dirty cow!
> I'll get my own back. I know how [Woods 69].

Chaucer then sends Absolon across town to Gerveys's blacksmith shop for a conversation with his friend and the loan of the hot coulter. Woods, however, because he cannot send his Absolon off to a location away from John's house, says nothing about where the poker comes from:

> ABSOLON: *(Re-enters with a red-hot poker).*
> She thinks she's a joker.
> Just wait till she feels my red-hot poker.
> Alison! I've got a gift for you!
> Please kiss once again, oh do [Woods 69].

It may be a flaw that Woods does not tell us or show us where Absolon acquired a hot poker in the middle of the night, but we should recall that the Miller's performance is set in modern, not medieval, times. Farmers no longer use coulters with their plows, and there are no longer blacksmith shops in most towns, so perhaps it is just as well that Woods does not specify what kind of poker it is, where it came from, or how it got heated up. Any readers who are puzzled can imagine anything they like—for example, a dandelion fork heated in a hibachi—or just not worry about it.

Woods has another role for Absolon to play. In Chaucer's version of the story, the neighbors come in to ridicule old John and call him mad:

> The neighebores, bothe smale and grete,
> In ronnen for to gauren on this man.
> [...]
> The folk gan laughen at his fantasye.
> [...]
> They seyde, "The man is wood, my leeve brother."
> [3826–27, 3840, 3848].

Rather than try to introduce any new characters at this point in the tale, Woods has Absolon do the honors of calling John crazy for thinking a flood has come:

> ABSOLON: A flood, you fool? You've gone insane.
> It's three months since we had rain [Woods 70].

Woods makes many more changes in retelling Chaucer's *Miller's Tale*. Most involve cutting and simplifying. For example, Woods does not have Nicholas mention the parallel with Noah's flood and ark, does not have John build ladders, and does not have him break his arm when he cuts the rope holding up his basket. A few involve additions, such as Nicholas's obscene joke about getting his divine foreknowledge of the flood from the planet Uranus.

Arnold Wengrow (1979)

A more daring production of the *Miller's Tale* was staged a couple of years later at a theater on the campus of the University of North Carolina at Asheville. Written and directed by Arnold Wengrow, it was first performed in 1979, then was taken on the road for several more performances. It was not published until 1983. As directed by Wengrow, the actors all wear simple white costumes. The play has no stage scenery and no props—at least not scenery and props in the usual sense. Wengrow has the actors themselves provide the scenery and the props and lets the audience imagine the rest. For example, to show that John is a carpenter, two actors kneel in front of him to make a pair of sawhorses supporting a third actor who plays a log that John pretends to cut with an imaginary saw.

Wengrow gives detailed stage directions. Here is what he writes for the scene in which Nicolas and Alison have agreed to a plan whereby Nicholas will take food and drink up to his room. Note that the two principles here speak of themselves in the third person:

> ALISON: Nicholas should exercise his wits
> And give her jealous husband fits.
> *(She begins to load his arms with imaginary items of food; he almost staggers under the weight. At the same time, a group of actors enters and, by crouching on hands and knees at different heights, form a staircase. Two actors enter and stand at either side of the crouched actors to make bannisters and give support to Nicholas, who is going to walk across the actors' backs. As he does so, the actors make creaking noises.).*
>
> NICHOLAS: So Nicholas, not a moment did he tarry,
> But softly to his chamber did he carry
> Food and drink to last at least a day.[2]

In a subsequent scene, six actors pair off and hold each other's forearms, forming the three imaginary tubs that John, Alison, and Nicholas crawl into. Later still, during the bedroom scene, the actors form Alison's bedroom wall and window:

ALISON: She flung the window open then in haste.
(She uses the arms of the actors forming the wall.)
"Come on," she said, "There's no time to waste."
The night was dark, and thus it came to pass
That through the window she daintily stuck out her ...
(Absolon, his eyes closed, scurries closer to the wall on his knees. Alison turns her back to him and leans her rear-end through the actors' arms that form the window. As she does so, she lifts her skirt slightly, so that when Absolon rises to kiss her, she can quickly drop the skirt over his head. He makes loud smooching noises under the skirt. Nicholas has been watching with eager interest.)
NICHOLAS: Alas!
For Absolon, as unsuspecting as one who's blind,
Eagerly began kissing Alison's behind! [Wengrow 59].

As in Chaucer, Alison then utters her famous "Tehee" and claps the window shut. Predictably, Absolon angrily fusses like a child and vows revenge. He runs over to the blacksmith shop. The most original feature of that scene is the hot poker enacted by a small actress:

ABSOLON: With rapid step he went across the street ...
(He crosses to the opposite side of the stage where Gerveys and a small actress have entered. The small actress stands facing away from Absolon, her arms tightly against her sides. She is the poker standing by the fire.)
GERVEYS: To a smith called Gerveys [Wengrow 60].

Subsequent stage directions have the small actress *"give a giggle,"* have Absolon pick up *"the small actress in a horizontal position"* and carry her back across the stage and set her on her feet beside the window.

Then comes the climactic window scene where Absolon gets his revenge:

ABSOLON: [He] with his hot iron gave such a jump
He struck poor Nicholas straight up the rump!
(He picks up the small actress horizontally again and gives a run towards Nicholas, hitting him in the rear-end with the actress's head on the word "rump." Then he sets the actress down; they shake hands in glee, and run out together.) [Wengrow 61].

The production ends predictably enough, with Nicholas calling for water, John cutting the rope, and the neighbors rushing in to laugh at the old carpenter and call him mad.

Having an actress play the role of a hot poker is not only a clever bit of staging that no doubt got a good laugh and an enthusiastic applause at the end of the play, but it also let Wengrow eliminate Nicholas's fart altogether. It would scarcely do, after all, for Nicholas to fart in the face of a small actress who is about to butt him squarely in the butt. Nicholas's fart, then, is forever silenced—at least in Wengrow's production.

Martin Riley (1998)

Martin Riley's adaptation of the *Miller's Tale* comes last in his 1998 retelling of five of Chaucer's tales, after the *Pardoner's Tale*, the *Nun's Priest's Tale*, the *Wife of Bath's Tale*, and the *Knight's Tale*. When the Knight has finished, the Miller is invited to tell his tale: "*On hearing his name, the Miller staggers on stage. He is quite drunk, and carries a bottle in one hand and a sack of flour in the other.* [...]" He sees the audience and releases a series of burps and

Figure 28. Cover of Martin Riley's *The Canterbury Tales* (1998).

belches."³ After that inauspicious beginning, he starts narrating his tale, but almost immediately his characters, fed up with his drunken confusion as a teller, join in to move the story along:

> MILLER: Once upon a time . . [*He rings the story bell furiously and shouts at the audience*) Shush, will yer! I'm telling a story! Once upon a ... you know ...
> ALISON: Once upon a time, there lived in Oxford a rich, miserly, boring old carpenter, called John.
> MILLER: What a boring name!
> JOHN: Boring—but rich.
> ALISON: Yeah. So he paid my parents a load of money and I had to marry him.
> JOHN: Alison, my beautiful young wife! You've got a body like a polecat—or is it a stoat? No, a weasel, that's it, a body like a weasel.
> ALISON: The wedding night was a nightmare.
> JOHN: I had a bad back and a headache [Riley 84–85].

Riley obviously augments the storyline, but the basic features of Chaucer's tale are still present. Here is the way Riley presents the grab scene (the ellipses are in the original):

> JOHN: One day, while I was away on business ...
> MILLER: ... Nicholas ran downstairs ...
> NICHOLAS: ... and grabbed Alison firmly ... [*He does so*].
> ALISON: ... in a private place ...
> MILLER: ... the kitchen! Alison made a loud scream.
> ALISON: Eeeek! [Riley 86].

Riley is aware that while his tale is set in medieval times, his audience is a modern one that needs some explanations. Here is the way he uses the Miller to give the playgoers historical information so they will understand why Absolon cannot see or identify by smell what he is kissing in the first kiss-scene:

> MILLER: Nights were very dark in the early Middle Ages. There were no street lights and no glass in the windows *(ALISON turns her back and sticks her bottom out the front of the booth. A joke shop fake bottom will avoid embarrassment. Absolon comes downstage to talk to the audience).*
> ABSOLON: What kind of a kiss should I give my love? I know! A big wet sloppy one, a kiss that she will remember forever! *(Absolon practices some kisses as he approaches Alison.)*
> MILLER *(to audience as Absolon prepares himself)*: Remember! There hasn't been any decent water supply since the Romans left! There's no toothpaste with stripes, either. One part of the body smells just as bad as any other part [Riley 91].

Absolon gets his revenge with a hot poker. Riley explains in a stage direction how he gets the poker:

> MILLER: Absolon went straight away to see his friend, Gerveys—the blacksmith! *(Gerveys enters stage left. He carries a metal poker, a mallet, and a bench. He creates*

his blacksmith's shop and starts to hammer the poker on the bench with his mallet. Percussion instruments provide sound effects.].
ABSOLON: I say, Gerveys, may I borrow that red hot poker? [Riley 92].

The presence of "percussion instruments" indicates that Riley envisioned a small band of some sort to provide for such sound effects. It was apparently pressed into service a few minutes later as Absolon hears from Nicholas:

ABSOLON: Speak, pretty bird, for I know not where thou art!
MILLER: At once Nicholas let fly a fart—as loud as a thunderclap! *(There is an appropriate sound effect.)*
ALISON: Absolon was half-blinded by the blast!
ABSOLON: But I was ready with my red hot poker. I lunged out with it, aiming at the source of the terrible smell [*In slow motion, ABSOLON charges across the stage to the booth. Speaking in slow motion*] Ger-on-i-mo! [Riley 93].

It did not bother Riley that Absolon's cry "Geronimo" is neither medieval nor British. He apparently hoped that its very anachronism would fetch a good laugh, and it probably did.

John O'Connor (2001)

Designed for a high school drama club or classroom performance, John O'Connor's script of the *Canterbury Tales* is also heavy with stage directions, suggestions for classroom discussion or activities, and definitions of words like "gluttony," "adultery," and "slander." Like Riley's adaptation for the stage, but unlike Woods's, O'Connor's makes some attempt to place the tales in a medieval setting. The gathering at the Tabard Inn is said to take place in April, 1385, but much of the humor of the play is based on intentional anachronisms. The pilgrims meet at the Tabard on a "Spring Bank Holiday," for example, and some of the pilgrims are said to be "discussing the Stock Market."[4] Some of the tales are explicitly said to have modern settings. Near the start of Chaucer's *Tale of Sir Topaze*, O'Connor gives this stage direction: "*The setting is mid-twentieth century. SIR TOPAZE enters on a bike. He is dressed in pin-stripe suit and bowler hat, with umbrella*" (O'Connor 39). Sir Topaze turns out to be a cricket player who encounters a giant cricket-player dressed all in white. Except for this one tale, everything is written in prose.

The tales told and enacted are, in order, the *Pardoner's Tale*, the *Reeve's Tale*, Chaucer's *Tale of Sir Topaze*, the *Franklin's Tale*, and, finally, the *Miller's Tale*. Much of O'Connor's *Canterbury Tales* theatrical version is witty inter-tale byplay among the pilgrims: the Host, Chaucer, the Wife of Bath, the

Cook, the Scholar, the Nuns, the Doctor, the Summoner, the Reeve, the Pardoner, and of course the Miller. By the time the inebriated Miller gets to tell his tale—the last one before the pilgrims get to Canterbury—some of his fellow pilgrims—most prominently the Prioress—knowing what to expect, leave as the Miller comes to center stage playing his bagpipes. O'Connor gives the Miller a Cockney accent—or is it French?:

> MILLER: Well, as I've been trying to tell you, there's this old carpenter, see, and 'e goes an' marries this really gorgeous little young piece, right? And they set up home in a nice little flat above his workshop, [...] all alone except for a lodger. Yeh, bit of an artist 'e was, and 'e 'ad 'is eye on the carpenter's young wife from the moment 'e set foot in the 'ouse [O'Connor 61].

O'Connor renames two of the characters. Alison becomes Alice and John becomes Jean-Pierre, apparently a Frenchman. Curiously, O'Connor opens the play proper with some head-bashing dancing: *"Music: Something like "Jealousy" in French/accordion style. NICHOLAS sits sketching ALICE as she tidies the dinner table. When the music develops into something like a tango, he grabs her and they perform a violent and dramatic dance, during which ALICE's head is bashed on the table more than once"* (O'Connor 62). A few seconds later, O'Connor tells us in a stage direction that *"Nicholas rushes to Alice and embraces her from behind"* (O'Connor 63). That is as close as we get to the Chaucerian Nicholas's grabbing Alison's "queynte."

There seems to be no real reason to move the setting from Oxford to France, except that it may provide opportunities for humor:

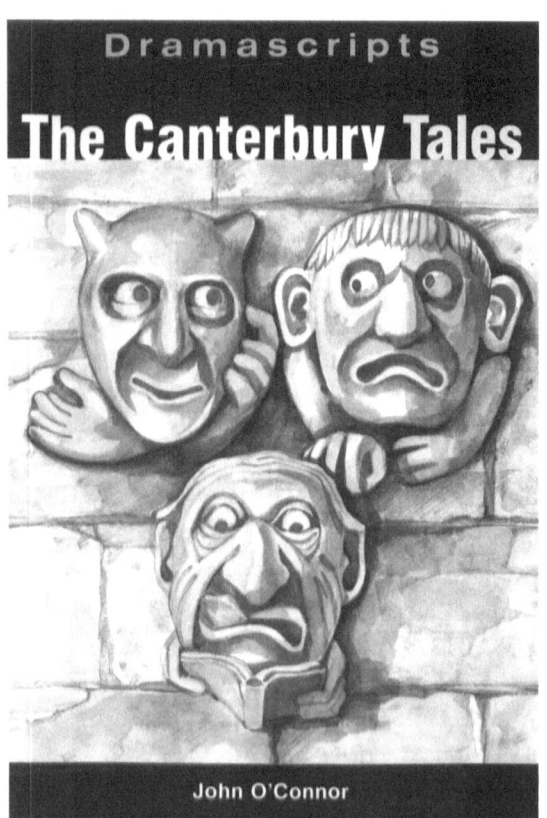

Figure 29. Cover of John O'Connor's *Canterbury Tales* (2001).

XVIII. In Theatrical Performance

NICHOLAS: Alice!
ALICE: Nicholas!
NICHOLAS: Je t'adore!
ALICE: Shut it yourself.
NICHOLAS: Mais, non. I love you [O'Connor 63].

When Nicholas tells Jean-Pierre about the coming flood, he mixes French and English:

NICHOLAS: "Tout est perdu! Ze world is coming to an end! It is written in ze stars! [...] A great flood. Un déluge! Thursday soir! It will cover ze 'ole world!" (O'Connor 65].

Because of the intended audience of high school students, O'Connor is discrete about what goes on the night of the flood. After old Jean-Pierre falls asleep in his tub we are told only that Nicholas and Alice "creep out of their tubs" (O'Connor 66). He says nothing about a bed or what they do there. Whatever it is, they are interrupted by Absolon, who is breezily introduced by the teller at this point in the play:

MILLER: Ah, what I haven't told you yet is that Nicholas isn't the only bloke with designs on the carpenter's wife. Down the road lives Absolon, a young vicar, and 'e's been trying to get off with her for months. Finally 'e's plucked up the courage. But some people have a knack of picking the wrong moment [O'Connor 66].

As for Absolon and his famous demand for a kiss, the script says: *"She draws the curtains across her window, so that we can no longer see her. Meanwhile, ABSOLON climbs the ladder"* (O'Connor 66). Then:

ABSOLON *(calling through her window)*: Alice! I love you. Give me a kiss, my little cabbage, and make me a 'appy man! (*The curtains are pulled apart to reveal a joke-shop fake bum representing Alice's. He kisses loudly and long. Pauses. Thinks. Touches the bum. And nearly falls off his ladder in horror.)* I have kissed a bim! *(Hearing their laughter as the bum is swiftly withdrawn behind the curtain, Absolon grinds his teeth in fury).* I must 'ave revenge! Honneur must be satisfied! [O'Connor 66–67].

Absolon soon returns from the blacksmith's shop with a hot branding iron. The fart scene is portrayed with humor and economy:

(The curtains whip open to reveal another rump, rather bigger than the first. As Absolon approaches, he cunningly checks on its exact whereabouts.)
ABSOLON: Speak to me, my little sparrow *(The bottom lets rip a terrifically rude noise—a trombone rendition of "La Marseilleise"—and its cheeks vibrate in time to it. Absolon thrusts home with the iron; the bottom disappears.)*
NICHOLAS *(screams)*: Water! Water!
JEAN-PIERRE *(wakes)*: Water? Ze flood 'as begun! *(He cuts the rope supporting his tub and plummets to the ground.)* [O'Connor 67–68].

O'Connor provides some sense of what the set should look like by suggesting an "Artwork" assignment:

> Draw a sketch of the set to show the three tubs hanging from the rafters and Nicholas's bedroom. (Don't show the characters.) So that the rest of the play can work, the bedroom should (a) be about two meters off the ground, and (b) have a small window. Save the sketch so that you can add to it in a moment [O'Connor 66].

It does not bother O'Connor that the set he describes is different from the one in Chaucer's tale, where the bedroom is at ground level and where Absolon never climbs a ladder to reach the window. On the contrary, he must kneel down to position himself for the kiss.

O'Connor's rendition of the *Miller's Tale* is short. The Miller does most of the talking, but he speaks only about 250 words, total. Nicholas speaks only about 100, Alice about 75, Absolon about 60, and Jean-Pierre about 50. Much of the effect of O'Connor's play is visual. For example, the play ends with Nicholas "*sitting in a chamber pot with steam rising round his bare haunches*" (O'Connor 68). It is not Chaucer, but it seems Chaucerian.

Lindsay Price (2002)

A year after O'Connor's acting adaptation of the *Miller's Tale* was published, another adaptation came out, also aimed at a young audience, probably also groups of high school students. Lindsay Price pays some attention to the staging of her play. The setting, she announces, should be "extremely simple": "Any props or set pieces should be flexible and interchangeable between the stories."[5] The play opens, as usual, in a tavern. The various pilgrims who tell tales—The Wife of Bath, the Pardoner, the Prioress, the Reeve, the Franklin, the Cook, and the Miller—all introduce themselves. Here is what the Miller says of himself:

> MILLER: First prize is mine in every wrestling match.
> I'm sure you can see why.
> I carry the mighty sword in one hand,
> The mighty bagpipe in the other.
> A bag of tricks and jokes is always by my side.
> The biggest trick of all is the corn that I will steal
> And sell back to all at triple the price
> As if it were the greatest deal! [Price 8–9].

To give more roles to female students, Price makes some of the characters women. The Host, for example, is the Hostess, the Cook is a female cook, the

Old Man in the *Pardoner's Tale* is an Old Woman, and the Nun's Priest becomes the Prioress. After the Prioress tells her tale of Chanticleer and Pertelote, the Miller tells his tale.

Part of Price's humor is to let the Miller talk to his actors as they play their roles in his tale. He also offers some direct addresses to the audience. Here is the byplay when John and Alison jump their cues and come out on the stage together too soon:

> JOHN: Welcome to your ...
> MILLER (*yelling at John*): Hang on! I'm not ready for you yet! Get off!
> (*John and Alison exit on the run.*) Now, the rich carpenter had a name. His name was ... his name was ... was (*he calls offstage*) Oye! What's your name?
> JOHN (*offstage*): John.
> MILLER: Of course it is. I knew that. It's my story, isn't it? Now. The carpenter, whose name was John ... (*calling offstage*) All right, you can come out now! John had just married a very young woman whose name was ... don't tell me ... Alison (*John and Alison enter again.*)
> JOHN (*to Alison*): Welcome to your new home [Price 24].

Because she was writing the play for a young audience, Price tells us not that Nicholas grabs Alison by the crotch or the haunches but that he "*grabs hold of her hand*" (Price 25). Price also adjusts the tub scene on Monday night, the night of the predicted flood. John, Alison, and Nicholas sit on the stage in pretend-tubs:

> MILLER: Each into their separate tubs they crept (*To the audience*): You can't see the tubs but they're there. You're not going to doubt me now are you? Not when I've been telling this story for so long! What a long story. A man should have a reward for telling such a story. Think on that, will you? (*He clears his throat.*) Now, John sat in silence waiting for rain.
> JOHN: Alas! Alas! Ohhhhh alas!
> MILLER: That's not silent! (*there is a pause*) Better. Zounds! John was so upset and filled with blind panic as he waited for the flood that he fell instantly asleep. Soon his snores filled the tub [Price 29].

As soon as John drops off to sleep, Nicholas and Alison make their exit. The Miller then tells us that the two "entertained themselves with much revelry and merrymaking all the night through until morning came" (Price 29). Price never specifies the kind of "revelry and merrymaking" they engage in offstage. When morning comes they come back onstage. That is when Absolon comes and asks for a kiss.

This is the first we have heard of Absolon, since in Price's version Alison does not encounter him at church and Absolon does not serenade Alison. Absolon makes his appearance just as the lovers return:

MILLER: At the exact same time as Alison and Nicholas were sneaking through the house, a young man named Absolon was walking by the cottage (*To the audience*): You didn't know there would be another person in the story, did you? Fooled you! Ha! [Price 29].

The first kiss-scene is described in a stage-direction: "(*Absolon leans forward with his eyes closed to kiss Alison. She turns her back to Absolon and leans over so that Absolon kisses her behind. Absolon jumps back with a start. Nicholas and Alison dissolve into hoots of laughter)*" (Price 30). Absolon resolves to exact his revenge. Price makes no mention of Gerveys, but provides an explanation—of sorts—for the availability of the weapon of Absolon's revenge. He literally trips over it after he kisses Alison's bottom:

ABSOLON: Ew, ew, ug, agh, yuck, yuck, phooey! Huh! How dare they! No one makes a fool of Absolon. My love for that woman has completely vanished! Gone! Departed! My love is nowhere to be found. I will have my revenge! (*He trips and falls*.) I will still have my revenge! Ah ha! What's this? A fire poker smouldering in the coals? Right here in the middle of nowhere? How very convenient! This will do just the trick! [Price 30].

In Price's polite adaptation for the stage, Nicholas does lean his bottom out the window towards Absolon but does not fart. Absolon jabs Nicholas, who then runs around the stage holding his bottom and screaming "Water!"

Mike Poulton (2005)

Another adaptation of Chaucer's *Miller's Tale* for the stage was written by Mike Poulton for the Royal Shakespeare Company. Poulton devised a play in two parts. At the start of the first part a character named Chaucer steps forward in the Tabard Inn to recite the opening lines. He is interrupted after his "And pilgrims were they all / That tóward Canterb'ry would ride" by the arrival of the pilgrims. Poulton gives this italicized stage direction: "*The* PILGRIMS *burst in, led by the low-life.*" They come in singing a song that starts out:

> *When the nightingale is singing*
> *The woods wax white and green*
> *With leaf and with blossom springing*
> *In April well I ween.*[6]

After the "low-life" come in, "*The Knight and the Squire come in leading the richer sort, and are greeted by the Host.*" Partway through Chaucer's description of the Knight and the Squire, the Host "*hands him a drink, which Chaucer drains*" (Poulton 9), and the Host proposes the tale-telling competition. After

XVIII. In Theatrical Performance   211

Figure 30. Cover of Mike Poulton's *Canterbury Tales* (2005).

a while the Wife of Bath asks Chaucer who he is. Chaucer replies, "Oh, I'm just—well—nobody—that is, nobody you'd know" (Poulton 10). When the Host proposes the tale-telling competition, Poulton provides this stage direction: "*The pilgrims are for the most part befuddled, unsure, or unwilling. Chaucer, who is drunk, speaks for them and is supported by the low-life who are drunker than he is*" (Poulton 11).

The next morning the Knight draws the short straw and tells his tale of chivalry (Poulton 15–32), part of which is enacted by others in the cast. The Knight is very much the teller of his tale, narrating 244 of the lines of this 592-line tale, more than 40 percent of the tale. When he is done, the drunken Miller insists on going next. He eventually prevails:

> CHAUCER: A warning, friends. I fear the tale he'll tell
> Will show us harlotry—bare flesh as well.
> A shame, I say! That things begun i'th'height
> (*Nods to the Knight*).
> Should sink so low so soon—just to delight
> The smutty-minded—those of simple wit.
> I say, good folk, let's stand no more of it:
> Those who are for high morals and good taste
> Should now be gone. Depart. Away. Make haste [Poulton 35].

The Miller then tells his tale, which runs to 356 lines in Poulton's edition, fewer than half the number of lines in Chaucer's *Miller's Tale*. The Poulton version has the Miller's running commentary woven with that of the personages in the tales. Here, for example, is the way Poulton handles the grab scene:

> MILLER: There comes a time—the husband he's away
>   Fetching some timber down in Oseney—
>   Young Nicholas puts on a playful front,
>   Goes to this wife, and grabs her by _____.
> NICHOLAS: I tell you straight—unless I have my will
>   Of you, my love, I'm going to burst and spill
>   My life before you here upon the floor—
>   Oh let me stroke your thighs—it's what they're for.
>   I have to have you now—Oh let me come
>   To you—I'll die! Or else I am undone.
> ALISON: Let be! Let go! Unhand me, Nicholas—
>   Or I'll cry out—Out harrow! Out alas!
>   Let go your hands—where is your modesty! [Poulton 36–37].

Part of the humor of the scene is that Poulton leaves that blank. Presumably the thing that Nicholas grabs would have been clear from his actions on stage, and the audience would have provided the word that rhymes with "front." Alison in this scene is more willing to cooperate than Chaucer's Alison is. In Chaucer, for example, she says, "I wol nat kisse thee, by my fey!" (3284). Poulton leaves off that line and four lines later provides this stage direction: "*She kisses him.*" Then a few lines later he gives Nicholas a new line, "Now kiss me close," followed immediately by this stage direction: "*She does. 'He thakkes hir about the lendes weel'*—i.e., they grope each other—kiss, and part" (Poulton 37). Chaucer says nothing about *her* kissing *him* or groping *him*:

> He thakked hire about the lendes weel,
> And kiste hire sweete [3304–05].

We should keep in mind that "groped" is not an accurate translation for "thakked"—a word usually translated as "patted." One wonders what the director of Poulton's play would have told Alison and Nicholas to do up there on the stage to enact their groping of each other. Immediately after that scene, Chaucer has Nicholas pick up his "sawtrie" and make "melodie" (3305–06). Poulton has Nicholas pick up his "Sawtrye" and sing three stanzas of "I Have a Gentil Cock" (Poulton 37–38). He may have taken the idea for that from the Starkie musical version of the tale played thirty-five years earlier on London's West End and New York City's Broadway. He did not take it from Chaucer.

Like most of the dramatists that I discuss in this chapter, Poulton cuts both the scene in which Alison encounters Absolon at church and the scene in which Absolon serenades his "dear lady" while she is in bed with John. Like the others, Poulton found those bits both awkward to stage and unnecessary. Poulton, however, made a unique adjustment. We should recall those two scenes in Chaucer's *Miller's Tale*. Early in the tale Chaucer has Alison go out to the parish church, where she encounters Absolon, who sees her and longs for her. Soon thereafter Absolon pays a nocturnal visit to John's house, where he serenades Alison from outside the couple's bedroom window with a song to "my deere lady" (3361). John and Alison, in their bed, hear Absolon. John speaks first:

> "What! Alison! Herestow nat Absolon,
> That chaunteth thus under oure boures wal?"
> And she answered hir housbonde therwithal,
> "Yis, God woot, John, I heere it every deel.
> This passeth forth; what wol ye bet than weel?"[7] [3366–70].

Then Chaucer tells us all the things Absolon did to win Alison—acting in plays, sending gifts, and so on. Poulton cuts all that, some ninety lines. He does not introduce Absolon until the Monday night of the predicted flood.

Before we see how Poulton introduced Absolon, we should take a look at the first of those Monday night kiss scenes. Chaucer has John, Nicholas, and Alison all say "Clom":

> "Now, *Pater-noster*, clom!" seyde Nicholay,
> And "Clom!," quod John, and "Clom!" seyde Alison [3638–39].

With enviable cleverness, Poulton changes "clom," which means "shhh" or "silence," to "Amen," setting up a humorous variation for Alison:

NICHOLAS: Pater-noster, Amen.
MILLER: This Nick'las says.
CARPENTER: Amen! Amen!
MILLER: The carpenter replies.
ALISON: Ahhhh! Men! Ahhhh! Men!
MILLER: Sighs naughty Alison [Poulton 40–41].

As soon as old John is snoring, Nicholas and Alison creep out of their tubs and climb down their ladders. This is the way Chaucer puts what happens next:

> And eft he routeth, for his heed myslay.
> Doun of the laddre stalketh Nicholay,
> And Alisoun ful softe adoun she spedde;
> Withouten wordes mo they goon to bedde,
> Ther as the carpenter is wont to lye.
> Ther was the revel and the melodye;
> And thus lith Alison and Nicholas,
> In bisynesse of myrthe and of solas,
> Til that the belle of laudes gan to rynge,
> And freres in the chauncel gonne synge [3647–56].

Poulton's Miller makes the scene both shorter and more explicitly orgasmic, with words like "strip," "thumping," "twineth," "straining," and "sweet release"—words that Chaucer did not use:

> MILLER: Without a word they strip and go to bed
> And, while the old man snores beneath the moon,
> The young are thumping out another tune.
> Thus twineth Alison with Nicholas
> Straining their limbs to reach each sweet release—
> Until the bell for Church begins to ring
> And friars in the chancel start to sing.
> *Enter* ABSOLON [Poulton 41].

This is the first we've heard of Absolon. Poulton introduces him with economical dispatch by having the Miller report that ever since Absolon had laid eyes on Alison he had loved her. Indeed, the Miller goes on, he would often at night sing at her window. Tonight was one of those nights. Then, borrowing John's words that Poulton had cancelled in the dropped ninety lines, Nicholas hears Absolon singing and, echoing John's words in the Chaucerian tale, says:

> NICHOLAS: Hush. Alison. Herestow nat Absolon
>   That chaunteth thus under the window's sill?
> ALISON: Yea, Nicholas. I hear him very well [Poulton 42].

Alison tells Absolon to go away, but at his insistence agrees to the kiss. She complies and Absolon kisses her bottom:

ABSOLON: Something's amiss? All rough and shaggy haired?
  I've never kissed a woman with a beard!
ALISON: Te hee! [Poulton 43].

Absolon goes to the blacksmith's shop and returns with the hot coulter. He taps on the window. Nicholas tells Alison that he has to have a piss. She stays in bed while he sticks his bottom out the window:

ABSOLON: Speak, my sweet bird. I know not where thou art.
NICHOLAS *lets out an iambic quatrametric fart, very loud and long on the eighth syllable.*
MILLER: A fart!
  As great as it hath been a thunder-dent—
  Absolon's half blind ere its force is spent!
But then: (*Absolon sticks the glowing implement up Nicholas's bum.*) [Poulton 45].

The play ends pretty much as Chaucer's tale had ended: Nicholas cries for water, John cuts the rope and breaks his arm in the fall, and the neighbors come in and laugh at John for spouting such nonsense about a flood.

Before we move in the next chapter to the several film versions of the *Miller's Tale*, we should note the rich variety of ways modern dramatists have adapted Chaucer's plot and characters to the stage. We saw in Chart 8 at the end of Part One above that Chaucer greatly increased the amount of dialogue in his tale. Only about 30 percent of *Heile of Beersele* was dialogue, while in the *Miller's Tale* about 40 percent is dialogue. In a full dramatization of the tale, we would of course expect that the percentages of dialogue would be considerably higher than in Chaucer. In Chart 9 I list comparative data for the six stage adaptations we have just been considering—the ones by Phil Woods, Arnold Wengrow, Martin Riley, John O'Connor, Lindsay Price, and Mike Poulton. I consider in Chart 9 only what I have called the "tale proper"—leaving off the Miller's Prologue and the closing five-line narrative summary, lines 3849–3854; compare, Woods 70, Wengrow 63, Riley 97, O'Connor 68, Price 31–32, and Poulton 46]). The category "Other" includes speaking characters like Robyn, Gerveys, and the neighbors.

Not surprisingly, the chart shows that all six dramatists gave proportionally more space to direct speech by the characters than Chaucer did and fewer to the Miller himself. The percentages of lines given to the four of the principal actors (John, Nicholas, Alison, and Absolon) all go up compared to Chaucer, with only one exception: for Price the percentage for Absolon goes down slightly. Woods and Wengrow so reduce the Miller's role as narrator that they increase the amount of non–Miller dialogue to more that 90 percent, as compared with Riley's almost 80 percent, Poulton's almost 70 percent, and

Chart 9. Percentages of dialogue in Chaucer's and six modern stage versions of the *Miller's Tale*.

	Chaucer	Woods	Wengrow	Riley	O'Connor	Price	Poulton
Miller	60.4%	8.8%	0.0%	23.1%	42.6%	41.0%	31.6%
John	7.9%	24.7%	15.3%	19.5%	9.8%	16.9%	12.9%
Nicholas	16.1%	30.8%	31.7%	16.6%	19.7%	29.1%	30.9%
Alison	4.2%	13.7%	19.0%	20.2%	16.4%	5.1%	9.0%
Absolon	8.4%	22.0%	26.3%	17.5%	11.5%	7.9%	12.9%
Others	3.0%	0.0%	7.7%	3.1%	0.0%	0.0%	2.7%
Totals	100%	100%	100%	100%	100%	100%	100%

O'Connor's and Price's almost 60 percent. The chart shows how differently the six modern dramatists accomplished that reduced role for the Miller. Nicholas, for example, gets the biggest percentage of lines in all versions except the one by Riley, who gives Alison more prominence than she has in any of the other versions. Woods gives more voice to John, while O'Connor gives him less. O'Connor gives more voice to Alison, while Price gives her less. Woods and Wengrow both give more than a fifth of the lines to Absolon, who gets smaller percentages in the other four versions. Only Wengrow, Riley, and Poulton give the minor characters speaking roles.

There is, then, wide variation in the ways modern dramatists have moved the *Miller's Tale* from the page to the stage, but all six build on the central fact that Chaucer wrote the *Miller's Tale* in such a way that it almost stages itself. Instead of having the narrator explain what the characters are doing, the dramatists place the characters up on the stage performing the roles that Chaucer gave them. Chaucer provided the theatrical seeds for these modern dramatists. All they had to do was water them and cultivate them to bring them to full theatrical flower.

XIX
In Filmic Performance: Pasolini (1972), Myerson (2000), Bowker (2003)

Chaucer could well have imagined that his *Miller's Tale* might someday be adapted for the stage. He could not have imagined, however, that it would ever appear on a television or movie screen. Centuries later, however, when the technology was ready, others were soon enough to imagine it.

Pier Paulo Pasolini (1972)

The Italian film director Pier Paulo Pasolini in 1972 produced a movie-length film he called *Canterbury Tales*.¹ The opening scene takes place at a tavern. A scraggly-looking innkeeper proposes to the group of pilgrims that he join them on their journey to pay homage to the blissful martyr, and that they each tell a tale on the way to Canterbury. They agree. There follow a series of short tales each based, in at least a general way, on one of Chaucer's tales. The tellers of the tales, however, are not further identified. For example, the first tale is based loosely on Chaucer's *Merchant's Tale*, but no narrator steps forward to tell the tale, and it is nowhere identified as the *Merchant's Tale*. Viewers who did not already know Chaucer's *Canterbury Tales* would have no way to know that a merchant was its teller. Occasionally we catch a glimpse of a man in a white skull cap putting pen to paper. This man is supposed to be Chaucer. At one point his shrewish wife tells him to get to work.

The tales run in no discernible order. After the segment based on the *Merchant's Tale* are segments based loosely on the tales of the Friar, Cook, the Miller, the Wife of Bath (her prologue, not her tale), the Reeve, the Summoner, and the Pardoner, though none of these is named or identified as being associated with a particular teller. The only pilgrims recognizable as tale-tellers are the Pardoner and the Wife of Bath. The former tries to sell pardons to passers-by (they ignore him). And the latter features herself in a very short sequence in which she flirts with Jankyn and then, after she has married him, tears up his book of wicked wives. There is much in his *Canterbury Tales* that Pasolini invents, such as the Wife of Bath's biting Jankyn's nose, the appearance in January's garden in the *Merchant's Tale* of Pluto and Proserpina totally naked, the scene in the *Friar's Tale* in which a reprobate sinner is burned alive for engaging in homosexual activities, and the opening scenes in the *Pardoner's Tale* where the three revelers consort with naked prostitutes in a tavern-bordello and where one of the revelers then urinates over the railing onto the other taverners below.

The story based on the *Miller's Tale* follows the plot of Chaucer's tale, but not closely. It opens with the brash, handsome, and priapic Nicholas watching to see when old John leaves for work, and then rushing down to the kitchen to attack Alison, lifting her skirt and making a grab in the general direction of her genitals. She resists, but not very convincingly, telling Nicholas that her husband is jealous and watchful. Nicholas then takes charge and tells her his plan to pretend to go into a trance.

Then the scene shifts to Absolon's bedroom, where he lies in bed listening to a song sung to him by a handsome young red-haired man. There is, of course, no such scene, no such man, in Chaucer. The two men go off, together, to sing a song to Alison outside the bedroom that she shares with her husband. On the way they pass a blacksmith shop, apparently the one where Absolon's red-haired friend works as an apprentice. When Absolon and his friend sing outside their bedroom, John and Alison both wake up and both recognize Absolon's voice. John identifies him as a sexton.

In the next scene, John and young Robyn go up to Nicholas's room to find out what is going on with Nicholas. Coming out of his pretend trance, Nicholas tells John about the coming flood and gives him instructions about the three tubs and how to provision them, giving particular instructions that there must be no carnality the night of the flood.

Then it is Monday night as the three climb into their tubs. Very soon John is snoring and Nicholas and Alison climb down their ladders and head for the bed, where they proceed to undress one another. While they are busy making love, Absolon's red-haired friend, runs to fetch Absolon, telling him that he has heard that John is out of town and that this is his chance to make his move for Alison. Absolon goes and raps on the window. Alison tells him to go away, but he asks for a kiss before he goes. Totally naked, Alison then puts her buttocks out the window and he kisses her, just as she farts.

The angry Absolon then goes to the local blacksmith where his friend is an apprentice and borrows a red-hot poker—and it is just that, not a coulter. He returns just as Nicholas, also totally naked, is urinating into a bucket. The rest is much as it is in Chaucer: Absolon asks Alison to speak, Nicholas farts, Absolon thrusts, Nicholas cries "Water," and John chops the rope and comes tumbling down.

Pasolini makes a number of puzzling departures from Chaucer in his reframing of the *Miller's Tale*. John is an old man in Chaucer, while Alison is a skittish eighteen. The difference in their ages—"she was wylde and ong, and he was old" (3225)—makes clear why Alison is eager to encourage the sexual offers of the randy young Nicholas. In Pasolini the ages of the husband and wife are never mentioned, but the carpenter is, while not young, certainly not what most of us would call old, and his wife, while not old, is played by an actress who is perhaps twice eighteen. Chaucer's Nicholas is "lyk a mayden meke for to see" (3202), but Pasolini's Nicholas is brash, loud-mouthed, and aggressive. He seems to enjoy ordering people around. He is "hende" enough, if by that we mean that he seems always to have a hand on his own overstuffed phallus or on Alison's breast—two locations that Chaucer does not mention.

Pasolini's most puzzling departure from his Chaucerian original is the addition of the unnamed red-haired blacksmith's apprentice. On the one hand, the addition makes sense because he provides the mechanism by which Absolon picks that particular Monday night to ask for a kiss from Alison: he learns from his friend that since John has dismissed his servants for the night, John may have left town also, leaving Alison quite alone and perhaps lonely in her bed. On the other hand, the close and apparently intimate nature of the friendship between Absolon and his musical companion makes us wonder if the two are lovers. If that is the case, why is Absolon eager to bed Alison, and why is his friend eager to help him?

Pasolini follows Chaucer fairly closely in the two Monday night window scenes, but we readily notice changes. First, he has Alison fart in Absolon's face just as he leans forward for the kiss. His doing so adds to the insult to Absolon, but it introduces some problems. It robs Nicholas's fart of its surprise element because Alison had already been there, done that. It also causes Pasolini to step away from one of Chaucer's best jokes—the joke about a woman's not having a beard. It appears that she farts in Absolon's face before he has a chance to get close enough to feel her "beard." More important, it makes questionable the likelihood that Absolon would come back for a second kiss. After all, since all three of them know that she farted on him, how can Absolon pretend not to know that she has rejected him? How can Nicholas possibly not know that if he pulls the same trick, his bottom will be vulnerable to the most painful and degrading punishment that the angry Absolon can dream up?

Jonathan Myerson (2000)

The only animated cartoon version of the *Canterbury Tales* produced so far is Jonathan Myerson's three-part sequence. The three parts are identified as "Leaving London," "Arriving at Canterbury," and "The Journey Back."[2] The *Miller's Tale* is for some reason saved for "The Journey Back," where it appears after various scenes in Canterbury that Chaucer never wrote: a bear-baiting, a cock fight, a visit to a dentist. "The Journey Back" comprises animated versions of four tales: the *Squire's Tale*, the *Canon's Yeoman's Tale*, the *Miller's Tale*, and the *Reeve's Tale*.

Two features of the Myerson *Miller's Tale* immediately stand out. The first is the method of depicting the faces of the characters by means of a process known as puppet stop-frame animation. The various characters in this tale have elongated faces—somewhat like concave horse's faces—with protruding jaws, lips, tongues, and teeth. They do not look at all like what Chaucer apparently meant them to look like. Few viewers would think this Alison is pretty or particularly desirable as she prances around the house on a hobby-horse. John, Nicholas, and Absolon perhaps find her attractive only because they look somewhat like her.

The other feature of the Myerson *Miller's Tale* that immediately stands out is that it is interwoven with the *Reeve's Tale*. That is, scenes from the *Miller's Tale* are cut-and-pasted alternately with scenes from the *Reeve's Tale*. In Chaucer's *Canterbury Tales* the Miller tells his tale, complete, and then the Reeve, annoyed at what he sees as the negative portrayal of the cuckolded carpenter in the *Miller's Tale*, tells his tale, complete, about a thieving miller. Myerson interweaves the two stories by cutting from one to the other with insertions from the pilgrimage showing the jovial Miller and the irascible

XIX. In Filmic Performance   221

Figure 31. Nicholas grabs a startled Alison in Jonathan Myerson's animated version (2000) of the *Miller's Tale*.

Reeve bickering about each other's plots and personalities as they ride along on their horses. Here is an outline of the various pieces:

1. Pilgrimage. The Miller on horseback begins his tale "about an Oxford scholar—a nice lad."
2. The Miller introduces Nicholas, Alison, and John. Alison is portrayed with huge red lips and huge, swaying breasts that provide a nesting place for her pet chipmunk.
3. Pilgrimage. The Reeve, annoyed at the portrayal of the carpenter, insists on starting his tale about a dishonest miller who lives near Cambridge.
4. The Reeve introduces John and Aleyn. They take a bag of grain to the mill, where Symkyn greets them as he plays his bagpipes. As the students carefully watch their grain being ground, a rat poops on a beam and kicks its turds into their bag of flour. Symkyn lets their horse loose. Leaving their bags of flour behind, John and Aleyn rush off to retrieve their horse.
5. Pilgrimage. The Miller objects to the Reeve's portrayal of millers and continues with his own tale.
6. The Miller shows Alison visiting the church, where Absolon, swinging his smoking censer, sees her and is smitten with her beauty. He prances around to get her attention and offers her mead, honey, and hotcakes. She accepts and consumes them all, then says a curt "Goodbye" and goes home. There, Nicholas

makes a grab for her, but she protests that her husband is jealous and watchful. Nicholas steps on the cat's tail, then says to himself that as a smart college boy, he will be able to trick a carpenter. He goes to his room and pretends to go into a trance. John investigates by following the cat, which enters the room through a small hole. John looks through the hole into Nicholas's room, then breaks the door down on top of the poor cat and comes in. Nicholas shows John a panoramic model of the flood to come and tells the gullible old carpenter to acquire and provision three tubs.

7. Pilgrimage. The Reeve angrily cuts in.
8. The Reeve shows John and Aleyn returning wearily with their horse. After they have supper, they all go to bed. Aleyn tells John that the law provides that if a man loses one thing he has a right to get something else in return. He then sneaks off and jumps into bed with the Miller's daughter. At the end of the bed a large rat looks puzzled.
9. Pilgrimage. The Miller protests once again.
10. The Miller shows Nicholas and Alison stealthily climbing down from their tubs, rushing into bed and enjoying themselves under the flopping covers. Absolon comes and knocks softly at the window. Alison tries to get him to leave, but he refuses until she gives him a kiss. She sticks her bottom out the window and Absolon eagerly kisses it. Then, shocked, he says, "Women don't have beards!"
11. Pilgrimage. The other pilgrims laugh, further angering the Reeve [Note: This is the last transitional cut to the horseback pilgrims until both tales are finished (see scene 18 below)].
12. The Reeve shows Symkyn's wife getting up and going outside to use the toilet. Not to be outdone by Aleyn, John moves the baby cradle so that when the wife returns, she gets into bed with John. Again the blankets quiver. As Aleyn prepares to leave Symkyn's daughter's bed, she weeps and tells him where he can find the flour and the cake she has made with part of it. John heads back to his own bed.
13. The Miller shows Absolon angrily smashing his guitar on the ground, then going off and returning with a red-hot knife-like tool. He asks for a second kiss. This time, after urinating into a chamber pot, Nicolas sticks his bottom out the window. Thinking it is Alison, Absolon asks her to speak so he can direct his kiss. Nicholas farts. When the red-hot knife lights the fart up like a blowtorch, Absolon's face gets scorched.
14. The Reeve shows Aleyn finding the cradle, changing course, and getting into bed with Symkyn. His bragging about his sexual exploits enrages Symkyn, who punches Aleyn and knocks him out against the wall.
15. The Miller shows Absolon striking Nicholas's bottom with the red-hot knife. Nicholas shouts "Water, water!" He then, to cool his scorched bottom, sits in the chamber pot that he has just urinated into. His cry for water wakes John up. Thinking the predicted flood has come, John cuts the rope holding up his tub and comes crashing down. He lands on the bed beside Alison.
16. The Reeve shows Symkyn's wife knocking her husband out with a staff. The boys take their flour and the cake and head back to Cambridge.
17. The Miller shows the neighbors looking in the window and laughing at old John.
18. The pilgrimage. Chaucer tries to make peace between the Miller and the Reeve,

XIX. In Filmic Performance 223

Figure 32. Absolon with his glowing poker in Myerson's animated version of the *Miller's Tale*.

but they are still fighting as the Myerson animated *Canterbury Tales* comes to an end.

There is much to like about the Myerson *Miller's Tale*. It is reasonably faithful to its Chaucerian original even as it eliminates characters like Robyn, Gille, and Gerveys. It is clever. It moves along fast. It makes comedic use of Alison's cleavage as a home for a pet chipmunk and it gives a wider role for the cat. It augments the scatology of the original by having Nicholas piss into a pot and then sit in it to cool his scorched bottom.

Although some scholars have praised Myerson for his interweaving of the *Miller's Tale* and the *Reeve's Tale*,[3] I am not so sure that much is gained, especially for first-time viewers. Those who already know both tales well can separate the two plots and follow the flipping back and forth from one to the other, with jumps also to the reactions of the pilgrims on horseback. Such viewers may enjoy the novelty of the intermixing, but first-time viewers watching the eighteen scenes can only be confused by what they see, particularly since several of the horse-face characters look pretty much alike. The eighteen shifts take place in a time-span of eight minutes, meaning that on average the film jump-cuts every thirty seconds. It is difficult enough to imagine any successful reduction of the *Miller's Tale* to four minutes, but then to have it chopped up by insertions from a different four-minute tale by a different teller—not to mention inserted scenes from the Canterbury pilgrimage—well, how can viewers not be confused?

Peter Bowker (2003)

On September 11, 2003, some eight million television viewers around the world watched a forty-five-minute BBC television drama called the *Miller's Tale*. In the next five weeks they would see modernized versions of five more of the *Canterbury Tales*: the *Knight's Tale*, the *Wife of Bath*, the *Shipman's Tale*, the *Pardoner's Tale*, and the *Man of Law's Tale*. The six tales all had different writers and directors. All were set in the twenty-first century. None had any connection with the other five except through the fact that each was based loosely—very loosely—on some feature of one of Chaucer's Canterbury narratives. None of the tales was part of a pilgrimage or a tale-telling competition.

The BBC *Knight's Tale* is about two working-class prisoners who both fall in love with one of their teachers. The *Wife of Bath's Tale* is about a fifty-something television actress who, after a series of failed marriages, weds a co-star thirty years younger than she. The *Sea Captain's Tale* is about an East Indian couple, Jetender and his unfaithful wife Meena, who live in Gravesend. The *Pardoner's Tale* is about three unemployed drunks who, out of greed, take part in a search for a missing teenager. The *Man of Law's Tale* is about a Nigerian refugee who drifts ashore in a small boat but remembers nothing about who she is or how she got there.

The BBC *Miller's Tale* was written not by Chaucer but by Peter Bowker. Directed by John McKay, it was not told by a miller, does not take place in a university town, has no carpenter, parish clerk, student of astrology, or blacksmith. It has no predicted flood, no suspended tubs. What it has are a pub owner and his wife, a barber who sings karaoke songs, three teenage boys, and a pharmacist. Any viewers familiar with Chaucer's original *Miller's Tale* must have been puzzled by what they saw on their television sets.

The tale opens with a handsome middle-aged man, played by John Nesbitt, driving his red sports car though the English countryside. His car breaks down just outside a karaoke pub in an English village in Kent. As he approaches the pub, he sees the irate old pub owner, played by Dennis Waterman, drag a customer out and threaten to beat him up for gawking at his wife. The sports-car driver leaves his car at the curb and goes into the pub. There he sees a handsome wavy-haired young man, played by Kenny Doughty, singing a karaoke duet with the pub owner's sexy young blonde wife, played by Billie Piper. We

XIX. In Filmic Performance

soon learn that the accidental visitor is a smart but self-centered con-man named Nicholas, that the jealous pub owner is named John Crosby, that the sexy young blonde wife is named Alison Crosby, and that the handsome wavy-haired young man is a local barber of ambiguous sexual preferences named Danny Absolon. If it were not for the four names and the title of this made-for-television drama, viewers would have little reason to think that they were in the world of the *Canterbury Tales* in general or the *Miller's Tale* in particular. For most viewers, only the window scenes at the end of the film would have connected this drama with the fourteenth-century tale that inspired it. The window, however, is not in a bedroom but in a recording studio.

Nicholas (usually referred to as Nick) exploits other people's character flaws—pride, greed, lust, ambition—to trick them into giving him what he wants. He convinces the naive Alison that she has genuine talent as a singer and can, with his help, make the big time. He convinces the rich old John that his wife has the potential to make him even richer. He convinces them both that he is a producer with a major music label and that he has the connections to make all three of them millionaires. Nick is so persuasive that John offers to let him stay in a room at the tavern, thus giving him ready access to Alison. Nick then capitalizes on that access by convincing Alison that he is deeply in love with her and by convincing John to give him a suitcase full of cash so that he can rent and outfit a recording studio to make a demo recording of Alison's singing.

When Absolon emerges as a potential rival and spoiler, Nick visits his barber shop and convinces Absolon that Alison has a crush on him and would respond well if he sang her a romantic love-song at the next karaoke night. Absolon does so, but angers the jealous John, who had all this while thought he was gay. With encouragement from Nick, John now angrily sees Absolon as a potential rival and forcibly ejects him from the pub.

Nick proceeds with the pretense that he is recording Alison's singing in the studio. He encourages John to come along to watch, but gives him drugs that make him pass out in his armchair. With John thus out of the way, Nick joyfully completes his seduction of Alison. After they have made love several times on the studio couch, they hear Absolon singing at the window. Absolon refuses to go away until she gives him a kiss. She then sticks her bottom out the window. Absolon kisses it, but immediately knows that he has been tricked. He fetches a steel pipe and a propane torch and comes back to request a second kiss, telling Alison that he wants to give her a special gift. This time Nick puts his bottom out the window and farts in Absolon's face. Absolon, who has been heating the steel pipe with his propane torch, thrusts the scalding pipe into Nick's backside.

Nich's screams wake old John out of his slumber enough that he can see Alison putting medicine on Nick's burned bottom. Still lost in his loopy drug world, however, John is easily convinced that he had merely dreamed that he saw Alison treating Nick's scorched bottom. John stumbles and falls, breaking his arm in the fall.

Danny Absolon decides to cut off his wavy locks. He shows up at John's pub wearing workman's overalls and a baseball cap, singing a new kind of song. John apparently does not recognize him in his new disguise. Nick and Alison are there watching. Nick's last words to Alison are, "No matter how this turns out, remember, you are better than this."

The next day John, his arm in a cast, is seen opening his bank statements. The statements show that Nick has cleaned out his bank account. He rushes to Nick's room to confront him, only to find that both Nick and his beloved Alison have left. We next see Alison standing, alone, along the highway, apparently hoping to hitch a ride to somewhere. A bus heading from Canterbury to London passes by. In the final scene we see that Nick has gotten on that bus and is starting his next con-man assignation, convincing a young couple about to be married that he works for a company that offers young newlyweds a chance to tell their story on television and make a lot of money. From Nick's sly grin in the closing scene we know that he plans to seduce the bride and rob the young couple of their money.

The BBC *Miller's Tale*, obviously, almost totally reinvents Chaucer's *Miller's Tale*. The silliness of its plot is mitigated by the skilled acting. Although Danny Absolon seems never to figure out who he is or what he wants, old John's fear, jealousy, and anger are convincing. Nick's totally self-serving cynicism is balanced by his cleverness and by his growing conviction that Alison really can sing well and deserves better than the sleazy pub life she gets as the wife of the town bully.

Alison alone grows in the course of the tale. She gains confidence in her own abilities. The genuine love she feels for Nick presents a nice contrast with the affection that Nick can only fake. And as she stands, alone, on the highway waiting for her next adventure, one senses that she is indeed on her way to a far better life than she had with John or than she would have had if she had run off with Nick. There is a huge sign on the pub in the opening sequence of the BBC *Miller's Tale*: "KARAOKE—Your chance to be somebody." Alison starts the tale voicing other peoples songs, pretending to be somebody she is not. By the end she is well-positioned to become somebody, not by lip-synching somebody else's songs, but by voicing her own.

This is not Chaucer's *Miller's Tale*, but it is a good tale nonetheless.

XX
In San Francisco and Southwark: Miller (2014), Machin (2014)

We are fortunate to be able to publish here for the first time two modern retellings of the *Miller's Tale*. The first is a non-dramatic verse tale set in modern San Francisco. The second is a dramatic production that was performed in the summer of 2004 in England. Both retellings are delightfully original in their use of Chaucer's tale as an inspiration for something quite different.

Peter N. Miller (2014)

In the introduction to his *Seven Canterbury Tales*,[1] Peter N. Miller, a retired professor of psychology at Plymouth State University in New Hampshire, describes his first and only academic exposure to Chaucer:

> I was introduced to Chaucer's *Canterbury Tales* the first semester of my freshman year at Antioch College in southwestern Ohio. The year was 1960, the course was Elements of Poetry, and the professor was Dr. Milton Goldberg. Elements of Poetry began with the Psalms of the Old Testament and continued through the medieval era and beyond. One of the texts we purchased for the course was Nevill Coghill's Penguin Classics translation of Chaucer's *Canterbury Tales*. I still have my copy of this book, one of only three books I have owned for more than fifty years. From the underlining and margin comments I made, I know that we were assigned the General Prologue, the *Knight's Tale*, the *Miller's Tale*, and the *Wife of Bath's Prologue* and *Tale*.
>
> I had never read anything quite like the *Miller's Tale*. I marveled at the storytelling art, as well as the absurd plot and intriguing characters. I was entranced with gorgeous Alison, of course. An eighteen-year-old who had not divested himself of his virginity, I was hung up on sex and everything connected with it. And

here was an eighteen-year-old medieval babe who seemed totally comfortable with her sexuality, the forerunner of the Playboy centerfold, a sex kitten.

I majored in psychology and never formally studied Chaucer again. I wrote my improvisation on the *Miller's Tale* around 1995 and revised it during the next several years. My story takes place in San Francisco in the late 1960s. I did my graduate work at Stanford, so I was familiar with the Bay Area during the height of the counter-culture movement. That was a crazy time. The conjunction of "anything goes" sexual liberation and the risk of a catastrophic earthquake sparked my imagination. I thought that Nicholas and Alison would feel right at home in the 1960s Bay Area. An earthquake was a ready-made substitute for Chaucer's flood.

I am grateful to Peter N. Miller for permission to quote from the introduction to his book and the first half of his improvisation of the *Miller's Tale*. Readers will immediately see in the nearly 600 lines quoted below the large departures that Peter Miller made in moving the tale from fourteenth-century Oxford to twentieth-century San Francisco. Most obvious are his changes in characterization: Old John's compulsive work habits and excessive concern with safety and security; Alison's growing conviction as a college student that her marriage to John was a mistake, her decision to select Nicholas as her lover, and her joyful management of the incident with Absolon; Nicholas's sensitivity to Alison's needs and his more passive role in his liaison with her; and Absolon's emphatic but perhaps self-deceptive homophobia. Readers will notice many plot changes as well, the most important being in the scene in which Alison directs Nicholas to disrobe and impersonate her in the bed in which Absolon is to massage her buttocks. But let's let Peter Miller tell the tale without further commentary from me.

The *Miller's Tale* in San Francisco
by Peter N. Miller

> Years ago, near the City by the Bay—
> don't ever call it "Frisco," natives say—
> lived a none-too-bright carpenter named John.
> His wife was young, but he was getting on.
> John's life was guided by a single theme:
> Take no risks! So he lived to the extreme.
> Life was a challenge in warding off threat
> from microbes, acid rain, communists, debt,
> meteorites, floods, drunken drivers, AIDS,
> tumors, thugs, and ultraviolet rays.
> Summed in a word, his personality
> was compulsive, to an absurd degree:
> Methodical, rigid, counting, checking,
> plodding, and predictably fun-wrecking!

XX. In San Francisco and Southwark

A place for all things, all things in their place;
disorder he'd not put up with a trace.
For adventure, he completely lacked thirst.
His hue and cry: Safety always comes first.
     As John was a tight-fisted sort of guy,
forever seeking out the cut-rate buy,
and an obsessive, workaholic bore,
scared the wolf would come calling at his door,
he had, by working long and hard and late,
amassed a goodly chunk of real estate.
He had bought up an entire city block.
Apartment rentals he owned by the flock.
And yet this seldom brought him any cheer.
That he'd end in the poorhouse was his fear.
     Like all obsessives, he was fright-ridden,
just ruthlessly anxiety-driven.
He'd burglar-proofed every window and door
with sirens that the dead could not ignore.
His water sprinklers would douse any flame;
they'd even put Niagara Falls to shame.
About health, he was a true fanatic,
and, disease prevention, most emphatic.
Why he wished a lengthy life was baffling.
Rarely did he know the joy of laughing.
Without gusto and spontaneity,
he was a foreigner to gaiety,
his expressiveness controlled and static
and, toward his wife, utterly pedantic.
His daily edicts were unforgiving.
He missed the point where it came to living.
     To finish presenting my description
of John's most peculiar disposition,
but one more instance shall I now relate.
Know why this man agreed to copulate?
He'd read that sex, engaged in frequently,
kept the prostate, in effect, cancer-free!
     This chucklehead's wife's name was Alison.
But eighteen years of age when she'd wed John,
she could not possibly have understood
that as people move on to adulthood
most of their wishes, wants, and needs mutate.
What once sufficed, at quite a later date
leaves a void, an emptiness, a longing,
that sets body, mind, and heart a-wandering,
causing a painful ache, a cruel distress,
that thrusts one toward another's warm caress.
She was too youthful then to have surmised

that human qualities possess two sides,
that what at first casts such a loving spell,
at a later date utterly repels.
The very traits initially adored
are precisely those soon enough abhorred.
She who seems devoted, so attendant
becomes clinging, stintingly dependent,
and he who seems the pinnacle of strength
flaunts an abusive, domineering bent.
She of beautiful, beguiling aura
soon is blinded by her own mascara,
and he of distant self-sufficiency
proves incapable of intimacy.
   And so it was 'twixt Alison and John.
For when he'd bird-dogged her hither and yon,
emotionally she was still a girl,
unprepared for the hardships of this world.
At eighteen, lacking in maturity,
she wed not for love but security.
In John's compulsively well-ordered life,
she thought she'd found a harbor free from strife.
She misperceived his dull rigidity
as the be-all of masculinity.
"Act in haste, be sad-faced," says wisdom's voice;
Alison soon enough did rue her choice.
By twenty-one, she'd reached that golden age
where feet are firmly planted on life's stage.
In the passage of but a few short years,
she'd rid herself of all her youthful fears,
and with firm hand and calm and steady gaze,
felt quite the queen of all that she appraised.
"Why, there's no challenge to this grown-up thing.
So, why does John his hands forever wring?"
   Soon, disrespect did fond esteem preempt,
and her regard convert to black contempt.
When she took harsh and realistic stock
of all the pros and cons of her wedlock,
she was forced to the bleak observation
that her marriage was without foundation.
She told John of this over and over,
begging and pleading him to grow with her.
He grasped not a word of her palaver.
It felt like speaking to a cadaver.
In these moments of darkest misery,
she wondered, "Is this all life holds for me?
Is it eternally to be my luck
to be a pretty flower left unplucked?"

XX. In San Francisco and Southwark

       The notion that her life represented
the apex of all that God intended
was repugnant. A kind of living death,
her marriage, sans heart, soul, and vital breath.
"Life is meant to be full of jollity,
joyous wonder and gay frivolity,"
she declared. "In this brief hour in the sun,
let us kick our heels high and have some fun.
Time is short, the moment is auspicious;
let's taste every fruit that looks delicious.
From these forms which shall betray us one day,
let's take such earthly pleasure as we may.
Life's what you make it, make the best of it;
so don't you dare just mopingly there sit!"
The blood coursed much too strongly in her veins
for her to be imprisoned by fear's chains.
No way would she accept the destiny
of being a peach left upon the tree.
       She decided, thus, to take a lover.
In this quest, she was more blest than others,
for she was, by far, the most comely lass
whose image ever graced a looking glass.
What a face! One could watch it all the day
and not tire for an instant of the play
of intellect and character on it.
Such coalescence of shape and spirit!
At times profound, at other mischievous,
then innocent or wise or serious,
she seemed like pure poetry in motion.
No artist, with even great devotion,
could have captured the mystery within
which she conveyed with but the subtlest grin.
Those eyes! The clearest penetrating blue,
imperious, yet full of laughter, too.
With confidence did she behold her land,
as only one sure of her beauty can.
One look sufficed to mesmerize most men,
who swore to be her vassals there and then,
Her gaze had the facility, you see,
of radical availability.
Her mouth: Now woundable then later bold,
with a smile such a wonder to behold,
mirth crinkling in the corners of her lips
hinting the phrasing of some clever quip.
Lucky the man to whom she'd give a kiss,
for he would have a taste of earthly bliss.
The hair that framed this most delightful face

fell down in wavy ringlets to her waist,
a lavish mane, conspicuously bold,
sheer lustrous brown, with flecks of red and gold,
done up in numerous distinctive ways,
depending on her mood each given day.
Straight nose, arched brows, high cheekbones, dimpled chin,
made everything symmetrically blend in.
After a single glance at her, one swore
that truth and justice were from beauty born.
   Her figure: tall, lissome, graceful, slender,
strong, fluid, the triumph of her gender,
with a glide as supple as a dancer's,
and a stride as well-knit as a panther's.
Her fool husband, in his compulsive style,
insisted that she daily walk six miles,
do calisthenics, pump heavy iron,
and run forever 'round the gridiron,
all to prevent future diagnosis
of arterial atherosclerosis.
And such was how she came to know apace
the earthy nature with which she was graced.
The more that she worked out to "Buns of Steel,"
the more supremely sexy did she feel.
Her model's body had the condition
of lovely muscular definition,
with the contours of her buttocks and breasts
protruding vividly in every dress.
She was one of those rare human beings
who looked more striking nude than in clothing,
marred not by love handles nor cellulite,
this vision of empyrean delight.
In a silken shift, her body's motion
could create a most distinct commotion.
When she walked by, men's necks turned like swivels,
their gawking, to her, just so much drivel,
for she wished to be cherished completely,
for mind and heart as well as her beauty.
Her future beau could find her form divine
provided that he knew she had a mind.
Not by feminism was she daunted.
She felt that real beauty should be flaunted.
"Hey, girls, what do you say, let's strut our stuff.
It's we who bear God's likeness, sure enough!"
Only the power of God Almighty
could have shaped this Venus Aphrodite,
gorgeous enough to rate a worldly "ten,"
or spark immortal lines from poets' pens.

XX. In San Francisco and Southwark

Do you know what I liked about her best?
She was not spoiled by her loveliness;
a regular gal, very down to earth,
just wanting to be valued for her worth.
  Now, Alison was enrolled at Berkeley,
studying drama and psychology.
For the cross-country team she ran the mile,
and she worked as a model all the while.
Also studying then at Berkeley was
a handsome hunk of guy called Nicholas.
Though Nick's parents believed he was pre-med,
'twas the dissolute sort of life he led,
the sole anatomy that he explored
being women's kind. Dames he did adore,
and they found him equally enchanting.
His appearance was indeed commanding.
Both tall and fair, his face like a Greek god's,
filled out, completely masculine in bod,
he fancied himself a lady-killer,
to mankind a monumental pillar.
On his muscular, broad, and hairy chest
he sported nothing save an open vest
to give his pectorals greater renown.
On his curly head, like a type of crown,
he wore a hat with a peacock feather,
which women found an attention-getter.
He acted like a popular rock star,
and where he wandered, so went his guitar.
When he felt so moved, he would play and sing,
especially amongst a gathering
of pretty coeds. Sweetly sorrowful
were his songs, or joyous, brash, or soulful,
whatever he assumed would best succeed.
That he had a lovely voice, all agreed.
To ensure that he's not been misportrayed,
permit me to immediately say
that he really was a decent fellow,
good-natured, considerate, and mellow,
with evil intentions not afflicted.
He just, to women, was quite addicted.
Black, white, old, young, single, divorced, or wed,
if she were pretty, he would share her bed.
  Acting on the stage was his life's passion.
That's where he first encountered Alison.
He fell in love with her head-over-heels,
and she with him, but kept it well-concealed
so he wouldn't know. That's how she wished it.

She'd make him be the first one to commit.
She knew his life to be a playboy fling;
she'd not be just the next bead on his string.
If a Romeo to her Juliette,
or her chocolate cream soldier, better yet
he'd be, he'd have to pass the stiffest test
and shoulder all the risks in this love-quest.
By the time she'd take him for her lover,
he'd have worked so hard he'd seek no other
fillies. No more roaming for this stallion!
He would learn to be her true companion.
No second place for this Queen of the Skies
in the age-old war between gals and guys.
Seduction in reverse was what she planned.
    So one summer's day, she wrote out by hand
a notice stating that she had for rent
a studio fit for a single gent
in the townhouse complex that she hosted.
This, on a bulletin board, she posted
smack dab in front of Nicky's very face,
as if naive to what was taking place.
She had the other day heard Nicholas
say to a joint acquaintance after class
that in a month his rental would expire
and more convenient lodging he desired.
She made like she'd not heard a whit of this,
nor did she seem, such was her artifice,
to see Nicky standing there beside her,
reading, as she hoped he would, her flyer.
That is how coolly she was playing it.
    Nick quickly made his opening gambit.
"Why, Mistress Alison! I truly say
Dame Fortune's being good to me today,
for is it not a wondrous circumstance
that you should have, by such peculiar chance,
available for rent the very place
that I would like to call my living space?"
"Why, Master Nicholas, what a surprise!
And here I'd just begun to advertise!"
So she described it all in great detail,
and he acknowledged that it was upscale,
especially the pool, which she let slip,
was where she nightly took a private dip.
When he discovered she lived right next door,
that settled everything. He asked no more,
advancing a month's rent right on the spot.
As for how it looked, he cared diddly-squat.

XX. In San Francisco and Southwark

He thought his victory sure as a lock.
Was this conceited guy in for a shock!
All partners past had made the first advance;
he knew not how to lead this kind of dance.
      How she baffled him, seeming like a friend,
yet distant, too, agreeing now and then
to pump heavy metal, take a long run,
play chess, go swimming, or baste in the sun,
like any good pal, just one of the guys.
He couldn't stop ogling her gorgeous thighs.
She'd play to win, then join him for a beer,
slapping his back in most hearty good cheer,
discoursing on subjects light and profound—
even sex! Oh my, how Nick was dumbfound
when she spoke about her sexual needs,
what gave her pleasure, how she liked to please,
not putting the move on him all the while.
Through it all, somehow, he kept up a smile,
although his testicles ached severely,
his ramrod penis showing most clearly.
When she'd do yoga in her leotard,
as quick as a flash, would his prick go hard!
Unmerciful was she with her teasing;
he didn't know if she found him pleasing.
      Finally, he could bear no more of this.
Pulling her close, he gave her a quick kiss,
bellowing with a most piteous cry,
"Babe, love me all at once or I shall die!"
First slapping his hand away from her hip,
she yelled, "Stop! You will ruin our friendship.
Would you throw everything we have away
just for a frivolous roll in the hay?
Where's your respect? Do you think I'm some tramp,
a harlot, a whore, or parading vamp,
a sexual object for men to grope?
To think in you I'd placed my trust and hope!"
      With that said, Nicholas dropped to his knees.
"No, no, my sweet; my apology, please.
I meant no harm. I love you, Alison.
You're the brightest star in heaven, bar none.
You are a queen, an angel from the sky,
and a mere, contemptible fool am I.
I only wished to tell you of my love.
I swear, as my witness is God above,
I've adored you since the day we first met
with a love that's as deep as love can get."
      "Come, come, Nicholas, how very absurd.

Excuse yourself with some four letter word?
And what is this 'love' about which you speak?
Talk man to man; no further hide-and-seek."
  "Umm, umm, umm, umm," stammered poor tongue-tied Nick.
  "Come out with it now," she declared, "be quick!"
  "Why, my love for you defies description.
True love always rejects definition.
Do you command I instantly provide
what even men of learning can't decide?"
  "How very clever, Nicholas, good chap.
Do you feed all your women this same pap?"
  "No other woman shall I take anon
if you'll grant me your love, sweet Alison."
  "I think that you have said these lines before.
Prove I can trust your word forevermore."
  "Alas, dearest heart, that no man can do;
you must take the risk that my love is true."
  "Twould help if we could have some honesty.
With which appendage do you most love me:
Your mind, your heart, or that thing in your pants?"
  "All three equally, for such is romance!
What is a body that hasn't a soul?
Inert, unlovely, an incomplete whole.
The spirit within that invigorates
only mind and heart can appreciate.
What is a soul that lacks an earthly shell?
Mute, without expression, invisible.
Because form and spirit are united,
my love and lust cannot be divided."
  "Very clever, Nicholas! Let me kiss
the mouth that temptingly just spoke all this."
She took him in her most tender embrace,
and then with silken lips caressed his face,
pressing herself against him. "I relent!
To be your eager lover, I'll assent,
if you have the mental ammunition
to meet one last perilous condition."
  "Tell me what it is, and it shall be done,"
he boasted, as he stroked her world-class buns.
  "You know how pleasure can be augmented,
and future interest-loss prevented,
when first one must some barrier surmount,
or delay's unending, pain-filled hours count.
When your challenge at last is overcome,
think of the depths of ecstasy you'll plumb,
anticipation's savory delight
making more sweet our grand, climaxing night.

XX. In San Francisco and Southwark

When this requirement causes you dismay,
consider it the start-up of foreplay."
　　　"I see you mean to put me to the test;
but what, my Alison, do you request?"
　　　"That our trysts take place in my very bed
while my husband, that trifling knucklehead,
is home. There must not be the slightest chance
of his discovering our dalliance.
Here is a hint to help you win the bet:
His life by fear is utterly beset.
Are you up to the task, my sexy man?"
　　　"To be sure, I've already got a plan,
but not a word of it shall I tell you.
You'll soon enough observe my derring-do."
He picked up his guitar and made to strum.
"What would you like to hear, my sugar plum?"
　　　Her impish humor showing not a trace,
she said, "April's in My Mistress's Face."
Nick gave a laugh and then played her request;
together they performed a few duets. They kissed and hugged and
stroked each other's loins.
Both looked forward to being fully joined.
　　　As it so happened, yet another gent
had long been sniffing 'round this minx's scent.
With this cute babe he, too, was most enthralled.
Absolon was what this fellow was called.
He was town clerk and justice of the peace,
and in a pinch would help out the police.
At all the weddings he gave far and wide,
he never yet had failed to kiss the bride
or grope her tits and ass, in point of fact,
"by accident," of course, to hide the act.
He'd dance with her, eyes filled with lechery,
then on the dulcimer play merrily
(if truth be told, but four chords did he know),
and sing in his high-sounding falsetto.
For many guys and gals he'd tied the knot,
but no wife of his own had he yet got,
for he was gangly, mostly skin and bone,
but for his innards, which were overblown.
Of his appearance, he was neglectful,
and, regarding hygiene, most forgetful,
so that, to get right to the point, he smelled,
and by his odor others were repelled.
His self-perception was so out of whack,
he thought for courting babes he had the knack,
and made a pass at every foxy dame,

not one of whom agreed to be his flame.
He hit on each new chick the self-same way,
not asking why his darts had gone astray.
  He carried on like some new-age guru.
Would you believe, mirabile dictu,
he could interpret tea leaves and I Ching,
cure both with herbs and past-life regressing;
teach you the secrets of the pyramids,
or how to free your ego from its id;
generate identical predictions
by reading palms or the stars' positions;
loudly drone the "Om" with finger cymbals,
and make known the use of diverse crystals?
But most of all, he liked to lay on hands.
The healing arts he claimed to understand,
shiatsu, reiki, rolfing, all the rest
(he surely could fling jargon with the best).
Souped-up back rubs, that is what he gave,
and, for pretty women, his fee he'd waive.
Men's bodies he would never touch a lick,
for he was wickedly homophobic.
  Now, this Absolon was the very one
who had married John to dear Alison.
No way did this stop him for a minute
from wanting to love her to the limit.
He'd filched a few quick feels at her wedding;
for lots more, he had for years been fretting.
He saw her fairly often at town hall,
where frequently she'd make a business call,
and she most positively had espied
his lecherously wanton, roving eye.
She'd parry his bawdy innuendo,
prematurely halting his crescendo
time and again. She thought it was a joke.
He felt the time had come to go for broke.
  So, while Nick and Alison were sporting,
Absolon saw fit to come a-courting.
Informed that John was out of town that day,
and thinking this his chance to make his play,
he put on what he called his poet's blouse,
and nonchalantly sauntered to her house.
Dulcimer in hand, he began to sing,
to "Dixie's" bouncy tempo of all things,
"Now, dear lady, if it be your pleasure,
grant this lovesick swain your fullest measure.
Don't dismay, don't dismay, poor Absolon.
For he can massage away your trouble

XX. In San Francisco and Southwark

and with proper herbs your good health double
right away, right away, dear Alison."
   Through his guffaws, Nick asked, "Who's this mooncalf?"
   "Hush," she said, "and we'll have a hearty laugh.
Quick, go and hide in my bedroom upstairs,
and don't show yourself 'til I dash up there."
With shirt unbuttoned, showing lots of skin,
she opened the door, saying "Come right in.
My good man, you must be telepathic!
For hours now, my backside has been spastic.
I'm doubled over in humongous pain.
Do you think you can set me right again?"
   Rubbing his hands, he said, "I guarantee
to immediately soothe your agony."
   "I'll go to my bedroom and get undressed.
Do not come up 'til you hear my request.
Be sure to touch me only where I say.
If with a cloth over my face I lay,
it's on account of my shy modesty."
Upstairs she bounced with barely suppressed glee.
"Come out of there," she whispered to her Nick.
"Take all your clothes off and hop in bed, quick.
Just you lie there; don't say a single word.
From underneath the bed I'll snare this nerd."
   She called him up, and he set right to work,
unaware she was playing him the jerk.
"Oh, my pet, such muscled definition!
You're an Amazon, my fluffy pigeon."
   "I think you're mixing metaphors," she cried.
Her Nicky laughed so hard he shook inside.
"Lower the covers and massage my bum,
for 'tis there that the pain seems coming from,"
she blurted out, "unless it makes you blush
to stroke and knead a lady's naked tush."
   "No, no my thoroughbred, my honeybee,
what you're asking for is my specialty."
Lowering the covers, his voice got coarse.
"What haunches," he snorted, "built like a horse!"
   Then Nicholas began to improvise.
While love-struck Absolon hyperbolized,
Nick shot a monumental burst of gas
from his immortal, gorgeous naked ass!
Now 'twas Alison's turn to bite her tongue.
Poor Absolon, he was so shocked, so stung
he was immobile, speechless for a bit.
He truly knew not what to make of it.
Only some sordid, low-life, little tart

would right into a man's face make a fart.
But Alison's a queen! At last he thought,
"The fault lies in this malady she's caught
that's giving her both pain and flatulence.
Poor dear! How wounded, then, must be her sense
of dignity." Now he would save the day;
her knight in shining armor he would play.
"Pet, don't concern yourself about my nose;
your wind is even sweeter than the rose.
I've got some herbs that can ease your troubles.
I'll run down and fetch them on the double."

    Out from under the bed sprang Alison.
"Keep still; our merrymaking's just begun!"
She scurried to the bathroom hastily,
stripping off her clothes, naked as can be.

    Back came Absolon. "Dearest one," he said,
"please yank that silly towel from your head.
Open up your mouth, turn sideways a bit;
I promise not to stare straight at your tits.
This medicine will cure you, have no fear."

    "I'm in the bathroom; give it to me here."
Absolon felt his pulse go very weak.
Toward the bathroom he crept to take a peak,
his mind fretfully wondering, "What's this?"
He sensed something was terribly amiss.
She stood so he could see her legs and more.
"Teehee," she cried, and BANG she slammed the door.

    What did he see? Was this his fair one's twin?
What dare he make of what he saw within?
And now at last the truth began to dawn
to this most hopelessly bamboozled pawn.
In a trembling voice, he asked, "Who lies there?
Is it you, my sweet, Alison mon cher?"
He snatched the cloth from Nicholas's face.

    "O damnation! What hideous disgrace!
To think that I have touched.—Oh God help me!
My hands are stained for all eternity.
And I have sniffed the fumes of— How perverse!
And my dingus went erect. O foul curse!
I'll get revenge on you someday," he swore.
Out of the house and down the street he tore,
for quite a while hearing the echoing
of Nick and Alison's loud bellowing.

    Then she leapt from the bathroom to the bed.
"Your 'modesty,' where is it now?" he said.

    "By heaven, you're a sprightly one, aren't you!"
And then he mocked, most deftly, impromptu,

XX. In San Francisco and Southwark

"My apple blossom, my ostrich feather,
your eyes like the owl's, skin pink as heather,
my centerfold playmate, my Valkyrie,
my chocolate bonbon, my honeybee,
what haunches, harumph!, built like a bull moose,
come suckle your lamb, my little papoose."
      She playfully gave his shoulder a cuff.
Then he saw that she still was in the buff.
"Hey, let's have a look at you," he exclaimed.
"Great glory be! Not even one as famed
as Michelangelo himself could match
your flowing, graceful lines, my splendid catch."
      "You're not so bad yourself, you handsome jock;
we're like two chips cut from the self-same block."
She asked him to get checked for HIV,
and, 'til they coupled, practice chastity.
That being said, she got quite frolicsome
as a foretaste of what was yet to come.

What was yet to come was the second half of the tale. I cannot take the space to quote it here, but here are a few hints about what happens. To prove that he is worthy of Alison, Nicholas convinces John that the dreaded Big One—the massive earthquake that will destroy San Francisco—is about to happen. Ever obsessive about safety, John builds three reinforced concrete bunkers in the basement. While he sleeps in his, Nicholas and Alison rush upstairs and have mutually satisfying sex. Absolon returns with a hot branding iron in a bucket of coals. This time Alison gets into bed naked. But whereas before Nicholas had impersonated her in bed, this time she impersonates Nicholas by wearing a false phallus made of a foot-long sausage. In his excitement Absolon brands his own buttocks with the branding iron and spills the coals. The resulting fire sets off the fire alarm and the sprinkler system. These wake John, who rushes out to tell the neighbors the earthquake has come. They think he is nuts. The next day Alison files for divorce. Here are the closing six lines:

      That's how Nick and Alison met their match,
      And became one another's true love catch,
      And John let himself be made a cuckold
      (he soon remarried an eighteen-year-old),
      and Absolon scorched himself on the bun.
      God save you all! This tale is done!

Gareth Machin (2014)

In the summer of 2004 Gareth Machin adapted a selection of the *Canterbury Tales* for an outdoor promenade production at the Duke's Playhouse, Lancaster, UK. It was so successful there that he then directed the same play for Southwark Playhouse on London's South Bank, not far from the stop where the original Canterbury pilgrims had gathered the night before their departure. In private correspondence with me Machin said, "We took our audience down Borough High Street on the route the pilgrims would have traveled. The *Miller's Tale* was performed in an adventure playground. It was not a faithful, scholarly adaptation, but worked very effectively for our audiences." Machin is now artistic director at the Salisbury Playhouse in Salisbury, UK.[2]

Machin's *Miller's Tale* is unusual in that it has the individual pilgrims both narrate the tale and take on speaking parts in it. In other words, an actor/pilgrim might refer to himself as "he" in one line and as "I" in the next. Machin distinguishes the two by the use of quotation marks. When a pilgrim tells a part of the tale—that is, acts as co-narrator with the Miller—the lines are not in quotation marks. When a pilgrim delivers lines as a character in the tale, those lines are enclosed in quotation marks. As co-narrators, the other pilgrims not only help the Miller tell his tale, but steal it from him and recreate it to their own liking. This *Miller's Tale*, then, might more accurately be called the *Miller's, Prioress's, Pardoner's, and Nun's Priest's Tale*. Some of the confused authorship of the tale is the result of the Miller's being too drunk to remember the tale he meant to tell. Some of it is the result of his decision to play the role of John the carpenter. He apparently had in mind a more heroic role for himself-as-John, but the other characters refuse to let him play that role. At one point the Miller says of his own tale, "I don't remember this at all."

Of particular interest in this version is the way Machin handled the practical problem of the tubs: how in an outdoor production was he to manage the suspension of the three tubs? His solution was to have Nicholas direct John to build a boat—just one—and made no effort to have John hoist it into a picnic shelter or hang it from a tree limb. Readers will also want to notice the way Machin eliminated the visit to Gervey's blacksmith shop from his version to the *Miller's Tale*. American readers may have some difficulty with the modern British slang—words like "snog"—but they will have no trouble figuring out from context the meaning.

The *Miller's Tale*
by Gareth Machin

MILLER: Now listen, one and all, to what I have to say. But first I'm bound to say I'm drunk. If the words get muddled, just put it down to too much Southwark ale *(Reeling a little.)* Actually, I might need a little help with this.

HARRY *(to audience as* Miller *prepares to speak)*: Ladies and gents, I feel bound to warn you that this'll be a tale of harlotry and sin. If there are those amongst us of a more refined disposition, do pass along. I'm sure there'll be tales of a better sort told further down the road.

MILLER: I shall play John, the carpenter, a rich, handsome fellow from Oxford. And I've got a wife. Someone who's young as blossom, sweet as honey and slender as a weasel *(He smiles lecherously at the Prioress.)* Why, good day, fair Alison!

PRIORESS: Non! Non! Non!

HARRY: You'd better help him along or we'll be here all night.

PRIORESS as ALISON *(gives a big sigh)*: If this is the only way to reach the tavern then so be it. But it will not be the story he wants. For this wife has a roving eye.

MILLER: What?

ALISON: And though the carpenter loves his wife, he is old and she is wild and young.

MILLER: By Jacob's intestines! This is a travesty!

HARRY: Shhh. It's begun.

ALISON: Observing her lecherous eye, the droopy old carpenter kept her locked within the house as if in a cage *(She claps her hands and her minions start to decorate the playing area.)*

PARDONER: I remember now. The carpenter wasn't particularly good at his trade, money was tight, so he took in a lodger.

MILLER: He's a *good* carpenter. Excellent by god!

WIFE OF BATH: Be quiet you Yorkshire pudding. I can't hear a word they're saying.

PARDONER as NICHOLAS: The lodger was a poor student who went by the name of Nicholas the Gallant. Now Nicholas had two particular talents. First, he was a superb astrologer, able to forecast the weather with unnerving accuracy. Second, he was a masterful lover.

WIFE OF BATH: Ooh, I can feel a tickling in my root.

NICHOLAS: He was particularly skilled at seducing women in secret. To that end, he decked his room with herbs and fruit—a concoction that produced a fragrant odor *(His room is suitably furnished.)* Then, as night fell, he would play the harp and sing in melodious voice:

> *I love love, love loves me.*
> *I love you, you love me.*
> *Love, love, love, all around.*
> *Up above, on the ground.*
> *I love love, love loves me.*
> *I love you, you love me.*
> *Love, love, love, blows your mind,*
> *From the front, and ... you've got a dirty mind!*

It didn't take long before Nicholas's promiscuous gaze settled upon Alison's pretty rump. One day, while the older, uglier, and fatter man was out buying wood, the young lover began to romp and frolic. In a mood of play he caught her by the queinte. "O Alison, love me all at once or I shall die!"

ALISON: "Give over, Nicholas."
NICHOLAS: "I will have my wicked way or else die of unrequited love!"
ALISON: "Let me go or I shall scream! Where are your manners? Take away your paws!"
NICHOLAS: "Swear you love me."
ALISON *(still struggling)*: "All right, I love you!"
NICHOLAS: "You do?"
ALISON *(thinking about it)*: "Actually, I do. Quite!"
NICHOLAS *(swooning)*: "Oh Alison!"
ALISON *(likewise)*: "Oh Nicholas!" *(They go into a big snog.)* "But Nicholas, my husband is full of jealousy. If he discovers our love, he will kill me."
NICHOLAS *(cocky)*: "Then I will hatch a fiendishly clever plan so that we can love the night away."
ALISON: "Oh Nicholas!"
NICHOLAS: "Oh Alison!" *(A further snog.)*
MILLER: I don't remember this at all.
WIFE OF BATH *(to Nun's Priest)*: I think it's time you joined in little lover boy. Don't want to be left out of the fun, do you?
NUN'S PRIEST: Yes, quite, erm.... Well, Alison also had another admirer who went by the name of Absolon. He was a bit of a singer too—a chorister indeed at the local church:

> *I wrote this tune, and sing it now,*
> *With furrowed brow, for Alisoon.*
> *She makes me swoon, she makes me sigh,*
> *She makes me cry, oh Alisoon.*

Though perhaps not as accomplished as his rival, he sang and pined and sang and pined until his heart was in an unrequited whirl. One night, with the moon full and fierce, he made his way to the carpenter's house. Bursting with slightly off-key song, he placed himself under the carpenter's bedroom window (*We see John and Alison tucked up in bed. John snores loudly. The Nun's Priest as Absolon sings his love song.*)

JOHN *(awakening)*: "Alison! Wife! Do you hear him? It's Absolon chanting away under our chamber wall."
ALISON: "Yes, John. God knows I hear it all. He's a little twerp. Go back to sleep."
JOHN: "He's singing about love—very badly."
ALISON: "I think he's got a crush on that young lodger, Nicholas. You know what these church people are like."
JOHN: "Oh aye. Well, fair enough."
ALISON: "Go back to sleep."
JOHN: "Aye, that'll be best" (*They both turn over and go back to sleep but Alison immediately springs up.*)

XX. In San Francisco and Southwark

ALISON: Truth to tell, Alison was not much interested in the affections of the local choir boy. Nicholas's geomancing genius had cut her to the quick.
ABSOLON: The more Absolon wooed, the more he became woe-begone. He sent her gifts *(hands her a parcel)*.
ALISON: "No ta."
ABSOLON: He offered her money *(gets out his money pouch)*.
ALISON: "No ta."
ABSOLON: He trilled and roulated like a nightingale *(does so)*.
ALISON: "Will you bloody shut up!"
ABSOLON: Once he even played the part of Herod on the stage in the hope that his, not inconsiderable, talent might win her over. But all to no avail. For Alison was in love with Nicholas.
NICHOLAS: And so it happened that one Saturday, with the carpenter out buying nails, Nicholas and Alison agreed at last on what was to be done.
ALISON: "If this plan works then I will sleep with you all night long!" *(They snog.)*
NICHOLAS: And Nicholas took to his room where he lay upon his bed without a sound.
JOHN: When the carpenter returned and asked after Nicholas, Alison replied:
ALISON: "I have not set eyes on him all day. I think he must be ill."
JOHN: "That'll be his book-studying. How blessed are we that are simple!" *(He charges into Nicholas's room and discovers him lying flat on his back, gaping upwards into air.)* "What, Nicholas! Hey! Look down! Wake up!"
NICHOLAS *(sitting bolt upright, as if possessed)*: "And must it come to pass? Must all the world be cast away?"
JOHN: "You've over-heated your brain, you daft bugger."
NICHOLAS: "I must speak of something touching you and touching me."
JOHN: "Uh-huh?"
NICHOLAS: "It concerns your, it concerns your ... "
JOHN: "My ... ? What are you saying man?"
NICHOLAS: "Your wife. I forget her name."
JOHN: "My Alison."
NICHOLAS: "Your Alison."
JOHN: "What is it?"
NICHOLAS: "I can tell you, John, my dear, my excellent host, but first you must swear on your honor not to repeat a syllable I say. For these are divine intentions I have glimpsed."
JOHN: "Divine?"
NICHOLAS: "John, I have been looking at the moon when it was bright and strange patterns in the spheres are apparent. Believe me when I say that tomorrow night, in the dead still hours, rain is to fall in torrents twice as bad as Noah's Flood."
JOHN: "That's a lot of rain."
NICHOLAS: "So much rain that this world, in little more than an hour, shall all be drowned."
JOHN: "Drowned?"
NICHOLAS: "Drowned."
JOHN: "But ... but ... my wife! My little Alison! Is she to drown?"

NICHOLAS: "Loss of life shall be total."
JOHN: "You swear this on your favorite bed-time read?"
NICHOLAS: "I swear it on Chaucer's *Canterbury Tales*."
JOHN: "You speak in truth then. But is there no remedy?"
NICHOLAS: "Thanks be to God, there is. If you will do exactly as I say. In order to survive the flood, you must build a boat."
JOHN: "A boat?"
NICHOLAS: "Aye."
JOHN: "You go to university for that kind of wisdom, do you?"
NICHOLAS: "Hear me out. You must build this boat and let it rest on the ground outside the house. Tomorrow night you will have to sleep in the vessel to wait for the rain."
JOHN: "What about ... ?"
NICHOLAS: "I'm coming to that. It will be very, very cold tomorrow night. Too cold for myself in this sickly state, and too cold for the delicate Alison. That is why you must stake out the vessel alone."
JOHN: "What about me? I don't want to catch a chill."
NICHOLAS: "That is why you must fortify yourself with alcohol. You must consume an entire bottle of strong spirits in order to keep the chill at bay."
JOHN: "That sounds wise."
NICHOLAS: "Then, when you hear the rain falling, you must shout for Alison and myself and we will come running to the boat. Together we can float until the waters drain away, a time when we shall be lords of all the world."
JOHN: "Fancy!"
NICHOLAS: "These are your orders. Get building and tomorrow night, when everyone's asleep, creep into the boat and await Heaven's grace. Now go, save our lives. God's speed!"
ALISON: And so the silly carpenter went on his way, telling his wife in strictest secrecy. "Alas! Whatever it may cost, hurry and help or we shall all be lost. I am your honest, true and wedded wife, so go, dearest husband and save my life!"
NICHOLAS: All through the night and following day he worked. Finally, as dusk began to fall on the night of the flood, the boat was complete (*The "boat" sits on the ground outside the house. The carpenter has also lined up an impressive supply of alcohol.*)
JOHN: "I name this boat the *Alison*" (*Nicholas makes to smash a bottle of whiskey against the boat.*) "Hey! What do you think you're doing?"
ALISON: "John! It's traditional."
JOHN: "My arse! That's good liquor!" (*He drinks from the bottle.*)
NICHOLAS: "It's getting a bit chilly."
JOHN: "You'd best be getting inside then. Leave the man's work to the man."
ALISON: "Oh John, I'm so proud of you. But be sure to drink up, we don't want you dying of a chill."
JOHN: "Cease your mithering and get inside. I'll call when the first drops start to fall" (*Alison and Nicholas go inside and watch John.*)
NICHOLAS: Just as the amorous couple had planned, exhausted by his work and aided by drink, the carpenter was soon sound asleep (*John starts to snore.*)
ALISON (*softly*): Nicholas and Alison moved to the bedchamber.

XX. In San Francisco and Southwark

NICHOLAS: And where the carpenter was wont to lie, the revels began! *(They disappear into the bedroom.)*
ABSOLON: Now Absolon, having received intelligence that the carpenter was away buying a new hammer, resolved to force his affections upon the reluctant Alison that very night: "I shall tap upon Alison's window and tell her all about my love-longing. My mouth is itching for a kiss. I must feel her lips upon mine or I'll go mad. Tongues would be nice too" *(He chews upon some liquorice to sweeten his breath and straightens his hair before advancing upon the house and taking up a position beneath the window which stands no higher than his breast. He coughs and sings):*

> "Pretty sparrow, let my love-lorn dart,
> A burning arrow, pierce your heart.
> Where 'er I go, I sweat for love,
> I croon with longing, like a turtle dove."

ALISON *(at window)*: "Go away, you tuneless church mouse! I want to get some sleep."
ABSOLON: "Alas! True love is always mocked."
ALISON: "Go to hell!"
ABSOLON: "For Jesu's love kiss me, sweetheart."
ALISON: "And if I do, will you clear off?"
ABSOLON: "I promise you, my darling."
ALISON: "Get ready then. Wait while I put something on" *(Absolon turns away in ecstasy and Nicholas appears at the window. To Nicholas.)* "Hush. This'll get rid of the strangled cat."
ABSOLON *(upon his knees)*: "A kiss! I am a lord! And there may be more to come!" *(Alison hangs her arse out of the window.)*
ALISON: "Get on with it then, the neighbors here are always peering through their shutters."
ABSOLON *(climbing to the window)*: "Mercy, my love! Your mouth, my chicken!" *(He kisses her arse but starts back.)* "What!? Rough and hairy? This woman's got a beard! Can that be you Alison?"
ALISON *(removing her arse)*: "Tee hee!"
NICHOLAS: "A beard! A beard!"
ABSOLON *(shocked)*: "Nicholas!"
NICHOLAS: "You just kissed her arse, old chum!" *(He dissolves in laughter.)*
ABSOLON: "Ughh!" *(He begins to frenetically scrub his lips clean.)* "I'll pay you back for that. I'll take my soul and sell it to the Devil but I'll be revenged upon you! O God, why did I let myself be fooled?" *(He exits, enraged.)*
NICHOLAS: "An excellent trick, my little carpenter's wife" *(They start to kiss again. Absolon re-enters carrying a red-hot poker. He coughs just like last time.)*
ABSOLON: "Oh Alison!"
ALISON: "Not again?"
ABSOLON: "It is I. Your own Absolon, my little flower-leaf. Look what I've brought you, a big shiny ring my mother gave me. It's very fine and prettily engraved. I'll give it to you, darling, for one more kiss."
NICHOLAS *(unheard by Absolon)*: "Saucy Alison, I think I can improve upon our jape! Tell him you agree."

ALISON: "Oh all right, Absolon. If you must" *(Nicholas hangs his arse out of the window. Absolon climbs to the window, unable to see clearly in the dark.)*
ABSOLON: "Speak, pretty bird. I know not where thou art!" *(Nicholas lets out an enormous fart—as loud as a thunder-clap—which half blinds Absolon, who whacks Nicholas on the arse with the hot iron.)*
NICHOLAS: "Ahhh! Help! Water! Water! Help! For Heaven's love!"
ALISON: "Water! Water! Help us! We need water!" *(As Absolon staggers around from the force of the fart and Nicholas and Alison attempt to cool the pain on his buttocks, John wakes up in a drunken state.)*
JOHN: "What's that? Water? Heaven help us! Here comes Noah's Flood! Alison! Nicholas! Come quick, the waters are rising" *(He starts to hoist a sail and paddle furiously. A large crowd, attracted by the noise gathers around him.)*
CROWD: "What? What's he saying? Something about Noah?"
JOHN: "Hoist the main sail, scrub the decks, weigh the anchor, man the life boats, full speed ahead!" *(He stops seeing everyone around him. Nicholas steps forward, with Alison still attending his burnt bum.)*
NICHOLAS: "Dear friends, I have to report that the poor fellow's crazy. And drunk. Smell his breath."
CROWD: "Disgusting. Silly old fool. He's lost his marbles."
JOHN *(as it slowly dawns on him)*: "I've been duped! God bring the two of you to Kingdom come."

Interest in the *Miller's Tale* shows no signs of abating. There is something about this tale that fascinated the Middle Dutch author of *Heile of Beersele*, that fascinated Chaucer, that fascinated early readers, and that continues to fascinate modern ones. Is it the foray into sexuality and scatology that captures us? Is it foolish old John who convinces himself that he is both man enough to satisfy a pretty young wife and virtuous enough to be selected by God to be a second Noah? Is it raunchy Nicholas who is too sure both of his own intellect and of his sexual superiority? Is it foppish Absolon who refuses to accept refusal and sees rejection as a call for revenge? Is it the lovely Alison who is both animal enough to enjoy her body and human enough to know how to use it to reward the men she likes? Is it the cleverness of the plot in which a thunderclap of a fart directs the thrust of a hot coulter, which calls forth an anguished cry for water, which causes a man to chop a rope? Is it that the tale stands in stark contrast with both the refined morality of the tale that it follows and with the nasty immorality of the tale that follows it?

It is, of course, all of those, and much more. A major thesis of this book is that much of the appeal of the *Miller's Tale* is its theatricality. In Part One I have showed some of the ways Chaucer transformed the quite undramatic anecdote he found in *Heile of Beersele* into something very like a play. In Part Two I have showed how, following Chaucer's lead, later retellers of the *Miller's Tale* have transformed it into all sorts of genres, but most dramatically into plays and films.

XX. In San Francisco and Southwark

In Part One we saw that the *Miller's Tale* is a thing of the past. In Part Two we have seen that it is thing of the present. Surely it will be a thing of the future, as well. Who can guess in what format, in what setting, with what people, and on what stage it will next appear? Who can guess how many more lives this lively story will live?

Chapter Notes

Introduction

1. George Lyman Kittredge, *Chaucer and His Poetry* (Cambridge: Harvard University Press, 1915, 1972).
2. The Miller picks up the phrase in line 3126, probably spoken with more than a hint of sarcasm. Unless otherwise noted, all of my Chaucerian quotations in this book are taken from the Miller's prologue and tale in Fragment A (I) of the Larry D. Benson, ed., *The Riverside Chaucer*, 3rd edition (Boston: Houghton Mifflin, 1987). When I quote from something not in the first fragment, I give the appropriate fragment designation. Where I depart from the *Riverside* wording or punctuation, I call attention to the departure in my notes. Where I quote a passage in which I leave out some words, I use brackets and three unspaced dots: [...]. Where I cut whole lines or paragraphs the bracketed three dots exist on their own line. Where I quote a passage in which there is already an ellipsis, I use unbracketed spaced dots: .... To avoid confusion, I have regularized the spelling of names. Alison (rather than Alisoun or Allison or Alisoon), Nicholas (not Nicolas), Absolon (not Absolom or Absalon), Robyn (not Robin), Gille (not Gill or Jill), and Gerveys (not Gervais or Jarvis).
3. For discussions of some possible implications of the reference to Pilate, see Edmund Reiss, "Chaucer's Miller, Pilate, and the Devil," *Annuale Mediaevale* 5 (1964): 21–25; Peter F. Mullany, "Chaucer's Miller and Pilates Voys," *American Notes and Queries* 3 (1964): 54–55; and Sandra Pierson Prior, "Parodying Topology and the Mystery Plays in the *Miller's Tale*," *Journal of Medieval and Renaissance Studies* 16 (1986): 71–73.
4. In "Chaucer's Records of Early English Drama," published in volume 2 (1988) of *Records of Early English Drama*, Ruby Wallrich reports that "Absolon's performance on a scaffold high is, in fact, emerging as the more usual method of production from fifteenth-century records" (p. 15). It had earlier been thought that pageant wagons were the dominant method of staging medieval plays. As V. A. Kolve points out, this reference to Absolon's role is the "only evidence that Oxford had plays in the fourteenth century" (*Chaucer and the Imagery of Narrative: The First Five Canterbury Tales* [Stanford: Stanford University Press,1984], p. 205).
5. It is not a part of my scheme here to analyze in detail the selection of Herod as the person Absolon portrays. Readers interested in considering the appropriateness of Herod to the actions and personality of Absolon will want to consult the work of Tracey Cummings in Peter G. Beidler et al., "Dramatic Intertextuality in the *Miller's Tale*: Chaucer's Use of Characters from Medieval Drama as Foils for John, Alison, Nicholas, and Absolon," *Chaucer Yearbook* 3 (1996): 1–19. In that article we argue that characters in various medieval plays provide an implied backdrop against which the four central characters in Chaucer's tale, by comparison, appear to be comically diminished. Cumming's ideas on Absolon as Herod appear on pp. 13–16. See also Claire Sponsler's *Drama and Resistance: Bodies, Goods, and Theatricality in Late Me-*

dieval England (Minneapolis: University of Minnesota Press, 1997), pp. 140–46. My own view is that Absolon's supposition that Alison, who is in various ways a comic representation of the Virgin Mary, could be impressed with the rantings of Herod, shows his utter foolishness. It was Herod, after all, who murdered the male children in Bethlehem in an effort to destroy the baby Jesus, son of Mary. It is interesting, incidentally, that Alison fears that the person knocking at her window is a thief: "Who is ther / That knokketh so? I warante it a theef" (3790–91). As Sponsler points out, in more than one of the Herod plays, Herod and his henchmen were portrayed as thieves of children (see p. 144). Sponsler does not discuss Chaucer's reference to Herod, but Alison's thinking that Absolon is a thief may be a veiled allusion to the role that Absolon plays on the scaffold to impress her.

6. See the sections by Jennifer McNamara Bailey and Christine G. Berg in Beidler et al., "Dramatic Intertextuality," pp. 1–5. For an attempt to determine the exegetical significance of Noah's wife in medieval plays, see Alfred David, "Noah's Wife's Flood" in *The Performance of Middle English Culture*, ed. James J. Paxson, Lawrence M. Clopper, and Sylvia Tomasch (Woodbridge, Suffolk: D. S. Brewer, 1998), pp. 97–109. David's central point that Noah's wife is in league with the devil has no obvious bearing on the *Miller's Tale*.

7. See the sections by Sister Elaine Marie Glanz and Anne M. Dickson in Beidler, et al., "Dramatic Intertextuality," pp. 7–13.

8. Beryl Rowland presents evidence for reading "game" as play or drama in "The Play of the *Miller's Tale*: A Game within a Game," *Chaucer Review* 5 (1970), especially pp. 141–42.

9. Several scholars have noted certain broad "dramatic" qualities of the *Miller's Tale*. Charles A. Owen, Jr., for example, notes that in the *Miller's Tale* "scenes are permitted dramatic fullness. Dialogue and action present repeatedly the surprisingly characteristic facet of character" (*Pilgrimage and Storytelling in the* Canterbury Tales: *The Dialectic of "Ernest" and "Game"* [Norman: University of Oklahoma Press, 1977], p. 100). I am preceded in connecting the *Miller's Tale* more specifically with the drama by several studies. The third footnote of Beidler, et al., "Dramatic Intertextuality," cites several of the more important studies, including the ground-breaking article by Kelsey B. Harder, "Chaucer's Use of the Mystery Plays in the *Miller's Tale*," *Modern Language Quarterly* 17 (1956): 193–98. I refer to specific portions of that article in my next several notes. Published since my students and I wrote "Dramatic Intertextuality" is a stimulating article by Enrico Giaccherini, "Theatrical Chaucer," in *European Medieval Drama* 2 (1998): 85–98. After a general discussion in which he tries to show that "a pervasive theatricality was characteristic of the Middle Ages, to the extent that it often renders excessively difficult, and sometimes futile, our efforts to distinguish and categorize poetic texts and genres that share fundamentally homogeneous techniques of performance" (p. 87), he focuses several pages on the general theatricality of the *Miller's Tale*. His article makes no reference to Chaucer's source for the tale or to the various comparisons that *Heile of Beersele* leads us to. Sandra Pierson Prior's "Parodying Topology and the Mystery Plays in the *Miller's Tale*," *Journal of Medieval and Renaissance Studies* 16 (1986): 51–73, is useful, though I am not persuaded that in the *Miller's Tale* Chaucer is constructing an elaborate parody of medieval mystery plays.

10. Kathleen Forni; *Chaucer's Afterlife: Adaptations in Recent Popular Culture* (Jefferson, NC: McFarland, 2013). See especially chapter 1, "Modes of Intertextual Engagement," pp. 21–60.

11. We sometimes have reason to suspect that writers may have economic reasons for seeking to establish a connection with Chaucer's *Miller's Tale* even when none exists. Margaret Silf's *The Miller's Tale and Other Parables* (London: Darton Longman and Todd, 2000) has nothing to do with Chaucer. Margaret Silf is a spiritual writer. G. A. Hauser's *Miller's Tale* (Lexington, KY: The G. A. Hauser Collection, 2007), has no connection with Chaucer's famous story. Rather, it is about the adventures of a Los Angeles policeman named Steve Miller who falls in love with a beautiful African American lawyer.

Chapter I

1. Many and varied are the possible influences on the *Miller's Tale*. It is widely accepted now that Chaucer was familiar with Boccaccio's mid-fourteenth century *De-*

cameron and that it influenced the *Miller's Tale*. See, for example, Donald McGrady, "Chaucer and the *Decameron* Reconsidered," *Chaucer Review* 12 (1970): 1–26, and my "Just Say Yes: Chaucer Did Know the *Decameron*," pp. 25–46 in Leonard Michael Koff and Brenda Deen Schildgen, eds., *The Decameron and the Canterbury Tales* (Madison, NJ: Fairleigh Dickinson University Press, 1999).

2. For my extended argument that Chaucer may well have known and been influenced by *Lippijn*, and for Therese Decker's literal translation of the full play, see "*Lippijn*: A Middle Dutch Source for the *Merchant's Tale*?" in the *Chaucer Review* 24 (1989): 236–50. For translations and discussions of two more of the Hulthem manuscript farces, see two special issues, edited by me and Therese Decker, of the *Canadian Journal of Netherlandic Studies*, volumes 15.2 (Spring 1995) and 17.2 (Fall 1997).

3. For a more extended account of the evidence for considering *Heile of Beersele* as the probably source of the *Miller's Tale*, see Peter G. Beidler, "*The Miller's Tale*" in *Sources and Analogues of the Canterbury Tales*, ed. Robert Correale and Mary Hamel (Woodbridge, Suffolk: D.S. Brewer, 2005), II, 249–75. The summary of *Heile of Beersele* given below is based on the text and translation provided in that chapter. All quotations from the Middle Dutch tale are from this edition. The bracketed translations of those quotations, sometimes simplified, are generally my own. Frederick M. Biggs and Laura L. Howes in "Theofany in the *Miller's Tale*," *Medium Ævum* 65 (1996), have suggested that "the author of *Heile* was influenced by Chaucer's version" (p. 273) rather than that it was itself the source for the *Miller's Tale*, or that both descended from a common French original. Biggs argues that view again in "The *Miller's Tale* and *Heile of Beersele*," *Review of English Studies*, n.s. 56 (2005): 497–523. For reasons that I present in the chapter in *Sources and Analogues*, however, I think it unlikely that *Heile of Beersele* was written after Chaucer wrote the *Miller's Tale*. In any case, the general similarity of the two tales and, more important, the many differences between them, provide a basis for the comparisons that I discuss in this and the following chapters. Whichever came first, the *Miller's Tale* is infinitely more drama-like than *Heile of Beersele*.

4. My calculations are necessarily rough. To find comparable lengths for the Middle Dutch eight-syllable as opposed to the English ten-syllable lines, I have estimated the number of syllables in each scene. That is, I multiplied the 177 lines of *Heile of Beersele* by eight, the number of syllables per line, for a total of 1416 syllables. I multiplied the 668 lines of the *Miller's Tale* by ten, for a total of 6680 syllables. The ratio of the syllables in the Middle Dutch and the English versions is roughly 1:5. I must emphasize, of course, that these are estimates, not exact figures. We all know that Chaucer sometimes gives us a nine-syllable line and more often gives us eleven-syllable ones. Still, rough though my estimates are, they give us a useful approximation of the comparative lengths of the two tales, excluding in both cases the pre-narrative prologues.

Chapter II

1. Thomas J. Farrell in "Privacy and the Boundaries of Fabliau in the *Miller's Tale*," *ELH* 56 (1989), hints at part of what I am getting at in this section: "Nicholas clearly stages a fabliau" and Absolon makes a "comically inept effort to compose a courtly romance" (p. 781). Farrell, however, makes little of the contrasting genres and suggests none for John or Alison.

2. Gerald Thomas Chambers, *Four Domestic Farces of Medieval France* (Ann Arbor: Xerox University Microfilms, 1975), pp. 29–30.

3. Sandra Pierson Prior, in "Parodying Typology and the Mystery Plays in the *Miller's Tale*," *Journal of Medieval and Renaissance Studies* 16 (1986), refers to Nicholas as "a play inventor and play director" (p. 65).

4. For a discussion of Absolon's confusion of Alison with the Virgin Mary, see my "'Now, deere lady': Absolon's Marian Couplet in the *Miller's Tale*," *Chaucer Review* 39 (2004): 219–22.

5. In "The Misdirected Kiss and the Lover's Malady in Chaucer's *Miller's Tale*" (in Julian N. Wasserman and Robert J. Blanch, eds., *Chaucer in the Eighties* [Syracuse: Syracuse University Press, 1986], pp. 223–33), Edward C. Schweitzer points out that for certain medieval authorities the best way to cure a man of his love "malady" was to confront him with the physical horrors of women, espe-

cially old women: their ugliness, their drunkenness, their odors, their bodily fluids like urine and menstrual blood. One questions, of course, whether a man who could be so easily horrified by exposure to a woman's nether parts was ever all that interested in real women to begin with. Nicholas is not horrified at all. It may be that Absolon's interest in being Alison's lover is mere pretense—in short, playacting.

6. In *The Staging of Drama in the Medieval Church* (Cranbury, NJ: Associated University Presses, 2002), Dunbar H. Ogden says that "acts showing awe, homage, humility, respect, or reverence almost always involve bowing the head, kneeling, or prostration" (p. 165).

7. Anyone familiar with the Herod of biblical drama, of course, would have seen reflected in Absolon's genuine anger at the misdirected kiss the play-anger he would have performed as Herod. According to Ogden, anger was not only one of the seven deadly sins, but was also associated in the drama with Herod: "Displays of anger belong almost exclusively to Herod's province, to his discovery of prophecies concerning the Christ Child, his reaction to the detour taken by the Magi, and his threat of murdering the innocents" (p. 167). Chaucer's selection of the angry Herod as Absolon's stage-role was surely made in careful anticipation of his role as the angry spurned lover later in the story.

Chapter III

1. We recall here the detailed description of Sir Thopas, the effeminate knight whom Chaucer spends several lines describing (see particularly VII 725-35).

2. Dunbar H. Ogden in *The Staging of Drama in the Medieval Church* (Cranbury, NJ: Associated University Presses, 2002) talks about the use of costume as a "major means of characterization" (p. 164). Ogden bases his statement on printed stage directions in biblical dramas designed to be played in the churches.

3. Others have discussed the role of music in the *Miller's Tale*. R. E. Kaske in "The Canticum Canticorum in the *Miller's Tale*," *Studies in Philology* 59 (1962): 479-500 sees in the tale humorous parodic allusions to the *Song of Songs*. Jesse M. Gellrich in "The Parody of Medieval Music in the *Miller's Tale*," *Journal of English and Germanic Philology* 73 (1974): 176-88 suggests that Chaucer provides "musical imagery to juxtapose the erotic action in the tale, a juxtaposition which establishes—I take it—a basic comic incongruity between spirituality and carnality" (p. 176). More useful is William F. Woods's suggestion in "Private and Public Space in the *Miller's Tale*," *Chaucer Review* 29 (1994): 166-78, that there is a structural element to the references to music. Even so, I find myself not quite convinced by Woods's thesis that "each of the five episodes begins with one of the characters leaving or having left the house, creating an apparent opportunity for Nicholas or Absalon to approach Alyson. Each time, the following interaction ends with a kind of music" (p. 167). For one thing, I see more than five "episodes" in the tale, and I find that Chaucer's references to music are not quite so carefully positioned. I agree with all three writers, of course, that music plays an important role in the *Miller's Tale*.

4. I am not persuaded by Gellrich's suggestion that there is exegetical significance to Nicholas's use of a psaltery: "Since the instrument is made of gut stretched over wood, it represents the body of man (his 'flesh') or the crucified body of Christ whose flesh was stretched across the wood of the cross" ("Parody" 179).

5. The identification of these two songs has occupied a number of Chaucerians over the years. See the "Parody" article by Gellrich and his note 6 on p. 177. The "Kynges Noote" has never been persuasively identified. See the helpful notes to lines 3216 and 3217 in the *Riverside Chaucer*, p. 844. In addition to the more obvious references to music, there are other possible ones. In the *Riverside* notes Douglas Gray reports that phrases like "deerne love" in line 3200 and "love-longynge" in 3349 were common in medieval verses.

Chapter IV

1. The term "Chaucerian realism," of course, is fraught with ambiguous meanings. In his *Chaucerian Realism* (Cambridge: D. S. Brewer, 1994), Robert Myles identifies some of the kinds of realism that philosophical and semiological semanticists talk about: foundational realism, epistemological realism, ethical realism, semiotic and linguistic realism,

intentional realism, psychological realism, Cratylic realism, scholastic realism, and so on (see pp. 1-2 for some preliminary definitions). By "realism" I mean something much simpler: that the actions of the characters would have been recognized as plausible by readers, who would be more likely to say, "Yeah, that is possible" rather than "Hey, no way would people I know do that." My thinking here is more in line with that of Dieter Mehl, who speaks in *Geoffrey Chaucer: An Introduction to His Narrative Poetry* (Cambridge: Cambridge University Press, 1986) of "the precise details of observed every day life" in the *Miller's Tale*. We get, Mehl says, "a sense of watching a more familiar world, a world that does not demand abstract reflection but only an immediate human fellow-feeling" (p. 175).

2. By not mentioning the number here, Chaucer is consistent with his behavior elsewhere. In three of the four most likely sources for the *Reeve's Tale* (conveniently gathered together and translated in volume 1 of *Sources and Analogues of the Canterbury Tales*, ed. Robert M. Correale and Mary Hamel (Cambridge: D. S. Brewer, 2002) the first lover brags that he has made love to the young woman six or seven times. Chaucer tells us only that Aleyn and Malyne "were aton" (4197). To be sure, Aleyn later brags that he has "swyved" Malyne "thries" (see lines 4265-66), but the context suggests that that number is almost certainly the result of a bragging college-boy exaggerating his prowess to his college chum. There is no bragging in *Heile of Beersele*, where the number is stated by the narrator as a fact.

3. J. A. W. Bennett tells us in *Chaucer at Oxford and at Cambridge* (Oxford: Clarendon Press, 1974) that "blacksmiths customarily worked at night to early morning—the best time to repair gear or 'tip' ploughshares that were needed on the morrow" (p. 41).

4. I cannot agree with the thread of criticism that sees Absolon's act as sodomitic. See, for example, Roy Peter Clark, "Christmas Games in the *Miller's Tale*," *Studies in Short Fiction* 13 (1976): "The 'kultour' is a phallus-shaped weapon. [...] Absolon's thrusting of the hot iron up Nicholas's rear is an act of symbolic buggery" (p. 283). More recently, Mark Miller, in "Naturalism and Its Discontents in the *Miller's Tale*," *ELH* 67 (2000), speaks of "the humiliation and pain of anal penetration by Absolon's hot borrowed blade" (p. 18). There is no penetration in the *Miller's Tale*.

5. A minor change in the direction of realism in the *Miller's Tale* is that Nicholas has John provide the tubs with "an ax to smyte the corde atwo" (3569), and that John at the appropriate time uses it: "And with his ax he smoot the corde atwo" (3820). Willem is not said to have any cutting instrument in the trough with him, but, manages in his panic to produce a knife from somewhere: "Sijn mes hi gegrepe / Ende sneet ontwee den repe" (161-62) [He gripped his knife and cut the rope].

6. For example, see Robert A. Pratt, "Was Robyn the Miller's Youth Misspent?" *Modern Language Notes* 59 (1944): 47-49, and Charles Long, "The Miller's True Story," *Interpretations* 6 (1974): 7-16. Long thinks that the events of the *Miller's Tale* actually took place "on a dark night, some twenty years ago in the home of John from Osenay, that is of Osewold" (pp. 8-9). Long discusses some of the changes that I discuss here, but reaches quite a different set of conclusions: "Chaucer intends for the story to be biographical or even autobiographical. [...] The Miller [...] had observed the events in his youth" (p. 9). According to Long, although Robyn was himself off in London with Gille on the fateful Monday night in question, he "could easily have satisfied his curiosity by gleaning the varying tidbits of information from the stories of neighbors or from Nicholas and Alison as well. The Miller's story, then, is almost certainly based on a real episode in his life, and Robyn the Miller is Old John's young apprentice, also named Robyn, who would have been a near 'eye' witness' of the Nicholas-Alison-John triangle" (p. 10). Long's argument is variously flawed. He never explains why a future miller would have apprenticed himself to a carpenter, for example, and the name and age of Osewald the Reeve do not work out well with those of old John of the twenty-years-past events of the tale. Long's argument is made even more tenuous when he surmises that John has long since separated from Alison and married "a new young wife," while Alison is currently the Wife of Bath on the pilgrimage to Canterbury. My own reasoning requires no such house of cards. A useful counter-reading to the Pratt-Long kind of "realism" is that of Charles A. Owen, Jr., "One Robyn or Two," *Modern Language Notes* 67 (1952): 336-38.

Chapter V

1. I am indebted particularly to six books for much of the information, and for models for some of the illustrative sketches in Figures 1 through 7: Margaret Wood, *The English Medieval House* (London: Studio Editions, 1994 [first published 1965]); Anthony Quiney, *The Traditional Buildings of England* (London: Thames and Hudson, 1990); Jane Grenville, *Medieval Housing* (London: Leicester University Press, 1997); Richard Harris, *Discovering Timber-Framed Buildings* (Buckinghamshire: Shire Publications, 2000 [first published 1978]); Geoff Egan, *The Medieval Household: Daily Living c. 1150–c. 1450* (Woodbridge: Boydell Press, 2010); and L. F. Salzman, *Building in England Down to 1540: A Documentary History* (Oxford: Clarendon Press, 1997 [originally published 1952]). This last has been particularly helpful for detailed technical information. Beginners will find the facing illustrations following page 196 in Salzman's book to be particularly interesting. The first is an illustration showing carpenters building a timber-framed building, and opposite it one labeling the various structural units of such a building. I have consulted, but found less useful, other books, such as Hugh Braun's *An Introduction to English Mediaeval Architecture* (London: Faber and Faber, 1951 [republished 1968]), which deals mostly with stone buildings, and J. T. Smith, *English Houses, 1200–1800: The Herfordshire Evidence* (London: Royal Commission on the Historical Monuments of England, 1992), which deals mostly with postmedieval houses.

2. See W. A. Pantin, "The Development of Domestic Architecture in Oxford," *Antiquaries Journal* 27 (1947): 120–51. Pantin discusses architecture in Oxford from the fourteenth to the eighteenth century. Virtually all of the fourteenth-century houses in Oxford have been replaced by more recent structures, but Pantin makes some surmises about them. See also Pantin's "Medieval English Town-House Plans," *Medieval Archaeology* 6–7 (1962–63): 202–39. A useful glossary of structural and carpentry terms appears in Cecil A. Hewett, "Structural Carpentry in Medieval Essex," *Medieval Archaeology* 6–7 (1962–63): 240–71. The appendix on pp. 267–70 contains definitions of terms like "collar-beam," "gable," and "ground-sill."

3. There has been some scholarly confusion about where old John is when he sleeps that Monday night while Nicholas and Alison are below in his bed. Larry D. Benson and Theodore M. Andersson suggest in *The Literary Context of Chaucer's Fabliaux* (Indianapolis: Bobbs-Merrill, 1971) that he sleeps on top of the roof, since they say that he "pitches off the roof" (p. 5) at the end of the tale. Patrick J. Gallacher also refers to him as "falling off the roof" in "Perception and Reality in the *Miller's Tale*," *Chaucer Review* 18 (1983): 38. Roger D. Sell in "Tellability and Politeness in the *Miller's Tale*: First Steps in Literary Pragmatics," *English Studies* 66 (1985) tells us that John sleeps "in his tub up in the attic" (p. 509). Linda Harte Holley in *Chaucer's Measuring Eye* (Houston: Rice University Press, 1990) thinks the tubs are "hung under the ceiling" (p. 95). That is misleading because we usually think of ceilings as horizontal. Chaucer is quite clear: Nicholas tells John to hang the tubs "in the roof ful hye" (3565) not *on* the roof, and the actions at the end of the tale make sense only if he is hanging from beams in the open smoke bay of the central hall, not in the attic.

4. V. A. Kolve in *Chaucer and the Imagery of Narrative: The First Five Canterbury Tales* (Stanford: Stanford University Press, 1984), calls attention to a hint at John's animal nature in Nicholas's comparison of him to "a white doke" swimming "after hire drake" as an image connecting him to the animals in the ark (pp. 183–85). My own suggestion connecting John with animal life—or rather non-life—of course, is quite different. We might recall here the Wife of Bath's reference to "bacon" in her discussion of the experience of sex with her old husbands: "And yet in bacon hadde I nevere delit" (III [D] 417).

5. Anthony Quiney in *The Traditional Buildings of England* (London: Thames and Hudson, 1990) reminds us that the smoke from open-hearth fires was often used to cure meat in medieval houses: "Smoking required an open fire and a hook in the roof above, where the meat could be cured by the smoke, yet not get hot enough to cook" (p. 101). It is possible, of course, that the three tubs were suspended from such meat hooks in John's house, though Chaucer makes no mention of them.

6. Other scholars are confused about the kind of beams from which the three tubs are suspended. Enrico Giaccherini, in "Theatrical Chaucer" (*European Medieval Drama* 2

[1998]: 92) tells us that John hangs the tubs "on a rafter," while William F. Woods in "Private Space and Public Space in the *Miller's Tale*" (*Chaucer Review* 29 [1994]: 166) says that John is "up in the rafters." The rafters are the sloping or slanted roof timbers that rest on the large beam at the top of a wall. Typically they join another rafter at the peak of the roof (see Figure 7). They are not referred to as balks or beams. John is far more likely to have suspended the three tubs from a collar beam or crown plate than from a rafter. Curiously, Joseph A. Dane in "The Mechanics of Comedy in Chaucer's *Miller's Tale*" (*Chaucer Review* 14 [1980]: 216) says that the "cuckolded carpenter is diligently awaiting Noah's second flood in a tub tied to the rafters of his barn." Chaucer never mentions any barn on John's property. The comparison of Alison's singing to that of "any swalwe sittynge on a berne" (3257) cannot be taken as evidence that John owned a barn. The tubs are clearly to be understood as suspended in the house itself and not from rafters. In his "translation" of the *Canterbury Tales* (New York: Viking, 2009), Peter Ackroyd says that the tubs are "suspended from the rafters of the ceiling (p. 92)." Chaucer makes no mention of rafters, and in any case ceilings do not have rafters.

7. In volume 5 of his monumental edition of *The Complete Works of Geoffrey Chaucer*, 2d ed. (Oxford: Clarendon Press, 1894–97), Walter W. Skeat, admitting his own confusion about the term, concludes that "I would therefor read *selle*, with the sense of 'flooring' or 'boarding' and *floor* to mean the ground beneath it" (p. 112). The *Riverside* note to these lines repeats the notion that "celle" is "flooring." The house, however, may not have had wooden flooring because of the danger of fire. It is interesting that in *Heile of Beersele* Heile's house has an earthen floor, if we can assume that Willem's fall "ter erden" (168) can accurately be translated as "to earth" or "to the ground."

8. A knowledge of the way the central living area or hall often functioned in medieval times as sleeping quarters for the servants helps us to understand why Nicholas thinks that it is important that John send Robyn and Gille away to London. It would scarcely do, after all, to have them observe the nocturnal doings of Nicholas and Alison as they climbed down the ladders to have their frisky young-animal sexual encounter in the master's bedroom.

9. Salzman, p. 373, quotes a document about the building of the cathedral at Canterbury which records the accidental fall of some 50 feet during construction: "Thus sorely bruised by the blows from the beams and stones, he was rendered helpless alike to himself and for the work.... The master, thus hurt, remained in his bed for some time under medical care ... but his health amended not."

10. Illustrations of such hinges appear on pp. 46–47 of Geoff Egan's *The Medieval Household*.

11. There is considerable confusion about prying open and closing the door to Nicholas's room. Derek Pearsall, for example, in *The Canterbury Tales* (London: George Allen and Unwin, 1985), says that when we try to figure out the architecture of John's house in the *Miller's Tale*, "we might find ourselves stumbling into some unexpected obstacles. That door, for instance, crashed off its hinges into Nicholas's bedchamber with such a deal of heaving from Robyn (3470), is back in position without a word a few lines later (3499) so that Nicholas and John can have their *tête-à-tête* (p. 183)." Chaucer never said that the door "crashed off its hinges." Richard Daniels agrees with Pearsall that Chaucer "nods" here: "John and Robyn knock down Nicholas' door to find him gaping (3468–71), but a few minutes later the young scholar is able to push that door firmly shut (3499)" (see his "Textual Pleasure in the *Miller's Tale*," in *The Performance of Middle English Culture: Essays on Chaucer and the Drama in Honor of Martin Stevens*, ed. James J. Paxon, Lawrence M. Clopper, and Sylvia Tomasch [Woodbridge, Suffolk: Boydell and Brewer, 1998], p. 116). Daniels is confused about other architectural features of the house, as well. He says that John was supposed to "chop a hole in the roof" with the ax (p. 116) and "chop his way through the roof" (p. 122). It is the gable John is supposed to chop through, not the roof itself.

Chapter VI

1. Many modern editors, including the editor of the *Riverside Chaucer*, hyphenate it as "shot-wyndowe," but we should remember that the hyphen does not appear in the man-

uscripts. I generally use the hyphen unless I am quoting someone who does not.

2. In private correspondence, in May 2010, Professor N. H. G. E. Veldhoen of the department of English at Leiden University wrote, in response to my query: "In Middle Dutch a *venster*, and by implication also a *vensterkijn*, refers primarily to the opening in a wall. It can be open to the air, or covered over by glass or parchment, and it may or may not have a shutter—but the shutter would be a separate item. In other words, *venster*, by itself would not refer to a window that could itself be opened and shut as a frame within a frame. That does not mean, of course, that it is not occasionally used loosely for any kind of window; but that is not its original meaning. '*Hij opende het venster*' is, technically, incorrect, and should read '*hij opende het raam*,' but people are, and no doubt were, rather careless in this usage" (printed with his kind permission).

3. Walter W. Skeat's long note in his six-volume *The Complete Works of Geoffrey Chaucer* (Oxford: Clarendon Press, 1894), volume 5: 103–04, lays out what he calls "the right sense" by defining a shot-window as "a hinge-shutting window" (p. 104), a designation adopted by many other glossators. In the glossary to the Modern Library *Canterbury Tales* (New York, 1929) based on Skeat's text, the term is defined simply as "casement" (p. 598)—another definition that appears in many later editions.

4. William F. Woods, "Private and Public Space in the *Miller's Tale*," *Chaucer Review* 29 (1994): 174.

5. J. A. W. Bennett, *Chaucer at Oxford and at Cambridge* (Toronto: University of Toronto Press, 1974), p. 38.

6. "Lamkin" in *The Oxford Book of Ballads*, ed. James Winsley (Oxford: Clarendon Press, 1969), p. 314.

7. Compare these original lines with three recent translations of the *Miller's Tale*: Peter Tuttle (Barnes and Noble Classics, 2007), "And took his place near an open window" (p. 179), "And still he stood under the open window" (p. 197); Peter Ackroyd (Viking, 2008), "he stood beneath one of the casement windows" (p. 86), "and stood beneath the bedroom window" (p. 93); Burton Raffel (Modern Library, 2009), "He posted himself beneath a small hinged window" (p. 92), "Standing under the window, still as a mouse" (p. 101). Chaucer does not say that the window is open, that the room has a casement window, let alone more than one of them, that the window is small or hinged, or anything about a mouse.

8. See Betsy Bowden, *Eighteenth-Century Modernizations from the Canterbury Tales* (Woodbridge, Suffolk: D. S. Brewer, 1991), pp. 172, 174.

9. *The Canterbury Tales Done Into Modern English by Frederick Clarke* (London: J. C. Hotten, 1870), volume 1, pp. 191, 209.

10. My quotations from Scott's *The Monastery* (originally published in 1820) are from the illustrated Adam and Charles Black edition (London, 1893). In the Glossary at the end of the volume we find this entry: "SHOT-WINDOW, a small projecting window" (p. 392).

11. John Trotter Brockett, *A Glossary of North Country Words* (Newcastle-upon-Tyne: E. Charnley, 1825). Brockett (1788–1842) published a second edition in 1829. His son W[illiam] E[dward] Brockett brought out, after his father's death, a co-authored third edition (Newcastle-Upon-Tyne: E. Charnley, 1846). The definition is on p. 125. It is likely that Thomas Wright, in his 1847 edition of the *Canterbury Tales* for the Percy Society (see vol. 1, p. 134), consulted the 1846 Brockett glossary before proclaiming the shot-window to be a projecting window.

12. I quote from John Jamieson, *An Etymological Dictionary of the Scottish Language*, rev. John Longmuir and David Donaldson (Paisley: Alexander Gardner, 1879), p. 158. I have not seen Jamieson's original 1808 edition.

13. The online, searchable, massive *Dictionary of the Scots Language* (Dundee: University of Dundee, 2001), http://dsl.ac.uk, combines electronically two earlier historical dictionaries, the twelve-volume *Dictionary of the Older Scottish Tongue* and the ten-volume *Scottish National Dictionary*. In it the noun *shot* is defined as "a small opening in the wall of a house [...] acting as a window but closed by hinged wooden shutters. [...] Also given, but prob. erron., as 'a projected window.'" The noun *schot-wyndo* is defined as "a partition, a board for closing an opening." We should recall, of course, that Scots usage is later than Chaucer's usage, and that the earlier Middle English meaning may—or may not—have been different.

14. This idea goes back to Thomas Tyr-

whitt, who said in his gloss to shot-window, "That is, I suppose, a window that was 'shut' " (*The Canterbury Tales of Chaucer* [Oxford, 1775]). It is echoed by Frederick Clarke, who renders Chaucer's "And stille he stant under the shot-wyndowe" (3695) as " 'Neath the closed window there he stood quite still" (Clarke 209).

15. "Clerk Saunders" as we know it now first appeared in Child's *Border Minstrelsy* in 1802, though it drew on motifs already known in other Scottish ballads, like "Sweet William's Ghost." I quote here lines 13–16 and, just below, lines 97–100.

16. I quote from the Lippincott edition (Philadelphia, 1920), p. 338. It is interesting to speculate, once again, that Scott picked the term up from Chaucer and used it in *Kenilworth* to lend an air of antiquity to that novel. In the first chapter a chubby innkeeper named Giles Gosling is compared with the Host: "Since the days of old Harry Baillie of the Tabbard in Southwark, no one had excelled Giles Gosling in the power of pleasing guests of every description" (p. 2). Near the end of the chapter in which Jane Thackham jumps out of the shot-window, Scott describes a garrulous traveler "who, from her jolly and laughter-loving demeanour, might have been the very emblem of the Wife of Bath" (p. 347).

17. *The Works of Geoffrey Chaucer*, 2d ed. (Boston: Houghton Mifflin, 1957), p. 977.

18. I quote from the prologue to Book Seven, as presented in *Virgil's Aeneid Translated Into Scottish Verse by Gavin Douglas, Bishop of Dunkeld*, ed. David F. C. Coldwell (Edinburgh: Blackwood, 1964). For my translation I have profited from Coldwell's glossary. He glosses both "schot" and "schot wyndo" as "a window that can be opened or shut on its hinges" (p. 375). Interestingly, Gavin Douglas says nothing of hinges.

19. I quote lines 193–98 of Frederick J. Furnivall's edition of *A Royal Historie of the Excellent Knight Generides* (Hertford: Stephen Austin, 1865).

20. Benson 70. In this designation the *Riverside* was perhaps taking the lead of Norman Davis, et al., in *A Chaucer Glossary* (Oxford: Clarendon Press, 1979). There a shot-window is defined as "a hinged window which can be opened or closed like a shutter" (p. 133).

21. Peter Brown, "'Shot Wyndowe' (*Miller's Tale* I.3358 and 3695): An Open and Shut Case?," *Medium Aevum* 69 (2000): 96–103. The quotation is taken from pp. 98–100.

22. Lethbridge Kingsford, "A London Merchant's House and Its Owners, 1360–1614," *Archaeologia* 74 (1925): 151.

23. Edith Rickert, et al., *Chaucer's World* (New York: Columbia University Press, 1948), pp. 6–7.

24. Mark Girouard, *Life in the English Country House: A Social and Architectural History* (New Haven: Yale University Press, 1978), p. 2.

25. The term "gnof," Chaucer's word for John, is usually translated as "churl," which suggests a rude, boorish, low-class person.

26. See Ernest L. Sabine, "Latrines and Cesspools of Mediaeval London," *Speculum* 9 (1934): 303–21. Sabine reports, for example, that in 1421 "the privy of a certain tenement [...] was indicted by the wardmote jury because of the great stench coming from it into the public street, to the great nuisance of the people" (319). Also, "for the majority of prosperous citizens [...] privies with pipes and cesspools were the best available arrangement; and these it was impossible to keep entirely free from tainted air" (321).

27. Gregory Heyworth, "Ineloquent Ends: *Simplicita*, Proctolalia, and the Profane Vernacular in the *Miller's Tale*," *Speculum* 84 (2009): 976n32. Heyworth apparently did not read "Art and Scatology in the *Miller's Tale*," *Chaucer Review* 12 (1977): 91–102. "I am seemingly the first to suggest that this fart is not merely scatological but eschatological" (968–69). Compare "Nicholas's farting in Absolon's face [was] Chaucer's means of demonstrating that the reward for such worldly behavior is not heavenly bliss but scatological, as well as eschatological, unpleasantness" (99).

28. L. F. Salzman, *English Life in the Middle Ages* (London: Oxford University Press, 1927), p. 89. The drawing is reproduced also by Geoff Egan in *The Medieval Household*, p. 42. Salzman says this of windows: "In the houses of the nobles the windows might be filled with stained glass, but in ordinary houses they would be unglazed, and until the sixteenth century glass was considered a luxury. Sometimes the window opening would be filled with a lattice of wood or metal, occasionally oiled linen would be stretched across it, but most often it would be open to the wind and rain, which could, however, be

excluded by closing the oak shutters with which the window was provided" (p. 94).

29. J. A. W. Bennett rejects the usual meaning of "up" in his zeal to read the shot-window as a hinged casement: "The 'shot-window' that Nicholas 'up dide' (3801; 'threw open,' not 'up') was evidently a small casement" (p. 38).

30. From the E.E.T.S. edition, No. 268, by O. D. MacRae-Gibson (London, 1973), lines 1123–32 (italics added). There has been speculation that Chaucer knew the Auchinleck manuscript, but I do not wish to take up that argument here.

31. For photographs of working models of the top-hinged and the sliding windows described, see my "Performing Academic Papers" in *Interpretation and Performance: Essays for Alan Gaylord*, ed. Susan Yager and Elise E. Morse-Gagné (Provo: The Chaucer Studio Press, 2013), pp. 160 and 162.

32. Francis Henry Stratmann, *A Middle-English Dictionary, Containing Words Used by English Writers from the Twelfth to the Fifteenth Century*, rearranged, revised, and enlarged by Henry Bradley (Oxford: Oxford University Press, 1891), p. 533.

33. See especially pp. 255–58. "Schot" is one of a dozen terms with Middle Dutch cognates that Chaucer use only once, and that one time being in the *Miller's Tale*: "lendes" (3237, 3304), "tapes" (3241), "popelot" (3253), "strouted" (3315), "brewhaus" (3334), "squaymous" (3337), "capyng" (3444), "kiked" (3445), "haspe" (3470), "tubbe" (3621, 3627), "shaar" (3763), "kultour" (3763, 3776, 3785, 3812). There I identify the noun "schot" as "a wooden board with which a door or window is closed." I here extend my thinking to identify the adjectival use of the term as suggesting "sliding."

34. I am grateful to Professor Veldhoen of the University of Leiden, for permission to quote from his April 2010 letter to me in response to my query about Middle Dutch *schotdore* and *schotporte*: "After consulting a colleague in the Dutch Department, I have come up with the following solution: a *schotdore* is a small vertically sliding door or hatch or panel in a big gate, a kind of wicket. A *schotporte* is the same, but is also used for a lock-gate in a river or canal. I hope this makes sense in your text." Indeed, it does.

35. Richard Harris, *Discovering Timber-Framed Buildings* (Buckinghamshire: Shire Publications, 2000), p. 25. Some useful diagrams appear on the facing page 24. Harris illustrates a horizontally sliding panel, but not a vertical one of the kind I think Chaucer may well have meant. He uses the modern term "shutter"; the term used in actual documents for wooden window panels was almost always "fenestra" or "leaf"—as in the documents Salzman quotes just below.

36. L. F. Salzman, *Building in England Down to 1540: A Documentary History* (Oxford: Oxford University Press, 1952), p. 256. Salzman mentions coming across the Middle English term variously spelled "schatbord," "schotbord," "schotebord" and "scocbord," in the fifteen hundred or so medieval manuscripts he consulted. According to Salzman, " 'Shooting' being a medieval term for planing, we may probably identify these shotboards with the 'planebord for repair of the roof of the leaden-covered chamber' at Westminster in 1402" (pp. 243–44). The *MED* defines the noun "shot-bord" as "a kind of board of small size often used for roofing" (p. 761). It was presumably made a kind of wood that would resist the rains, so it might also have served a useful purpose in a window panel.

Chapter VII

1. J. A. W. Bennett, in *Chaucer at Oxford and at Cambridge* (London: Oxford University Press, 1974), p. 38.

2. I discuss this matter in a little more detail in my "Art and Scatology in the *Miller's Tale*," *Chaucer Review* 12 (1977): 90–102.

Chapter VIII

1. Bennett, p. 41, suggests that Gerveys, and therefore his close neighbor John, would probably have lived within the city walls at the north edge of Oxford, in Smithgate, on a street called Catte Street. There is no solid internal evidence in the tale for so specific a location, of course, but contemporary readers might have thought that they could locate it. At the time we speak of, Oxford was a small town indeed, with a population of around four thousand.

2. Bennett tells us that these lines "provide much the fullest inventory of a scholar's belongings before the sixteenth century" (p. 32). I find it telling that while historical writers saw no reason to record this kind of detail,

a poet interested in setting the stage for the action in his tale did. Chaucer wants us to visualize Nicholas's room. Other writers saw no need for anyone to.

3. Mark Miller in "Naturalism and Its Discontents in the *Miller's Tale*," *ELH* 67 (2000) assumes that it is a real stone: "when Alison wants to chase Absolon off, there is a stone lying about in her bedroom" (p. 6). I call it a false prop because she merely threatens to throw a stone. There is no evidence that she actually has one in hand or at hand, any more than that Absolon actually has his mother's ring.

4. For an alternative explanation of the image of selling bread and ale, see the note to the lines in Benson, p. 848: Cf. the Fr. "ne trouva point de pain a vendre"—itself a reference to the notes of earlier editors. My own explanation picks up the bread and ale of the earlier line 3628.

Chapter IX

1. Again, the comparative lengths are based not the number of lines, but on the number of syllables. I calculate roughly 1056 syllables in the 132-line bedroom scene in *Heile of Beersele*, as compared with 2170 syllables in the corresponding 217 lines of the *Miller's Tale*. The ratio is about 1:2.

2. This estimate is based on a calculation of 264 syllables for the thirty-three lines of the setup of the pre-bedroom scene in *Heile of Beersele*, as compared with 4460 syllables for the 446 lines setting up the bedroom scene in the *Miller's Tale*. The ratio is almost 1:17.

3. Using syllables, the whole of the tale proper is 1320 syllables in *Heile of Beersele* as compared with 2100 for the first two pre-bedroom sequences in the *Miller's Tale*. That is a ratio of roughly 1:1.6.

4. There is, of course, some subjectivity in my counting. If a line has only one spoken word, I count it as the narrator's line; if it has more than one, I count it as belonging to a character. If there are two different speakers in the same line, I assign it to the character whose speech seems to be more important in context. I count directly-reported thoughts as a character's speech. That is, when we are told, "he thought, 'I shall get my revenge,' " that counts as that character's line, but when we are told more generally "then he sat down and carefully planned his revenge," I count the words as the narrator's.

5. This point has been made often, but perhaps first by J. Burke Severs, "Appropriateness of Character to Plot in the *Franklin's Tale*," in *Studies in Language and Literature in Honor of Margaret Schlauch* (Warsaw: PWN-Polish Scientific Publishers, 1966): "Absolon is the very type whose sensibilities will be most revolted" (p. 387).

6. I am aware that I punctuate the line differently from other editors, including Benson in the *Riverside*. Every edition I have checked puts the second line (3370) in the mouth of the narrator, not Alison. Virtually all punctuation in modern editions, of course, is added by the editors. In Chaucer's time the quotation mark had not yet been invented. I give the second line to Alison because the "ye" seems more appropriate as her address to her husband, who has just addressed her. The sense of her speech, then, is "Yes, God knows, John, I hear it well enough. He'll go away. You can expect no better from him." The "ye" is problematical in the usual way of punctuating the line, for it is then the only direct address by the narrator to the listening audience in the *Miller's Tale*. In my punctuation, the "ye" refers more logically to the character whom Alison is addressing. For more on repunctuating Chaucer, see my "Where's the Point: Punctuating Chaucer's *Canterbury Tales*" in "*Seyd in forme and reverence*": *Essays on Chaucer and Chaucerians in Memory of Emerson Brown, Jr.*, ed. T. L. Burton and John F. Plummer (Provo: Chaucer Studio Press, 2005), pp. 193–203; reprinted in *Chaucer's Canterbury Comedies*, pp. 55–71.

7. For more on that couplet, see my "'Now, deere lady': Absolon's Marian Couplet in the *Miller's Tale*," *Chaucer Review* 39 (2004): 219–22; reprinted in *Chaucer's Canterbury Comedies*, pp. 23–28.

Chapter X

1. See note 4 in the preceding chapter for a description of the way I assign lines to each of the speakers. The number 132 does not include the 12-line moral summary at the very end.

2. The category "Others" includes three different speakers in the *Miller's Tale*. In the Oseney scene it is the cloisterer, in the smithy scene it is Gerveys, and in the neighbor scene

it is, collectively, the various neighbors. The number 217 does not include the closing five-line moral commentary at the very end.

3. J.A.W. Bennett, in *Chaucer at Oxford and at Cambridge*, p. 52, says that Oseney was a place of "public resort." He speculates that the cloisterer whom Absolon encounters at the abbey would have been "an ordinary monk, perhaps a novice" (p. 54).

4. Enrico Giaccherini for some reason assumes that Absolon "wakes him up" ("Theatrical Chaucer,") in *European Medieval Drama* 2 (1998): 85–98 (p. 93), though it is evident that Gerveys is already up and working. Chaucer tells us that Gerveys "in his forge smythed plough harneys" and that he specifically is busy sharpening "shaar and kultour" (3762–63)—quite typical nighttime activities for blacksmiths on a spring night.

5. In terms of syllables, the Middle Dutch second window scene, at 8 × 35 lines is 280 syllables, as compared with the English second window scene, at 10 × 36 lines, or 360 syllables.

Chapter XI

1. I quote from Betsy Bowden's excellent *Eighteenth-Century Modernizations from the Canterbury Tales* (Woodbridge, Suffolk: D. S. Brewer, 1991), p. 168. I give page numbers for subsequent quotations in parentheses. Bowden conveniently republished the three versions that I discuss in this chapter. Samuel Cobb's retelling appears on pages 15–22 of Bowden's book, John Smith's on pages 24–30, and the anonymous 1791 one on pages 171–76. All lines are renumbered starting with line 1. Cobb's version is 729 lines long, Smith's 828 lines, and the anonymous one 613 lines. None of the three versions, then, is a line-by-line translation of Chaucer's 668-line tale. Where I quote from these three versions, I give the line numbers from Bowden's edition.

Chapter XII

1. Francis Storr and Hawes Turner, *Canterbury Chimes, or Chaucer Tales Retold for Children* (Cambridge: John Wilson and Sons, 1889), p. v.

2. For a helpful discussion of William T. Stead and his Penny Poets series, see Christina von Nolcken, " 'Penny Poet' Chaucer, or Chaucer and the 'Penny Dreadfuls,'" *Chaucer Review* 47 (2012): 107–33. She also tells about Edith Johnstone, who did the actual writing of the Penny Poets volume on Chaucer.

3. F. J. Harvey Darton, *Tales of the Canterbury Pilgrims Retold from Chaucer and Others*, illus. Hugh Thomson (New York: Frederick A. Stokes, 1904), p. 54.

4. *Tales from Chaucer: The Canterbury Tales Done into Prose by Eleanor Farjeon* (London: Medici Society, 1930), p. v.

Chapter XIII

1. *The Canterbury Tales of Geoffrey Chaucer Done into Modern English by Frederick Clarke* (London: J. C. Hotten, 1870), volume 1, preface. Subsequent parenthetical references are to pages in this edition. In September 1870, just after the first volume of his edition-translation appeared, Frederick Clarke was struck by an express train and killed. None of the proposed second through eighth volumes was ever published.

2. *Chaucer for Children: A Golden Key* (London: Chatto and Windus, 1877).

3. *Tales from Chaucer* (London: George Routledge and Sons, 1887). The title page announces that the book was "Adapted by Mrs. Haweis" and was "Edited by the Rev. Hugh Reginald Haweis, M.A."—her husband. Mrs. Haweis's given name was Mary Eliza. The *Miller's Tale* occupies pages 54–64. I give page references to quotations in parentheses.

4. Geoffrey Chaucer, *The Canterbury Tales: A New Unabridged Translation by Burton Raffel* (New York: Modern Library, 2008), p. xxxi. Raffel renumbers the lines. The lines I quote correspond to lines 3223–41 in most editions of the *Canterbury Tales*.

5. Peter Ackroyd, *The Canterbury Tales by Geoffrey Chaucer: A Retelling by Peter Ackroyd* (New York: Viking, 2009), p. 84. Subsequent page references are indicated parenthetically.

Chapter XIV

1. *The Canterbury Tales*, by Geraldine McCaughrean, illus. Victor G. Ambrus (Oxford: Oxford University Press, 1984), p. 18. Subsequent page references are to this edition.

2. Selina Hastings, *A Selection from the Canterbury Tales*, illus. Reg Cartwright (New York: Henry Holt, 1988), p. 26. Subsequent page references are included parenthetically.

Chapter XV

1. My quotations from George Milburn's *Julie* are from the 35-cent Lion Library Edition published in March 1956. These lines are from pages 178–79. Subsequent page references, included parenthetically, are from this edition. *Julie* has not previously been discussed by medieval scholars, with the brief exception of a note by James T. Bratcher and Nicholai von Kreisler in "The Popularity of the *Miller's Tale*," *Southern Folklore Quarterly* 35 (1971): 325–35. The note consists mostly of plot summary and the judgment that in Milburn's novel, "Gone, in a word, is Chaucer's art and his surpassing comic vision" (334). That statement misses the point. It is not that Milburn's tale lacks art or comic vision, but that it shows a different notion of narrative art and envisions a different kind of comic vision.

2. Mencken was the editor of the magazine *American Mercury* from its start in 1924 to 1933. As editor he published original literature by such writers as Eugene O'Neill, Carl Sandburg, William Faulkner, Sinclair Lewis, F. Scott Fitzgerald, Langston Hughes, W. E. B. Du Bois, James Weldon Johnson, Conrad Aiken, Sherwood Anderson, Edgar Lee Masters, and William Saroyan. Mencken also published a number of Milburn's stories, as did the editors of *Scribner's Magazine*, *Harper's Magazine*, and the *New Yorker*. The *New York Times* obituary makes no mention of *Julie* or *Old John's Woman*.

3. *Shivaree* is a simplification of *charivari*, a mock serenade sung to newlyweds.

4. Milburn does, however, incorporate some elements of the Miller into other characters. His short-shouldered, wide-nosed simian features (see General Prologue, lines 547–49, 557) are reflected in old John's "apelike arm" (Milburn 9). His red-hair-tufted nose (see lines 554–56) is picked up in Virgil Pruitt's "hair-sprigged, purple-veined nose" (Milburn 12). His knife-brandishing (see line 558) is picked up in Pearl Pruitt's "jackknife" and Jewel Pruitt's "switch-blade knife" (Milburn 10). Milburn also blends in characteristics from other tales than the *Miller's Tale*: like the Wife of Bath, John has been married five times and now welcomes Julie, the sixth; like January he jealously keeps a hand on his young wife (see pages 28–29, 89, 111).

5. References in *Julie* to Roosevelt's New Deal (1933–1936), the WPA (Works Progress Administration, 1935), the REA (Rural Electrification Act, 1935), and the FHA (Federal Housing Authority, 1934) suggest that the novel is set sometime after the mid–1930s. Two references suggest a later date, however. Dexter Nichols is said to have "restless gray eyes [...] as bleak as zinc pennies" (Milburn 22). Zinc pennies were the grey pennies minted in 1943 because copper was being used in the war effort. The most specific hint about the temporal setting of the novel comes in Dexter Nichols's reference to "that giant telescope on Mount Palomar" (Milburn 85). He apparently refers to the 200-inch reflecting telescope built there in 1949.

6. Dexter Nichols's "You're from Missouri" (84) places the unnamed town in that state. At the end of the novel, Dexter Nichols leaves town on "the northbound bus for Joplin" (185). That tells us that the town he leaves from is south of Joplin, which is in the southwest corner of Missouri. We know that Julie is from Joplin and that John can drive her from there in his beat-up truck in time to get to the courthouse by early afternoon. Except for Joplin, Kansas City, Tulsa, Sallisaw, Smackover, and a few big cities like New York and Los Angeles, the place names mentioned in the novel are made up, including McKenzie County. That county, though, may have been meant as a McStand-in for McDonald County, the southwestern-most county in Missouri. In McDonald County we find Honey Lake Hollow, Big Sugar Creek and, nearby, Little Sugar Creek. Perhaps these real names in McDonald County suggested to Milburn the fictional names he used for Big (or Upper) Honeybucket Creek and its smaller tributary, Little Honeybucket Creek.

7. It is not entirely clear why Milburn give so many of his characters physical or mental disabilities. It serves no immediately apparent function for Jarvis Gerveys to be deaf and dumb, able to produce only "stuttering grunts" (99), or for Absolon Kendall to become for Milburn a one-legged cripple nicknamed "Caterpillar." It is particularly puzzling that for Milburn, Robin becomes a drooling half-wit, a "mush-headed bastid"

(129). For one thing, Robin Goodkind at times seems to be unusually bright, as when he cleverly makes money by selling information about John and Julie to the townspeople. He is smart enough to challenge John Bundix about filling the rain barrel during a drought, and, on his own initiative, to fetch Doc Sinclair to treat Dexter Nichol's scorched buttocks and John Bundix's broken arm.

8. I count as neighbors in the *Miller's Tale* Robyn, Gille, and Gerveys. For *Julie* I count as neighbors Robin Goodkind, Jilladeen Mapes, Jarvis Gerveys, Pearly Pruitt, Jewel Pruitt, Virgil Pruitt, Judge Throgmorten, Granny Gosnell, Orpheus Clark, Nadine Jones, August Schultz, Doc Sinclair, Troy, and Lyman, as well as a few unnamed men and women who also speak.

Chapter XVI

1. Bellerophon Books published *The Miller's Tale by Geoffrey Chaucer and Also Rendered New by Lieuen Adkins* in 1973. Bellerophon Books was located at 153 Stewart Street, San Francisco. Neither the lines nor the pages are numbered. For ease of reference, I have provided line numbers for the Middle English passages and [bracketed] page numbers for the modern English passages. The Middle English text differs in small ways from the one in the *Riverside Chaucer*.

2. *Scornful Simkin, Retold and Illustrated by Lee Lorenz* (Englewood Cliffs, NJ: Prentice-Hall, 1980). The thirty pages of text and pictures are not numbered.

3. *Pinchpenny John, Written and Illustrated by Lee Lorenz* (Englewood Cliffs, NJ: Prentice-Hall, 1981). The pages are not numbered, but they total thirty pages of text and drawings. I provide bracketed page numbers for my quotations from this edition.

4. *Chaucer's Canterbury Tales, Retold and Illustrated by Marcia Williams* (Cambridge, MA: Candlewick Press, 2007), p. 16.

5. *The Canterbury Tales Adapted by Seymour Chwast* (New York: Bloomsbury, 2011), p. 10. Subsequent quotations, from the tale itself (pp. 25–31) are from this edition.

Chapter XVII

1. A shorter version had been presented at the Oxford Playhouse in 1964. Martin Starkie had conceived and directed the earlier performance as well as the expanded later one. He had worked with Nevill Coghill on the book for both. The music was written by Richard Hill and John Hawkins, with the lyrics by Nevill Coghill. One-page essays on "The Story" and on "Geoffrey Chaucer," some photographs of the Broadway performance, and some of the lyrics were published in a twenty-four-page booklet called *Vocal Selections from Canterbury Tales* (Boston: Frank Music Corp., 1969).

2. *Some Canterbury Tales Freely Adapted from Geoffrey Chaucer by Ken Pickering with Music by Derek Hyde* (London: Samuel French, Ltd., 1988), p. 1. The *Miller's Tale* occupies pages 41–46. Subsequent quotations are from this edition. The musical scores do not appear in this edition, but are available in a separate thirty-page booklet of the same title and date by Samuel French. The ISBN for the play and the lyrics is 0-573-08077-1. The ISBN for the booklet with the musical scores for the seven songs and three dances is 0-573-08679-X.

3. Baba Brinkman, *The Rap Canterbury Tales*, illus. Erik Brinkman (Vancouver, B.C.: Talonbooks, 2006), p. 6. Subsequent page numbers to Brinkman's book are included parenthetically. His book includes four tales, those of the Knight, the Miller, the Pardoner, and the Wife of Bath, without Chaucer's General Prologue or Chaucer's prologues to the individual tales. Brinkman does not number the lines of his version of the *Miller's Tale*, though he does for the facing-page Chaucerian Middle English version. Readers who want to listen to Brinkman performing the *Miller's Tale* can order the *Rap Canterbury Tales* CDs from Brinkman's website at http://www.bababrinkman.com/rap-guides/canterbury.tales-remixed/. A longer version of this section appeared as "It's Miller Time: Baba Brinkman's Rap Adaptation of the *Miller's Tale*," *LATCH* (Literary Artifact in Theory, Culture, or History) 3 (2010): 134–50.

4. Brinkman on pages 190–91 defends his decision not to use what he takes as the modern vulgar descendant of "queynte." He does not defend his decision to say that Nicholas grabs Alison with "perverted intentions" except to say that "[p]artially this was necessary to follow my rhyme scheme." The preceding four line-endings are *senses*, *against us*, *circumstances*, and *defenceless*. Few readers would see Nicholas's grab as "perverted."

5. *The Rap Canterbury Tales* is illustrated by inventive cartoons drawn by the author's brother Erik Brinkman. For the *Miller's Tale* there are more than twenty-five such drawings, all on the right-hand pages where they act as fillers of the white space occasioned by Brinkman's version's being so much shorter than the Chaucerian original on the left-hand pages. To give only one example, the drawing for page 193, presenting the first dozen lines of Brinkman's *Miller's Tale*, shows a cocky-looking Nicholas in his bedroom. A guitar stands against the wall. At the open window is a telescope of sorts. A mobile showing various stars and planets is suspended from the ceiling. No telescope or mobile, of course, is mentioned in the Chaucerian version or, for that matter, in Baba Brinkman's rap version.

Chapter XVIII

1. Phil Woods and Michael Bogdanov, *Canterbury Tales: Chaucer Made Modern* (Manchester: Iron Press/Signature Books, 1980), p. 7. Subsequent page references are to this edition. The *Miller's Tale* itself comes at the end, pages 63–70.
2. Arnold Wengrow, *The Canterbury Tales: A Contemporary Theatrical Adaptation of the Works of Geoffrey Chaucer* (Worcestershire: Hanbury Plays, 1983), p. 52. Subsequent quotations, given parenthetically, are from this edition, in which the *Miller's Tale* is found on pages 46–63.
3. *The Canterbury Tales Adapted by Martin Riley* (Oxford: Oxford University Press, 1998), pp. 83–84. The *Miller's Tale* occupies pages 84–99. Subsequent quotations from Riley's retelling of the *Miller's Tale* are from this edition. A curious feature of Riley's version of the *Canterbury Tales* is the role that Geoffrey Chaucer plays. In the early part of the drama, before the tale-telling begins, he is portrayed as a lifeless shrouded manikin carried along from place to place on the pilgrimage. After the *Miller's Tale* is finished he comes to life. At first he thinks he is in hell, being punished by demons out to torment him for telling lewd stories, but in the end he is applauded as the author of the *Canterbury Tales*.
4. John O'Connor, *The Canterbury Tales: A Play Based on the Poem by Geoffrey Chaucer* (Cheltenham: Nelson Thornes, Ltd., 2001), pp. 1, 4. The *Miller's Tale* runs from page 62 to 68. Subsequent page references are to this edition.
5. Lindsay Price, *The Canterbury Tales: A Comedy in Two Acts Adapted by Lindsay Price from the Original by Geoffrey Chaucer* (Crystal Beach, Ontario, CA: Theatrefolk, 2002), p. 5. The *Miller's Tale* runs from page 23 to 31. Price does not number the lines. Parenthetical references are to page numbers in this edition.
6. Mike Poulton, *The Canterbury Tales: An Adaptation in Two Parts* (London: Nick Hern Books, 2005), pp. 8–9. Poulton's edition is very much an acting version. One would not call this stage adaptation a musical, but the script provides the lyrics for several songs, none of which appeared in the original *Canterbury Tales* musical. Poulton does not provide musical scores for the songs. Wherever he can, Poulton uses Chaucer's Middle English, altering only the spelling and guiding the actors with some accents to suggest a Chaucerian way of pronouncing the lines. Because Poulton does not number the lines in his version, the parenthetical numbers in the text are to page numbers. The *Miller's Tale* occupies pages 36–46.
7. Virtually all editors put the quotation mark at the end of the previous line, giving line 3370 to the narrator. I believe, however, that the "This passeth forth" makes more sense as Alison's weary response to her husband, with a meaning something like "Yes, I hear him all too well. He won't stay long; leave well enough alone."

Chapter XIX

1. Copies of the 121-minute original, uncut version were made available through the cooperation of the Pier Paulo Pasolini Foundation in Rome and the Museum of Modern Art in New York. The jacket of that edition announces that "Pasolini's startling candor and ribald humor illuminate these classic tales of romance, deception, murder, and lust. Photographed on location in rural England." An American X-rated video called *The Ribald Tales of Canterbury* was produced by Hyapatia Lee in 1985, but because it does not present the *Miller's Tale*, I make no further mention of it.
2. Jonathan Myerson (b. 1960) is a British dramatist and novelist. His *Canter-

bury Tales was nominated for an Oscar in 1999. It won an award for best animated film of the year and four Emmys. It is available in both Middle English and modern English. The *Miller's Tale* and the *Reeve's Tale* were directed by Deiniol Morris. They were published by Aaargh! in Cardiff.

3. Kathleen Forni, for example, in *Chaucer's Afterlife: Adaptations in Recent Popular Culture* (Jefferson, NC: McFarland, 2013), speaks of the "brilliant climactic montage of the *Miller's Tale* and the *Reeve's Tale*" (p. 103).

Chapter XX

1. Peter N. Miller, *Seven Canterbury Tales Retold: Improvisations on Chaucer*. Although the book has not been published by a commercial press, Miller has made bound copies available through Amazon, eBay, and the Payloadz store. Readers who would like to see the rest of this tale or the other six of his improvisations should write directly to him at petermiller@metrocast.net.

2. I am grateful to Gareth Machin for permission to give here a slightly edited version of his *Miller's Tale*. Anyone interested in staging a performance of this *Miller's Tale* should of course apply to him for permission. He can be reached at Gareth.Machin@salisburyplayhouse.com.

Bibliography

Ackroyd, Peter. *The Canterbury Tales by Geoffrey Chaucer: A Retelling by Peter Ackroyd.* New York: Viking, 2009.

Adkins, Lieuen. *The Miller's Tale by Geoffrey Chaucer and Also Rendered New by Lieuen Adkins.* San Francisco: Bellerophon, 1973.

Beidler, Peter G. "Art and Scatology in the *Miller's Tale.*" *Chaucer Review* 12 (1977): 90–102.

_____. *Chaucer's Canterbury Comedies.* Seattle: Coffeetown Press, 2011.

_____. "It's Miller Time: Baba Brinkman's Rap Adaptation of the *Miller's Tale.*" *LATCH* (Literary Artifact in Theory, Culture, or History) 3 (2010): 134–50.

_____. "Just Say Yes: Chaucer Did Know the *Decameron.*" In *The Decameron and the Canterbury Tales,* ed. Leonard Michael Koff and Brenda Deen Schildgen. Madison, NJ: Fairleigh Dickinson University Press, 1999, pp. 25–46.

_____. "The Miller's Tale." In *Sources and Analogues of the Canterbury Tales,* ed. Robert Correale and Mary Hamel. Woodbridge, Suffolk: D. S. Brewer, 2005, II, 249–75.

_____. " 'Now, deere lady': Absolon's Marian Couplet in the *Miller's Tale.*" *Chaucer Review* 39 (2004): 219–22.

_____. "Performing Academic Papers." In *Interpretation and Performance: Essays for Alan Gaylord,* ed. Susan Yager and Elise E. Morse-Gagné. Provo: The Chaucer Studio Press, 2013, pp. 149–68.

_____. "Where's the Point: Punctuating Chaucer's *Canterbury Tales.*" In *"Seyd in forme and reverence": Essays on Chaucer and Chaucerians in Memory of Emerson Brown, Jr.,* ed. T. L. Burton and John F. Plummer. Provo: Chaucer Studio Press, 2005, pp. 193–203.

_____, Elizabeth M. Biebel, Tracey Cummings, Anne Dickson, Jennifer McNamara Bailey, Christine Lynch Berg and Sister Elaine Marie Glanz. "Dramatic Intertextuality in the *Miller's Tale*: Chaucer's Use of Characters from Medieval Drama as Foils for John, Alison, Nicholas, and Absolon." *Chaucer Yearbook* 3 (1996): 1–19.

_____, and Theresa Decker. "*Lippijn*: A Middle Dutch Source for the *Merchant's Tale*?" *Chaucer Review* 24 (1989): 236–50.

_____, and _____. "*Nu Nock* and *Boss for Three Days.*" *Canadian Journal of Netherlandic Studies,* volumes 15.2 (Spring 1995) and 17.2 (Fall 1997).

Bennett, J. A. W. *Chaucer at Oxford and at Cambridge.* Oxford: Clarendon Press, 1974.

Benson, Larry D., gen. ed. *Riverside Chaucer,* 3d ed. Boston: Houghton Mifflin, 1989.

_____. *The Canterbury Tales, Complete* [based on the *Riverside Chaucer*]. Boston: Houghton Mifflin, 2000.

_____, and Theodore M. Andersson. *The*

Literary Context of Chaucer's Fabliaux. Indianapolis: Bobbs-Merrill, 1971.

Biggs, Frederick M. "The *Miller's Tale* and *Heile of Beersele.*" *Review of English Studies,* n.s. 56 (2005): 497–523.

———, and Laura L. Howes. "Theofany in the *Miller's Tale.*" *Medium Ævum* 65 (1996): 268–79.

Bowden, Betsy. *Eighteenth-Century Modernizations from the Canterbury Tales.* Woodbridge, Suffolk: D. S. Brewer, 1991.

Bowker, Peter. *The Miller's Tale* [film]. London: BBC, 2003.

Bratcher, James T., and Nicholai von Kreisler. "The Popularity of the *Miller's Tale.*" *Southern Folklore Quarterly* 35 (1971): 325–35.

Braun, Hugh. *An Introduction to English Mediaeval Architecture.* London: Faber and Faber, 1951 [republished 1968].

Brinkman, Baba. *The Rap Canterbury Tales.* Illust. Erik Brinkman. Vancouver, B.C.: Talonbooks, 2006.

Brockett, John Trotter. *A Glossary of North Country Words.* Newcastle-upon-Tyne: E. Charnley, 1825 [2d ed. 1829; 3d ed. co-authored by W. E. Brockett, 1846].

Brown, Peter. "'Shot Wyndowe' (*Miller's Tale* I.3358 and 3695): An Open and Shut Case?" *Medium Aevum* 69 (2000): 96–103.

Chambers, Gerald Thomas. *Four Domestic Farces of Medieval France.* Ann Arbor: Xerox University Microfilms, 1975.

Child, Francis James. *Border Minstrelsy.* London, 1802.

Chwast, Seymour. *The Canterbury Tales Adapted by Seymour Chwast.* New York: Bloomsbury, 2011.

Clark, Roy Peter. "Christmas Games in the *Miller's Tale.*" *Studies in Short Fiction* 13 (1976): 277–87.

Clarke, Frederick R. *The Canterbury Tales Done into Modern English by Frederick Clarke.* London: J. C. Hotten, 1870, volume 1.

Cobb, Samuel. "The Carpenter of Oxford: Or the *Miller's Tale*" (1712). In Bowden, pp. 15–22.

Coldwell, David F. C., ed. *Virgil's* Aeneid *Translated into Scottish Verse by Gavin Douglas, Bishop of Dunkeld.* Edinburgh: Blackwood, 1964.

Dane, Joseph A. "The Mechanics of Comedy in Chaucer's *Miller's Tale.*" *Chaucer Review* 14 (1980): 215–24.

Daniels, Richard. "Textual Pleasure in the *Miller's Tale.*" In *The Performance of Middle English Culture: Essays on Chaucer and the Drama in Honor of Martin Stevens,* ed. James J. Paxon, Lawrence M. Clopper, and Sylvia Tomasch. Woodbridge, Suffolk: Boydell and Brewer, 1998.

Darton, F. J. Harvey. *Tales of the Canterbury Pilgrims Retold from Chaucer and Others.* Illust. Hugh Thomson. New York: Frederick A. Stokes, 1904.

David, Alfred. "Noah's Wife's Flood." In *The Performance of Middle English Culture,* ed. James J. Paxson, Lawrence M. Clopper, and Sylvia Tomasch. Woodbridge, Suffolk: D. S. Brewer, 1998, pp. 97–109.

Davis, Norman, et al. *A Chaucer Glossary.* Oxford: Clarendon Press, 1979.

Dictionary of the Scots Language. Dundee: University of Dundee, 2001 [online at http://dsl.ac.uk].

Egan, Geoff. *The Medieval Household: Daily Living c. 1150–c. 1450.* Woodbridge: Boydell Press, 2010.

Farjeon, Eleanor. *Tales from Chaucer: The Canterbury Tales Done into Prose by Eleanor Farjeon.* London: Medici Society, 1930.

Farrell, Thomas J. "Privacy and the Boundaries of Fabliau in the *Miller's Tale,*" *ELH* 56 (1989): 273–95.

Furnivall, Frederick J., ed. *A Royal Historie of the Excellent Knight Generides.* Hertford: Stephen Austin, 1865.

Gallacher, Patrick J. "Perception and Reality in the *Miller's Tale.*" *Chaucer Review* 18 (1983): 38–48.

Gellrich, Jesse M. "The Parody of Medieval Music in the *Miller's Tale.*" *Journal of English and Germanic Philology* 73 (1974): 176–88.

Giaccherini, Enrico. "Theatrical Chaucer." *European Medieval Drama* 2 (1998): 85–98.

Girouard, Mark. *Life in the English Country House: A Social and Architectural History.* New Haven: Yale University Press, 1978.

Gray, Douglas. Explanatory Notes to the *Miller's Tale*. In the Riverside *Canterbury Tales, Complete*, ed. Larry D. Benson. Boston: Houghton Mifflin, 2000, pp. 371–77.

Grenville, Jane. *Medieval Housing*. London: Leicester University Press, 1997.

Harder, Kelsey B. "Chaucer's Use of the Mystery Plays in the *Miller's Tale*." *Modern Language Quarterly* 17 (1956): 193–98.

Harris, Richard. *Discovering Timber-Framed Buildings*. Buckinghamshire: Shire Publications, 2000 [first published 1978].

Hastings, Selina. *A Selection from the Canterbury Tales*. New York: Henry Holt; 1988.

Haweis, Mrs. [Mary Eliza]. *Chaucer for Children: A Golden Key*. London: Chatto and Windus, 1877.

———. *Tales from Chaucer*. London: George Routledge and Sons, 1887.

Hauser, G. A. *Miller's Tale*. Lexington, KY: The G. A. Hauser Collection, 2007.

Heile of Beersele. Presented and translated in *Sources and Analogues of the Canterbury Tales*, ed. Robert Correale and Mary Hamel. Woodbridge, Suffolk: D. S. Brewer, 2005, II, 266–75.

Hewett, Cecil A. "Structural Carpentry in Medieval Essex." *Medieval Archaeology* 6–7 (1962–63): 240–71.

Heyworth, Gregory. "Ineloquent Ends: *Simplicita*, Proctolalia, and the Profane Vernacular in the *Miller's Tale*." *Speculum* 84 (2009): 956–83.

Holley, Linda Harte. *Chaucer's Measuring Eye*. Houston: Rice University Press, 1990.

Jamieson, John. *An Etymological Dictionary of the Scottish Language*. Rev. John Longmuir and David Donaldson. Paisley: Alexander Gardner, 1879.

Johnstone, Edith. *The Canterbury Tales*. Ed. William T. Stead. London: Penny Poets Series, 1895.

Kaske, R. E. "The *Canticum Canticorum* in the *Miller's Tale*." *Studies in Philology* 59 (1962): 479–500.

Kingsford, Lethbridge. "A London Merchant's House and Its Owners, 1360–1614." *Archaeologia* 74 (1925): 137–58.

Kolve, V. A. *Chaucer and the Imagery of Narrative: The First Five Canterbury Tales*. Stanford: Stanford University Press, 1984.

Long, Charles."The Miller's True Story." *Interpretations* 6 (1974): 7–16.

Lorenz, Lee. *Pinchpenny John, Written and Illustrated by Lee Lorenz*. Englewood Cliffs, NJ: Prentice-Hall, 1981.

———. *Scornful Simkin, Retold and Illustrated by Lee Lorenz*. Englewood Cliffs, NJ: Prentice-Hall, 1980.

Machin, Gareth. *The Miller's Tale* [first performed in 2004, published here for the first time]. For more information, Gareth. Machin@salisburyplayhouse.com.

McCaughrean, Geraldine. *The Canterbury Tales*. Oxford: Oxford University Press, 1984.

McGrady, Donald. "Chaucer and the *Decameron* Reconsidered." *Chaucer Review* 12 (1970): 1–26.

Mehl, Dieter. *Geoffrey Chaucer: An Introduction to His Narrative Poetry*. Cambridge: Cambridge University Press, 1986.

Milburn, George. *Julie*. New York: Lion Library, 1956. Republished as *Old John's Woman*. New York: Pyramid, 1960.

Miller, Mark. "Naturalism and Its Discontents in the *Miller's Tale*." *ELH* 67 (2000): 1–44.

Miller, Peter N. *Seven Canterbury Tales Retold: Improvisations on Chaucer* (privately available from the author at peter-miller@metrocast.net).

"The *Miller's Tale* from Chaucer" (1791). In Bowden, pp. 171–76.

Myerson, Jonathan. *Canterbury Tales* [animated film]. Cardiff: Aaargh!, 1999.

Myles, Robert. *Chaucerian Realism*. Cambridge: D. S. Brewer, 1994.

O'Connor, John. *The Canterbury Tales: A Play Based on the Poem by Geoffrey Chaucer*. Cheltenham: Nelson Thornes, Ltd., 2001.

Of Arthur and Merlin (Auchinleck MS). Ed. O. D. MacRae-Gibson. London: E.E.T.S. Number 268, 1973.

Ogden, Dunbar H. *The Staging of Drama in the Medieval Church*. Cranbury, NJ: Associated University Presses, 2002.

Owen, Charles A., Jr. "One Robyn or Two." *Modern Language Notes* 67 (1952): 336–38.

———. *Pilgrimage and Storytelling in the Canterbury Tales: The Dialectic of "Ernest" and "Game."* Norman: University of Oklahoma Press, 1977.

Pantin, W. A. "The Development of Domestic Architecture in Oxford." *Antiquaries Journal* 27 (1947): 120–51.

———. "Medieval English Town-House Plans." *Medieval Archaeology* 6–7 (1962–63): 202–39.

Pasolini, Pier Paulo. *Canterbury Tales* [121-minute film]. Rome: Pier Paulo Pasolini Foundation and the Museum of Modern Art, 1972.

Pearsall, Derek. *The Canterbury Tales*. London: George Allen and Unwin, 1985.

Pickering, Ken. *Some Canterbury Tales Freely Adapted from Geoffrey Chaucer by Ken Pickering with Music by Derek Hyde*. London: Samuel French, Ltd., 1988.

Poulton, Mike. *The Canterbury Tales: An Adaptation in Two Parts*. London: Nick Hern Books, 2005.

Pratt, Robert A. "Was Robyn the Miller's Youth Misspent?" *Modern Language Notes* 59 (1944): 47–49.

Price, Lindsay. *The Canterbury Tales: A Comedy in Two Acts Adapted by Lindsay Price from the Original by Geoffrey Chaucer*. Crystal Beach, Ontario: Theatrefolk, 2002.

Prior, Sandra Pierson. "Parodying Topology and the Mystery Plays in the *Miller's Tale*." *Journal of Medieval and Renaissance Studies* 16 (1986): 51–73.

Quiney, Anthony. *The Traditional Buildings of England*. London: Thames and Hudson, 1990.

Raffel, Burton. *The Canterbury Tales: A New Unabridged Translation by Burton Raffel*. New York: Modern Library, 2008.

Rickert, Edith Rickert, et al. *Chaucer's World*. New York: Columbia University Press, 1948.

Riley, Martin. *The Canterbury Tales Adapted by Martin Riley*. Oxford: Oxford University Press, 1998.

Robinson, Fred N. *The Works of Geoffrey Chaucer*, 2d ed. Boston: Houghton Mifflin, 1957.

Rowland, Beryl. "The Play of the *Miller's Tale*: A Game within a Game." *Chaucer Review* 5 (1970): 140–46.

Sabine, Ernest L. "Latrines and Cesspools of Mediaeval London." *Speculum* 9 (1934): 303–21.

Salzman, L. F. *Building in England down to 1540: A Documentary History*. Oxford: Clarendon Press, 1997 [originally published 1952].

———. *English Life in the Middle Ages*. London: Oxford University Press, 1927.

Schweitzer, Edward C. "The Misdirected Kiss and the Lover's Malady in Chaucer's *Miller's Tale*." In *Chaucer in the Eighties*, ed. Julian N. Wasserman and Robert J. Blanch. Syracuse: Syracuse University Press, 1986, pp. 223–33.

Scott, Sir Walter. *Kenilworth*. Philadelphia: Lippincott, 1920 [originally published 1821].

———. *The Monastery*. London: Adam and Charles Black, 1893 [originally published 1820].

Sell, Roger D. "Tellability and Politeness in the *Miller's Tale*: First Steps in Literary Pragmatics." *English Studies* 66 (1985): 406–512.

Severs, J. Burke. "Appropriateness of Character to Plot in the *Franklin's Tale*," in *Studies in Language and Literature in Honor of Margaret Schlauch*. Warsaw: PWN-Polish Scientific Publishers, 1966, pp. 387–96.

Silf, Margaret. *The Miller's Tale and Other Parables*. London: Darton Longman and Todd, 2000.

Skeat, Walter W. *The Complete Works of Geoffrey Chaucer*, 2d ed. Oxford: Clarendon Press, 1894–97.

Smith, John. "The *Miller's Tale* from Geoffrey Chaucer" (1713). In Bowden, pp. 24–30.

Smith, T. J. *English Houses, 1200–1800: The Herfordshire Evidence*. London: Royal Commission on the Historical Monuments of England, 1992.

Sponsler, Clair. *Drama and Resistance: Bodies, Goods, and Theatricality in Late Medieval England*. Minneapolis: University of Minnesota Press, 1997.

Starkie, Martin, and Nevill Coghill. *Canterbury Tales* [a musical produced in London in 1968 and New York in 1969]. No print version is known to exist, though there is a 24-page booklet entitled *Vocal Selections from Canterbury Tales*. Boston: Frank Music Corp. 1969.

Stoor, Francis, and Hawes Turner. *Canterbury Chimes, or Chaucer Tales Retold for Children*. Cambridge: John Wilson and Sons, 1889.

Stratmann, Francis Henry. *A Middle-English Dictionary, Containing Words Used by English Writers from the Twelfth to the Fifteenth Century*. Rearranged, revised, and enlarged by Henry Bradley. Oxford: Oxford University Press, 1891.

Tuttle, Peter, trans. *The Canterbury Tales*. New York: Barnes and Noble, 2000.

Tyrwhitt, Thomas. *The Canterbury Tales of Chaucer*. Oxford, 1775.

von Nolcken, Christina. " 'Penny Poet' Chaucer, or Chaucer and the 'Penny Dreadfuls.' " *Chaucer Review* 47 (2012): 107–33.

Wallrich, Ruby. "Chaucer's Records of Early English Drama." *Records of Early English Drama* 2 (1988): 13–21.

Wengrow, Arnold. *The Canterbury Tales: A Contemporary Theatrical Adaptation of the Works of Geoffrey Chaucer*. Worcestershire: Hanbury Plays, 1983.

Williams, Marcia. *Chaucer's Canterbury Tales, Retold and Illustrated by Marcia Williams*. Cambridge, MA: Candlewick Press, 2007.

Winsley, James, ed. *The Oxford Book of Ballads*. Oxford: Clarendon Press, 1969.

Wood, Margaret. *The English Medieval House*. London: Studio Editions, 1994 [first published 1965].

Woods, Phil, with Michael Bogdanov. *Canterbury Tales: Chaucer Made Modern*. Manchester: Iron Press/Signature, 1980.

Woods, William F. "Private and Public Space in the *Miller's Tale*." *Chaucer Review* 29 (1994): 166–78.

Wright, Thomas. *The Canterbury Tales*. London: Percy Society, 1847.

Index

Page numbers in ***bold italics*** indicate pages with illustrations.

Ackroyd, Peter 142–44, 257n6, 258n7, 262n5
Adkins, Lieuen 169–73, ***171***, 264n1
Andersson, Theodore M. 256n3
Anonymous, teller of 1791 *Canterbury Tales* 125–26, 128–31, 262n1
Angelus ad virginem 20, 35
The Art of Courtly Love 22

Bailey, Jennifer McNamara 252n6
Bennett, J. A. W. 61, 81–***83***, 255n3, 258n5, 260n29, 260n1, 260n1–2, 261n3
Benson, Larry D. 251n2, 256n3, 259n20, 261n4, 261n6
Berg, Christine G. 252n6
Biggs, Frederick M. 253n3
Boccaccio, Giovanni 252n1
Bogdanov, Michael 195–***96***, 265n1
Bowden, Betsy 258n8, 262n1
Bowker, Peter 224–26
Bratcher, James T. 263n1
Braun, Hugh 256n1
Brinkman, Baba 187–94, ***188***, 264n3–4
Brinkman, Erik 188, 265n5
Brockett, John Trotter 63, 258n11
Brockett, W. E. 258n11
Brown, Peter 68–72, 76–77, 259n21

Capellanus, Andreas 22
Chambers, Gerald Thomas 18, 253n2
Child, Francis James 64
Chwast, Seymour 180, ***181***, 182, 264n5
Clark, Roy Peter 255n4
Clarke, Charles Cowden 132
Clarke, Frederick R. 62, 138–39, 258n9, 259n14, 262n1
"Clerk Saunders" 61, 64–65, 259n15

Cobb, Samuel 126–28, 131, 262n1
Coghill, Nevill 184–***85***, 227, 264n1
Coldwell, David F. C. 259n18
Corpus Christi plays 4–5
Correale, Robert 253n3, 255n2
Cummings, Tracey 251n5

Dame Sirith 9–11, 26
Dane, Joseph A. 257n6
Daniels, Richard 257n11
Darton, F. J. Harvey 134, 262n3
David, Alfred 252n6
Davis, Norman 259n20
Decameron 253n1
Decker, Theresa 253n2
Dickson, Anne M. 252n7
Dictionary of the Scots Language 258n13
door to Nicholas's room 57, ***58***, 59
Doughty, Kenny 224
Douglas, Gavin 66–67, 259n18

earthfast house ***49–50***
Egan, Geoff 256n1, 257n10

Farjeon, Eleanor 134–37, 262n4
Farrell, Thomas J. 253n1
Forni, Kathleen 6, 252n10
Franklin's Tale 22
Furnivall, Frederick J. 259n19

Gallacher, Patrick J. 256n3
Gellrich, Jesse M. 254n3–5
Giaccherini, Enrico 252n9, 256n5, 262n4
Girouard, Mark 70
Glanz, Sister Elaine Marie 252n7
Gray, Douglas 254n5
Grenville, Jane 256n1

273

274 INDEX

Hales, Ada 132
Hamel, Mary 253n3, 255n2
Harder, Kelsey B. 252n9
Harris, Richard 78–79, 256n1, 260n35
Hastings, Selina 148, *149*, 150, 263n2
Hauser, G. A. 252n11
Haweis, H. R. 132
Haweis, Mrs. [Mary Eliza] 139–41, 262n2–3
Heile of Beersele 2, 6–7, 9, 12–14, 17–18, 20, 22–23, 24–25, 27–28, 29, 33, 35–37, 38–47, 57, 69, 84–85, 87–123, 154, 165, 193, 248, 252n9, 253n4, 257n7
Henryson 166
Herod 4, 24, 254n7
Hewett, Cecil A. 256n2
Heyworth, Gregory 71, 259n27
Holley, Linda Harte 256n3
Howes, Laura L. 253n3
Hulthem manuscript 11, 253n2
Hyde, Derek 184–87, 264n2

Jamieson, John 63, 258n12
Johnstone, Edith 133–34, 262n2
Joseph and Mary 5

Kaske, R. E. 254n3
Kelman, Janet Harvey 132
Kenilworth 61, 65, 259n16
Kingsford, Lethbridge 69, 259n22
Kittredge, George Lyman 3, 251n1
Knight's Tale 3, 224, 227
Koff, Leonard 253n1
Kolve, V. A. 251n4, 256n4
"Kynges Noote" 35, 254n5

"Lamkin" 61, 258n6
Lippijn 9, 11
Long, Charles 255n6
Lorenz, Lee 173, *174*, *175*–77, 264n2–3

Machin, Gareth 242–48, 266n2
Man of Law's Tale 224
McCaughrean, Geraldine 145, *146*–48, 262n1
McGrady, Donald 253n1
McKay, John 224
McSpadden, J. Walker 132
Mehl, Dieter 255n1
Mencken, H. L. 156, 263n2
Merchant's Tale 27, 70–71
Merode Altarpiece 73, *74*, 75
Milburn, George 151–68, *152*, *157*, 263n1–2
Miller, Mark 255n4, 261n3
Miller, Peter N. 227–41, 266n1
The Monastery 62–63, 258n10
Morris, Deiniol 266n2
Mullany, Peter N. 251n3

Myerson, Jonathan 220, *221*, *223*–24, 265n2
Myles, Robert 254n1

Nesbitt, John 224
Noah 4–5

O'Connor, John 205–08, 265n4
Of Arthour and Merlin 75, 260n29
Ogden, Dunbar H. 254n6–7, 254n2
Owen, Charles A., Jr. 252n9, 255n6

Pantin, W. A. 256n2
Pardoner's Tale 7, 224
Pasolini, Pier Paulo 217–20, 265n1
Pearsall, Derek 257n11
Pickering, Ken 184–87, 264n2
Piper, Billie 224
Pontius Pilate 4
Poulton, Mike 210–16, *211*, 265n6
Pratt, Robert A. 255n6
Price, Lindsay 208–10, 265n5
Prior, Sandra Pierson 251n3, 252n9, 253n3
Procol Harum 1

Quiney, Anthony 256n1, 256n5

Raffel, Burton 141–42, 258n7, 262n7
Reeve's Tale 27, 255n2
Reiss, Edmund 251n3
Rickert, Edith 69, 259n23
Riley, Martin 203–05, 265n3
Robinson, Fred N. 65, 259n17
Rowland, Beryl 252n8
A Royal Historie of the Excellent Knight Generides 67, 259n19

Sabine, Ernest L. 259n26
Salzman, L. F. 57, 72–73, 79–80, 256n1, 257n9, 259n28, 260n36
Schildgen, Brenda Deen 253n1
Schweitzer, Edward C. 253n5
Scott, Sir Walter 61–63
Sell, Roger D. 256n3
Severs, J. Burke 261n5
Shelton, Gilbert 169, *171*, 264n1
Shipman's Tale 27, 224
shot-window 60–80, *73*, *74*, *76*, *77*, *78*, *79*
Silf, Margaret 252n11
Skeat, Walter W. 257n7, 258n3
Smith, John 128–29, 131, 262n1
Smith, J. T. 256n1
Sponsler, Clair 251n5
Starkie, Martin 184–85, 264n1
Stead, William T. 133, 262n2
Stoor, Francis 132, 262n1
Stratmann, Francis Henry 76, 260n32

Thompson, Clara L. 132
timber-framed house **50**, 51, **52**, 53, **54**, **55**–56
Troilus and Criseyde 166
Turner, Hawes 132, 262n1
Tuttle, Peter 258n7
Tyrwhitt, Thomas 258n14

Veldhoen, N. H. G. E. 258n2, 260n34
von Kreisler, Nicholai 263n1
von Nolcken, Christina 262n2

Wallrich, Ruby 251n4
Waterman, Dennis 224
Wengrow, Arnold 201–02, 265
"A Whiter Shade of Pale" 1–2
Wife of Bath's Tale 7, 224, 227
Williams, Marcia 177, **178**–80, 264n4
Winsley, James 258n6
Wood, Margaret 256n1
Woods, Phil 195–201, **196**, 265n1
Woods, William F. 254n3, 257n6, 258n4
Wright, Thomas 258n11

www.ingramcontent.com/pod-product-compliance
Lightning Source LLC
Chambersburg PA
CBHW021342230426
43666CB00006B/370